THE
JEWISH
PRIMER

THE
JEWISH
PRIMER

Questions and Answers on Jewish
Faith and Culture

Rabbi Dr. Shmuel Himelstein

Facts On File®

AN INFOBASE HOLDINGS COMPANY

For Judy, Noam and Aytan

Words cannot express my love and gratitude for everything

Copyright © 1990 by G.G. The Jerusalem Publishing House, Ltd., 39 Tchernichovski St.,
P. O. Box 7147, Jerusalem 91071

Facts On File, Inc.
460 Park Avenue South
New York NY 10016

Himelstein, Shmuel.
    The Jewish primer / Shmuel Himelstein.
      p. cm.
    HC ISBN: 0-8160-2322-0
    PB ISBN: 0-8160-2849-4
    1. Judaism—Miscellanea.   I. Title.
    BM51.H49   1990
    296—dc20   90-2951
                      CIP

British CIP data available on request from Facts On File.

Facts On File books are available at special discounts when purchased
in bulk quantities for businesses, associations, institutions, or sales
promotions. Please contact our Special Sales Department in New York
at 212/683-2244 or 800/322-8755.

Manufactured by the Maple-Vail Book Manufacturing Group
Printed in the United States of America

10 9 8 7 6 5 4 3

This book is printed on acid-free paper.

Contents

Illustration Credits

Introduction

How does one boil down 3,500 years of a religion and culture into one small book? The answer, of course, is that one can't possibly cover more than a fraction of the total. What I have attempted to do, though, is to cover many of the major concerns of Judaism to a certain extent, touching on such diverse matters as prayer and organ transplants, the dietary laws and ecology. The fact is that while Judaism is the oldest of the monotheistic religions, it has something to say about all of today's concerns.

This book has been written for various types of people: for the Jew with little background of the Jewish heritage, with the hope that this may serve as an introduction to the glorious panorama of Judaism; for the Jew who is grounded in that heritage, but who will hopefully find much that is new and of interest to him or her as well; and for the non-Jew who would like to understand some of the basic beliefs, practices and views of Judaism.

My many years in education taught me that some topics lead almost automatically to others, and that a willingness to be flexible, rather than discussing only one specific issue at a time, can be most rewarding. I have thus on occasion allowed myself to digress – within careful limits – to topics of an allied interest to the main one at hand. These digressions sometimes consist of allied points of law and other times of illustrative anecdotes. Hopefully, the digressions will aid in elucidating the main topic, while serving to open other avenues of thought to the reader.

The form chosen is one with a long and distinguished history in Jewish annals: the question and answer. Many of the questions are the result of discussions with students and friends. (The two terms are not mutually exclusive.) Others were introduced by me in order to elucidate various points. The reader's indulgence is asked where the question seems too contrived.

I must add one *caveat*: While this book discusses a great number of aspects of Jewish law, it is not meant to be a substitute for an authoritative guide to that law. Thus, while every effort has been made to ensure that the statements dealing with the law are in accordance with definitive rulings, the reader is cautioned not to use this source as the sole arbiter in questions in this area.

It is my profound wish that this book will serve as a stepping stone in the pursuit of further Jewish knowledge. If the different answers to questions result in more questions being asked, I will feel amply rewarded.

At this time, I would like to express my gratitude to Shlomo (Yosh) Gafni, Rachel Gilon and the staff of the Jerusalem Publishing House, who were extremely supportive throughout the writing of this book, and to Dr Raphael Posner, who edited the completed manuscript; his comments and insights were invaluable. If there are any errors or omissions, they are, of course, purely mine.

Jerusalem,   Shmuel Himelstein
Hanukkah, 5750/1989

Chapter One

General Basics

Before we can delve into this book proper, we need to clarify certain terms and concepts. This chapter serves as an introduction to the subsequent chapters, and is especially important for those with little knowledge of Judaism.

Question Jews speak with great reverence of the Torah. What is the Torah?

Answer The word "Torah" is derived from a root indicating "to lead" or "instruct." In practice, it has a number of meanings. Most specifically, the word refers to the first five books of the Bible – the Five Books of Moses. It may also be used to refer to the entire Bible. By extension, it is often used to include all religious texts of the Jewish people. Thus, for example, a statement like "to study Torah" will normally encompass not only study of the Bible, but also the Talmud and its commentaries. Jews often differentiate between the *Torah she-Bikhtav* – the "written Torah" – which includes the entire Bible, and the *Torah she–be'al Peh* – "the oral Torah" – which, in essence, includes all works which came after the Bible, such as the Talmud and the Midrash.

Question What is the Talmud?

Answer A basic belief of Judaism is that, along with the Torah, the Five Books of Moses, an oral law was given as well, which was handed down by word of mouth from one generation to the next, each father teaching his children. The need for an amplification of the written Torah is an obvious one: There are numerous verses in the Torah, which command the Jew to do certain things or refrain from doing others, but with no explanation of what is involved. For example, one is not permitted to "work" on the Sabbath. What is considered "work"? Again, one must bind "them" on one's hand and between one's eyes, "them," as the rabbis explain it, referring to the *tefillin*.

What link is there between the verse to bind "them" and the square leather boxes containing specified paragraphs from the Torah, all of which are written by hand on parchment? Similarly, on Sukkot, one must take the "fruit of a goodly tree." Why should we assume that that is a reference to the citron? And so on and on. All of this indicates clearly that alongside the written Torah, an oral law was also given. Furthermore, new questions arose over the course of time. As an eternal law, the Torah had to supply a *mechanism* for solving future questions. That mechanism was a system of rules which could be used to interpret the verses of the Torah and deduce what the law was.

At first, the laws that were handed down were clearly defined. Later, over the course of centuries, doubts began to arise as to what the exact tradition had been. Furthermore, as different rabbis applied the rules of deduction, they might come up with different rulings. And all of these traditions and rulings and debates were handed down orally.

Eventually, though, the amount of material became immense and, given the fact that the Jews were suffering persecution and had been exiled all over the world with the resulting loss of knowledge of the tradition, various rabbis began writing down all that they had heard orally. This was done with great reluctance, because the oral law was meant to be exactly that. In fact, the rabbis consider the day when permission was given to commit the oral law to writing as one to be commemorated by mourning.

In any event, various rabbis made their own collections and as a result different versions of the oral law came into existence. Rabbi Judah the Patriarch (2nd century C.E.) collected all the different versions, edited and collated them and arranged them into six sections, known as Orders. This collection was known as the Mishnah, a word which may be translated either as "learning," or "repetition," in that it reviews all the laws of the Torah. This work was completed about 200 C.E.

Now that there was an authoritative, written *corpus* of the oral law in the form of the Mishnah, people began studying it and making various deductions from the text. At first, these deductions and comments were made orally, but history repeated itself. There came a time when the oral comments had to be written down. A new work was composed, the Talmud (from the root meaning "to learn"), which consisted of the Mishnah and, following each individual paragraph of the Mishnah, a kind of shorthand transcription of the discussions regarding that particular paragraph. The record of the different comments on the Mishnah was referred to as the *Gemara*, "the conclusion," the implication being that nothing would ever be added after the *Gemara*. In sum, then, the Mishnah and the *Gemara*, its expansion and interpretation, together make up the Talmud.

We should also mention that there are two Talmuds, the Jerusalem Talmud, completed in about 400 C.E. in the Land of Israel, and the Babylonian

Talmud, completed in Babylon in about 500 C.E. In most instances, when we refer to the Talmud, we mean the latter.

Question If, as stated above, the oral law is Divine, how is it that there are so many disputes among rabbis throughout the ages, as, for example, the hundreds of disputes between the School of Shammai and the School of Hillel?

Answer As we noted earlier, the oral tradition offers certain principles which one may use to deduce the law from the Torah text. God, as it were, allows man to use the greatest of all his powers, the power of his intellect, to shape the law, as it were, and He assents to these decisions. The proviso, of course, is that the decision must be reached after careful deliberation and according to all the ground rules. In fact, we are told that whenever two true Torah scholars disagree, "both these and those are the words of the living God." As paradoxical as it may seem, both scholars are correct – they have followed the rules as they understood them, and their conclusions are thus valid.

Of course, that doesn't solve matters for a person who wants a decision on a certain specific case: if one rabbi rules it is permissible and another rules it is forbidden, and both are "the words of the living God," what is the person to do? Here, the oral law steps in with a very simple solution. Granted, in the Torah sense, both views are correct, but there are rules as to how one must act in exactly such a case, i.e., how one must deal with such disputes. Thus, for example, there is a general rule that – everything else being equal – one follows the later (chronologically) authority, as one assumes that he was aware of the earlier ruling and nevertheless ruled the way he did. Another such rule is that in questions of Torah law (as opposed to rabbinic decrees), one must follow the more stringent of the rulings. (In questions relating to rabbinic decrees, one follows the more lenient ruling.) There is even a principle that – again everything else being equal – one follows the ruling that permits a certain action over a ruling that forbids it, the rationale being that anyone can forbid something, while to permit something, a person must have convincing evidence on his side. Of course, in the final analysis, these tools are not for the amateur, and when confronted by a question in Jewish law, each individual should consult with an authority whom he feels he can trust.

Question What aspects of life are covered by Jewish law?

Answer The story is told of a French king who offered one of his courtiers a royal reward if he could tell him where God is to be found. The courtier answered: "Your majesty, I will pay you twice that sum if you can tell me where God is not to be found." The same is true, in a way, for Jewish law, which, simply put, covers all aspects of human life, from the day a person is born until the day he is laid to rest; from the moment he wakes up in the morning and recites the prescribed prayer of thanks to God, to what he wears, how and when he prays, what he eats and what he does not eat, how he manages his business, how he spends his leisure time, how he behaves toward other people and down to what he recites before he falls asleep.

Question Much of Jewish literature refers to "the Sages." Who are they?

Answer As we noted, Jewish law is a combination of the written law, as embodied in the Torah, and the oral tradition and interpretations, as eventually recorded in the Talmud and thereafter. When we refer to the Sages, we generally mean the rabbis of the Mishnah and the Talmud, i.e., those who kept the Jewish tradition alive and transmitted it to the future generations. Sometimes it may be used for Talmudic scholars of later generations. As used in Jewish literature, the term is generally used to convey the majority (or consensus) view of the Jewish Sages on any given topic.

Question What is the *halakhah*?

Answer The word *halakhah*, which will be used extensively throughout this book – it is one of the basic words throughout Jewish literature – means the Jewish law, as accepted by observant Jews. Thus, we may state that the *halakhah* requires a person to perform a certain action at a certain time, or that the *halakhah* forbids one to perform another action. The word itself is derived from the Hebrew verb root letters *HLKh*, and is etymologically related to the Hebrew word for walking. In essence, then, the *halakhah* is the path that the Jew must follow throughout his life.

Question What is the *aggadah*?

Answer While the Talmud deals primarily with questions of Jewish law as deduced from the Torah, a parallel body of work developed at the same time, using the Torah as a source for homiletic discussions. The different works of the *aggadah* are generally (but not always) linked to specific books of the Bible. There are various aggadic works, many of them bearing the word *midrash* in their title (the word *midrash* comes from a root meaning "to enquire" or "to investigate.") Thus, for example, the most important work in the field, the *Midrash Rabbah* (the "Great Midrash"), is a commentary, as it were, on the Five Books of Moses. While the *aggadah* does on occasion contain items touching on Jewish law, its major purpose is homiletic, offering insights into both the Torah and human nature and giving guidance as to how a person should live and behave.

Question   What would be an example of *aggadah*?

Answer   As we noted earlier, Jewish law covers every aspect of Jewish life. One might imagine that this would be an onerous set of rules, limiting man's freedom drastically. Thus, on the verse, "The writing [on the two Tablets] was the writing of God, graven [Hebrew: *harut*] upon the tablets" (Ex. 32:16), the Sages comment (Tractate Avot 6:2), "Do not read the word as '*harut*', but as '*herut*' – freedom." (We must note that in the Torah text there are no vowels, so the word could be read either way.) Thus, as the Midrash explains the verse, what was given to the Children of Israel with the Torah was "freedom on the tablets." Observance of the commandments, then, is considered to make man free rather than to enslave him. The rationale for this is eminently logical: A person who does not adopt constraints is a slave to his every passing whim and passion. The only truly free person is the one who rules himself.

From the above example, then, we can see how the *aggadah* takes a verse, changes the vowelling somewhat, and comes up with a beautiful moral lesson.

Question   Why are Jews known as "the Chosen People"?

Answer   The Torah states, "For you are a holy people unto the Lord your God: the Lord your God has chosen you to be a special people unto Himself" (Deut. 7:6). Thus the origin of the name.

Question   Does this mean that the Jewish people are superior?

Answer   As history so clearly indicates, the life of the Jewish people throughout the centuries has hardly been a bed of roses. Until quite recently, the life of the Jews was one of constant humiliation and degradation. But that was not what the Jewish people were chosen for. Judaism sees itself as chosen for a mission – to bring the message of the One, Omnipotent God to mankind. In that, it has succeeded brilliantly. After all, between Judaism and its two offshoots, Christianity and Islam, monotheism has been brought to every corner of this globe.

When the Torah states that the Jews are to be holy, that is an unparalleled demand. Holiness is not something which comes of itself. It requires constant effort to strive to attain that level. It imposes an added burden on the individual, rather than endowing him with extra privileges. It is thus not surprising that the Torah lists a total of 613 commandments which the Jewish

people must perform, whereas the rest of the people in the world have only seven commandments.

Question Are the 613 commandments sub-divided in any way?

Answer Indeed, there have been a number of classifications, along different lines. We will only mention two of the most commonly accepted divisions:
1. Positive commandments and negative commandments. According to this division, all commandments that require a person to take a specific action (e.g., to eat *matzah* at the Passover *seder* meal) are known as *mitzvot aseh* – literally "commandments you are to do," while those that require a person to refrain from doing something (e.g., to refrain from eating pork) are known as *mitzvot lo ta'aseh* – "commandments you are not to do." These are divided numerically into 248 positive commandments, that, the Sages tell us, being the total number of bones and organs in the male body; and 365 negative commandments, equivalent to the number of days in the solar year.
2. In terms of the basic underlying reason for each specific commandment. According to this division, there are three types of commandments:

a) *Edot* – literally, "testimonies." This includes all commandments that are meant to bear witness. For example, the festival of Passover is a reminder of the Exodus from Egypt. Similarly, the four-fringed garment known as *tallit katan* or *tzitzit*, which men wear, is meant to remind them constantly of the presence of God.

b) *Mishpatim* – literally "judgments." This refers to those laws that one would expect people to develop on their own, even if they had not been commanded by the Torah. Included are such laws as honoring one's parents and the prohibition against stealing and against killing.

c) *Hukim* – usually translated (for want of a better term) as "statutes." These are the laws that are utterly unfathomable by man with his limited intelligence. They include laws such as the prohibition against wearing *sha'atnez* – a garment made of both wool and linen; and – according to many rabbis – all the dietary laws, such as not mixing milk and meat. What we must stress here is that it is not that the laws have no explanation, but that man is unable to fathom God's reasons behind these laws.

Question Does a Jew have to keep all 613 commandments?

Answer No Jew *can* keep all 613 commandments, for a simple reason: certain commandments apply only to certain people. As an example, some of the commandments apply only to the *kohanim* – members of the priestly clan.

★ *Two Torah scrolls in cases in the Sephardic style; Iran, 19th century.*

No Jew other than a *kohen* can observe these commandments. On the other hand, certain commandments *cannot* be observed by a *kohen*. An example of this is the positive commandment a person fulfills if he remarries a woman he once divorced (only, though, if she had not been married to anyone else after divorcing him). A *kohen* is forbidden to marry a divorcee, even if she was divorced from him. Similarly, there are certain commandments that can only be fulfilled by a king, and others that a king cannot fulfill. Then there are laws that apply only to men and not to women, and *vice-versa*. The number 613, then, reflects the total number of all commandments that the Jewish people – as a total unit – must fulfill. (Incidentally, Muslim law forbids a man to remarry his divorcee *unless* she has been married to someone else since he divorced her.)

Question As certain of the commandments cannot be fulfilled except in the Temple in Jerusalem, or, for example, only by a king, how many actual commandments apply to Jews today?

Answer Rabbi Israel Meir of Radin (1836-1933), known universally as Hafetz Hayyim ("He who Seeks Life"), the name of his first book, calculated that in our times there are 77 positive commandments that can be fulfilled, as well as 194 negative commandments, for a total of 271 commandments.

Question As noted above, Judaism has different requirements for men and for women in the observance of the commandments. What differences are there, and why?

Answer As a general rule, all the negative commandments, i.e., those things which are prohibited, apply equally to men and to women. As regards positive commandments, where one must perform a specific action, women are generally exempt if the action required must be done within a given time frame. Thus, since the wearing of *tzitzit* – a four-cornered garment with a special fringe in each corner – is limited to the daytime, women are exempt. There are certain positive commandments that women are obligated to perform, with each having its own individual rationale. As an example, women, just as men, are required to eat *matzah* at the Passover *seder* meal, for they too must celebrate being taken out of Egypt. A common explanation given for the general exemption is that women are involved with raising a family, and, as such, cannot possibly be expected to perform tasks at a given time. If an infant needs feeding, that takes precedence over anything else. We can therefore understand why women are required to pray once a day, but at whatever time they find convenient, rather than being required to do so at three fixed times each day, as men must do. Another rationale given for the difference between men and women (avowed feminists may cringe at this explanation) is that women are by nature more devout. Men must thus be given a greater series of constraints in order to ensure that they remain on the straight and narrow path.

Question Are there any other laws that Jews have to keep in addition to the 613 commanded in the Torah?

Answer In addition to the 613 commandments of the Torah, there are three other classes of rules which are binding, all of them man-made. These are:
1. The *gezeirah* – a rule instituted by the Sages as a type of "fence" to keep people from violating a Torah law. For example, while the Torah forbids a person from writing on the Sabbath, there is a *gezeirah* which extends the prohibition to even handling a pen on that day.
2. The *takkanah* – a rabbinic decree instituted without any basis in Torah law, for the public welfare. An example is the *takkanah* of the medieval Rabbenu Gershom forbidding a person to read anyone else's mail without permission. Another, much earlier example, was the *takkanah* instituted by Ezra (5th century B.C.E.), that the Torah is to be read publicly every Monday and Thursday morning, the traditional market days on which everyone would come to town from the surrounding villages. That was also the time the courts would be in session.
3. The *minhag* – any worthwhile custom which has been in effect for a sufficiently extended period of time, becomes obligatory. An example of this is the head covering required of men throughout the day, although the actual law only required this during prayer and while eating. In fact, we are told that "a Jewish custom has the binding force of law."

We stress "worthwhile customs," because there are also customs which have developed without any basis, or even with a faulty basis.

There is a story of a rabbi who once saw a congregant doing something which was clearly in violation of Jewish law. The rabbi, knowing the man to be observant in all his other actions, asked the man why he had done what he had done.

"It's my custom, Rabbi," the man replied.

"And where did you get it from?"

"I learned it from my father?"

"And where did your father learn it from?" the rabbi persisted.

"From my grandfather."

"Now I understand," the rabbi exclaimed with a smile. "He got it from his father and so on from one generation back to the next; all the way back to Terah, Abraham's father, the idol worshipper!"

Then there is the story – supposedly true – of the custom in a certain synagogue in Italy. Whoever entered the synagogue would walk up to a certain point, bow his head, and then continue on. No one could understand the origin for this custom, until someone discovered that there had once been a lamp at that particular point, which had forced everyone to bow in order to pass by. Although the lamp was gone, the custom remained!

Question Is there any flexibility in determining what the law is in any particular case?

Answer In many cases, the law is clear and unequivocal, and there is no possibility for ruling in more than one way. In other cases, the rabbis differentiate between the ideal ruling, known as *le–khatehilah* (literally translated, this means "from the outset," or *ab initio*), and a ruling where circumstances dictate that the original ruling be modified. The latter type of ruling is known as *be–di'avad* (literally: "if he already acted"), implying an *ex post facto* type of decision. An example will illustrate this. *Le–khatehilah*, one may not eat any dish which contains both meat (or meat products) and milk (or milk products). Let us say, though, that a person was cooking a dairy dish and a piece of meat accidentally fell into it. Here the law *be–di'avad* is that if there was more than 60 times by volume of the dairy dish than of the piece of meat, the dish may be consumed.

Another area where there may be flexibility is where a great financial loss may be incurred. The classic example is where a person slaughters a cow, and a question arises about a certain internal condition which may or may not render the cow non-kosher. Considering that at the time a person's entirely worldly goods might well have been invested in this single animal, the rabbis would often permit a person to adopt the more lenient view in the specific case, even though in general the decision would normally be to adopt the more stringent ruling. (Nowadays, much of this is academic, because kosher slaughterhouses are often linked up with non-kosher ones, and whenever any doubt arises in terms of Jewish law, the carcass is shifted to the non-kosher line. This way there is little or no financial loss for the owners of the cattle. Of course, we must stress that the fact that an animal is rejected by Jewish law does not necessarily render it unfit for human consumption, and all animal carcasses must in any event pass veterinary inspection. At the same time, one can understand why there are numerous non-Jews who generally buy kosher meat, for they consider it to be more wholesome.)

Question Are there any commandments that apply to non-Jews, similar to the 613 that apply to Jews?

Answer Indeed there are. There are seven laws which are required of all

humans. As these were given to the sons of Noah after the flood, they are known as the Noahide laws. The laws are:
1. To believe in the one God.
2. Not to blaspheme.
3. Not to kill.
4. Not to steal.
5. Not to be sexually immoral.
6. To set up courts of law.
7. Not to eat the flesh of an animal which was cut from it while it was still alive.

Question Are there any dogmas which Jews must believe?

Answer Judaism is much more a religion of deed than of creed. It is the deed – the *mitzvah* – which brings man to belief, rather than the reverse. A famous *midrash* has God stating, "Would that they would forsake Me and observe My Torah, for the light within it would return them to the proper way." In other words, God, as it were, is willing to resign Himself to people forsaking Him, provided they perform the commandments. By their deeds, they will then return to God.

There are nevertheless certain beliefs that Jews do have, although they have never been adopted as a formal catechism. Various rabbis, though, have given their own lists of basic Jewish beliefs. Probably the most famous of these lists is that of Moses Maimonides (1135-1204), who formulated what have become known as the Thirteen Principles of the Faith. These principles include the following beliefs: 1. God is the sole creator; 2. God is One; 3. He does not have a physical form; 4. He is eternal; 5. Man is to pray only to Him; 6. All the words of the prophets are true; 7. Moses was the greatest of all prophets; 8. The Torah which we have today is the same one given to Moses by God; 9. God will not replace this Torah with another; 10. God knows all of man's thoughts; 11. The good are rewarded and the evil punished; 12. The Messiah will come; 13. The dead will be revived.

Question It is often said that the Jewish view of God is that of a stern figure, whereas the Christian view is that of a kind God. What is the basis for this differentiation?

Answer Needless to say, this differentiation is not of Jewish origin. Nor does it hold water under even the most cursory examination. Unfortunately, this misconception arose because there were those who read the Torah and took it literally, without realizing that the written Torah is incomplete without the oral Torah, as later transcribed in the Mishnah, Talmud, etc. After all, as we showed above, parts of the written Torah are simply incomprehensible without the oral one.

Now, even though the Torah prescribes the death penalty for many offenses, including, in theory, for a person who strikes a match on the Sabbath, the oral law so circumscribes the law as to make it almost a "dead letter." Thus, for a person to be convicted and sentenced to death, two witnesses have to see him about to commit the punishable offense, have to warn him not to do so, have to specify the exact penalty for violating the law, and then have to hear the person state clearly, *immediately before taking the action*, "I am nevertheless going to do so." If any of these factors is missing – if there is only one witness, or if the witnesses did not warn the person, or if they did not indicate the exact punishment, or if the person did not state, "I am nevertheless going to do so," or if there was a delay of any kind between his statement and the actual offense – *there is no death penalty*. (In actuality, if all the conditions are met, there is a good case to judge the perpetrator insane!) The Talmud tells us that a court which judged a single person to death in seven years (another version has "seventy years") is considered to be bloodthirsty! Oh yes, one other factor: a court that has the power to sentence a person to death consists of 23 judges. If all 23 vote for conviction, the person cannot be put to death. Only if at least one of the judges is willing to acquit him, can the majority sentence a person to death. And the logic is impeccable. In Talmudic times, the judges acted as both prosecuting and defense counsel, in that they were charged with asking all pertinent questions in an effort to ascertain the truth. Now, the Talmud believes that if *all* the judges voted in favor of conviction, it meant that none of them had acted in the defense of the suspect, and thus he had been, as it were, unjustly convicted, without a defense counsel!

Question How about "an eye for an eye."

Answer Here too, the Torah law indicates clearly that the words cannot be taken literally. After all, the Talmud asks, how can we possibly guarantee, in taking out the guilty party's eye, that he will suffer no more than did the victim? Can we be sure that there will be no complications beyond those caused the victim? All in all, then, as the Talmud makes clear, the words simply imply that the *value* of an eye must be paid for damaging another person's eye.

Question What are the main branches of Judaism, and what are the differences between them?

Answer To answer this question, we can look at the American Jewish scene, for two reasons: a) The United States has the largest population of Jews in the world, and b) all the trends except Orthodoxy either began or developed in that country. A short history lesson will also help us answer this question.

In the beginning, there was Orthodoxy. Of course it was not called that. Being the only type of Judaism, it was called, understandably, "Judaism." Until the early 1800s, everyone was Orthodox, in the sense it is understood today. There was a general consensus on the divinity of the Bible and the need to observe all the commandments. There are those who go so far as to claim that a Polish Jew transplanted in the Moroccan *mellah* (as the ghetto there was called), would feel quite at home.

Then, following the French Revolution and the Napoleonic era, an upheaval began in the Jewish world, at first in Germany and then later in other European states and eventually the United States. There were those who began questioning the basic premises of the Judaism with which they had grown up. But they went further. They began modifying religious ceremonial and practice. At first, the modifications were minor, but eventually a new movement emerged, known variously as "Progressive," "Liberal" or "Reform" Judaism.

Reform Judaism, which at the end of the 19th century was predominant in the United States, began with the premise that the Bible is not divine. From this, it followed that a Jew may select the rituals he wishes to adopt. The stress was laid on the ethical character of the religion, while the practical commandments were generally ignored or allowed to lapse. The changes that were made were often far-reaching, including the transfer of the Sabbath prayer services from Saturday to Sunday.

The last decades of the 19th century were marked by a great influx of East European Jews to the United States, especially from Russia. These Jews, who had generally come from traditional homes, might abandon much of the ritual, but they nevertheless felt uncomfortable about Judaism as represented by the Reform.

At first, the more liberal elements of this East European influx worked together with the Reformers, and a non-denominational school was even established jointly by the groups to train rabbis that could better serve the needs of American Jewry. But there were clear sources of friction between the more traditional and the more radical groups who had banded together in this rabbinic school. This disquiet came to a head at the first graduation ceremony of the rabbinical school. At the graduation dinner, shrimp, a notoriously non-kosher fish, was served. The more conservative wing of the school and its supporters stormed out, and formed what later became the Conservative movement.

We know that Orthodoxy accepts the divinity of the Bible and Reform rejects it. Where, then does Conservatism stand? The answer to that question is very difficult, because the Conservative movement includes people with views more traditional than some Orthodox rabbis, and others with views as radical as those of many Reform rabbis. Officially, though, the Conservative movement views itself as accepting the divinity of the Bible and the basic authority of the *halakhah* and, accordingly, regards itself as an heir (some of its adherents would even say the only true heir) to the development of Jewish law throughout the ages. Where it differs with Orthodoxy is that it is willing to accept many more factors, such as sociological trends, in arriving at decisions on Jewish practice and observance. As an example, the Conservative movement has permitted Jews to drive to the synagogue on the Sabbath, seeing the need for synagogue attendance as overriding the prohibition of driving. The Orthodox, on the other hand, who regard driving on the Sabbath as a violation of the Biblical commandment not to make a fire on the Sabbath (by igniting the gasoline), cannot find any justification for such a practice.

But there is one more stream in Judaism – Reconstructionism, an offshoot of the Conservative movement. This is by far the youngest stream, having developed primarily in the last half-century under the direction of Mordechai Kaplan. Reconstructionism begins with one premise that effectively separates it from all the rest – it does not believe in God in the accepted sense. Instead, it believes that the universe as a whole has a tendency toward good – almost a type of "pantheism." Opponents of the movement have claimed that its slogan should be, "There is no God, and Mordechai Kaplan is His prophet." In essence, though, Reconstructionism sees Judaism as an evolving civilization, and sees all aspects of the Jewish experience – Jewish law, the Jewish diet, song, dance, etc. – as part of that civilization. Thus, attempts to foster any of these "folkways" are helping to maintain this civilization.

Question   If there have always been disputes among rabbis about interpretation of the law, why are the Orthodox rabbis not willing to acknowledge the rulings of the Conservative and Reform rabbinates?

Answer   Although all of Jewish law involves thousands upon thousands of disputes and disagreements and different, sometimes opposing, rulings, those involved in this dynamic process – one which continues to our day – have always had one thing in common: They all accepted certain basic fundamentals, as, for example, the divine origin of both the written Torah and the oral tradition. As long as a qualified and knowledgeable person works within the parameters of the law, any conclusion he reaches is considered to be a Torah ruling. Unfortunately, the Reform movement, and many members of the Conservative movement, deny the basic verities that Orthodoxy feels are divine. As a result, Orthodoxy feels that the rulings of the other movements are not merely differences of opinion within the same basic guidelines, but relate to entirely different sets of guidelines.

Question What are Ashkenazic Jews? Sephardic Jews?

Answer As Jews spread throughout the world, two major streams of practices and customs were evident. On the one hand, there were the Jews of Germany (in Hebrew, *Ashkenaz*), who later spread throughout Eastern and Western Europe. On the other hand, there were the Jews of Spain (*Sepharad* in Hebrew).

The year 1492, a date known by every American school child as the year Columbus discovered America, had a very different meaning for the Jews of Spain, for it was in that year that Spain banished all the Jews who would not convert to Christianity from its territory, forcing countless thousands – the number has been estimated to be 100,000 – into exile. In a desperate search for a more hospitable climate, Spanish Jews reached places such as Turkey, the Near East, and Northern Africa, and joined the existing Jewish communities there. In the course of time the descendants of the Spanish Jews were assimilated into the local Jewish communities who adopted many of the rites and customs of the Spanish Jews.

The two streams – one might almost refer to them as different cultures in many ways – showed marked differences, in Jewish practice, custom, prayer, and Hebrew pronunciation, etc. Some of these differences were no doubt traceable to the environments in which the groups lived. Sephardic religious practice, which is in many ways a more liberal one than the Ashkenazic practice, may have resulted partially from the open society in which the Sephardic Jews lived – at least this is the view of some scholars. There is no doubt that the differences in Hebrew pronunciation were to some extent due to the phonetic influence of the languages of the countries in which the Jews lived.

The Talmud records that there were numerous differences in ritual between those Jews who lived in Judah and those who lived in Galilee. There have been hypotheses that the differences between the Ashkenazic and Sephardic Jews may ultimately trace back to that division.

Today, probably 3/4 of all Jews are Ashkenazic. This includes the vast majority of Jews in the western world (France is an exception, for, following the attainment of independence in North Africa, many Sephardic Jews – possibly in the hundreds of thousands – opted to move to France from the newly independent North African Arab states). In Israel, which is of course a melting pot, somewhat more than a half of the Jewish population is of Sephardic origin, having arrived from countries such as Morocco, Iraq, Iran, Syria, Egypt, and Soviet Georgia. As over 20% of all Israeli marriages are of "mixed" Ashkenazic-Sephardic couples, there is reason to believe that the distinction between the two communities may well disappear in Israel within a generation or two.

Question Do all Jews fit into these two categories?

Answer Actually, no. Although most Jews throughout the world are descended from these two groups, there is at least one other distinct category, that of the Yemenite Jews.

Question What, then, is the background of the Yemenite Jews?

Answer According to the Yemenite Jewish tradition, the Jews arrived in Yemen already at the time of King Solomon, or about 3,000 years ago. While that obviously cannot be proven, there is no doubt that the Yemenite Jewish community dates back for thousands of years. As the country was quite isolated, Yemenite Jews are considered by many to have maintained their original characteristics with relatively little change throughout this time.

Question How is this manifested?

Answer As an example, the Yemenite Jews have their own distinctive pronunciation of Hebrew. In fact it is so distinct that an untrained ear – even of a person who speaks Hebrew fluently – may find it difficult to follow the Yemenite prayers. (In the case of Ashkenazim and Sephardim, although there are major differences of pronunciation, they are generally intelligible to one another.) What is interesting, though, is the Yemenite differentiation between certain consonants, a differentiation which has been lost by the other Jews. For example, it is commonly accepted by grammarians that there are six letters – *bet*, *gimmel*, *daled*, *kaf*, *peh* and *tav* – that have two pronunciations, one when the letter appears alone, and a different one when it appears with a dot in it. The *Ashkenazim* and *Sephardim* only indicate three or four differences of the possible six, whereas the Yemenite pronunciation has all six. Thus, the Yemenite has a *gimmel* and a *jimmel*, a *daled* and a *thaled*. The Yemenites also differentiate between various other letters that others pronounce the same way. Thus, their pronunciation has different sounds for the *samekh* and the *sin*, the *kuf* and the *kaf*, the *tet* and the *tav*. An advantage of this pronunciation, of course, is that one is less likely to make spelling mistakes when each letter has its own distinct sound.

Question What customs do the Yemenites follow?

Answer There are numerous customs that Yemenites have that are entirely their own; in fact, even different towns would have their own customs. That, of course, is not surprising when one considers how long the Jews may have lived in a given place. On the other hand, the Yemenite practice and custom was greatly influenced by Maimonides, whom they considered as their mentor. In fact it was Maimonides that wrote the Jews of Yemenite a famous epistle at a time of forced conversion to Islam, offering them solace and encouragement. As Maimonides was a *Sephardi*, there is a great deal in the Yemenite practice that is similar to, or identical with, the Sephardic practice. As an interesting sidelight, we should note that so great was the veneration of the Yemenite Jews for Maimonides, that during his lifetime they added a number of words to their *Kaddish* prayer, modifying it to read: "in our lives and in our days and in the life of our teacher Moses [Maimonides] and in the life of all of Israel." This is possibly the only case in Jewish history where a standard prayer was modified in such a way. It is not surprising, then, that the Yemenite Jews considers Maimonides' *Mishneh Torah* as the most decisive Jewish code, and as binding on them.

Question What is Yiddish?

Answer Yiddish is a language derived from medieval German, with the addition of various Hebrew words and phrases. As Yiddish spread throughout the world, it adapted to the language of the majority, both in terms of pronunciation and the addition of words. Yiddish is written phonetically in Hebrew letters, although it uses various letters or letter combinations to replace the Hebrew vowel points. Words which are derived from Hebrew are generally written in accordance with the Hebrew spelling rather the phonetic Yiddish spelling. In an attempt to divorce Yiddish from its Hebrew origins, the Jewish communists in the Soviet Union adopted a new spelling system, which spelled even words of Hebrew origin phonetically, and published books and magazines using this "reformed" spelling. This experiment was a failure. While there were 11,000,000 native Yiddish speakers in the before World War II, the Holocaust and the acculturation of Jews throughout the world in the period since that time has decreased the number drastically. There are nevertheless signs of revival of interest in Yiddish throughout the world, and it has become a popular college course in many areas.

Question What is Ladino?

Answer Just as Yiddish developed as a language among Jews living in countries where German was the language in general use, Ladino developed as a Jewish language among those Jews living in Spanish-speaking countries. Ladino, then, is a language derived from Spanish, but with an admixture of Hebrew words. To this day it is used by some of the members of the older generation of Sephardic Jews, and Israel radio has a daily news service in this language.

Question Who are the *Mitnagdim* and the *Hasidim*?

Answer Until the mid-1700s, all Ashkenazic Jews, regardless of where they lived, had a common tradition, prayer version and basically the same customs. The rabbis of the time laid great stress on the importance of Torah study, deeming it as the highest of values. This was also a specially trying time for Jews throughout the world, with city after city, country after country oppressing them. Many of the common folk, unable to study the holy books in depth and faced by their bleak lives, drifted deeper and deeper into despair.

It was at this time that there came on the scene Rabbi Israel Baal Shem Tov ("Israel of the Good Name"), who is also sometimes known by his Hebrew acronym as the Besht. The Besht preached a new doctrine: that there are different ways to approach God, and that studying the holy books is only one of these. Further, the Besht preached the importance of serving God in joy. His views soon spread like wildfire among the Jews of Eastern Europe. Those who adhered to this belief named themselves the *Hasidim* – the "pious ones" – while they named their opponents, i.e., those who still maintained the traditional beliefs, as *Mitnagdim* – "opponents." And those names have stuck to this day. Ironic as it sounds, those of the original view are known as "opponents," while those who adopted the almost revolutionary view are known as "the pious ones."

This argument had many ramifications. The *Hasidim*, for example, stressed content rather than form. Thus they might delay their prayers beyond the halakhically approved time in order to pray with greater devotion at a later time. The *Mitnagdim*, to whom halakhah is inviolate, of course regarded such deviations as no less than heresy. Thus the stage was set for a deep-seated enmity between the two groups, which has lasted almost to our day – and, in fact, is to a large extent responsible for the break-up of one of the ultra-Orthodox parties in Israel into two separate parties, which ran independent slates in the last Israeli elections.

Chapter Two

The Jewish Calendar

Question   What are the Biblically ordained festivals, and how many days are they celebrated?

Answer   Besides the Sabbath, there are five festivals ordained by the Torah. For reasons we will explain later, those living outside Israel are often required to keep extra days in addition to those ordained. The festival days are:

1. Rosh Hashanah – 1 Tishrei (September-October) 2 days
2. Yom Kippur – 10 Tishrei (September-October) 1 day
3. Sukkot/Shemini Atzeret – 15 Tishrei (September-October) 9 days (8 days in Israel)
4. Pesah (March-April) 8 days – 15 Nissan (7 days in Israel)
5. Shavuot – 6 Sivan (May-June) 2 days (1 day in Israel)

Question   Why is there a difference between the number of days the latter three festivals are celebrated in Israel and the number of days they are celebrated elsewhere?

Answer   In ancient times, there was no fixed calendar. Each month began with the sighting of the new moon. As the lunar cycle is of 29 1/2 days, the sighting of the new moon could only take place on the 30th night or the 31st night after the previous new moon had been observed. Now, people who had sighted the new moon would come to the Sanhedrin – the supreme rabbinic court – in Jerusalem and would testify to this effect. If the testimony of two witnesses was deemed reliable, the beginning of a new month would be proclaimed, and the festival/s of that month would be scheduled accordingly. Messengers were then sent out by the Sanhedrin throughout the Land of Israel to inform all the communities when to celebrate the festival/s of that month. A problem arose, though, for communities situated too far from Jerusalem for the messengers to arrive in time. These communities (i.e., those outside the Land of Israel) were never sure as to which day had been proclaimed the first of the month. As a result, they kept an additional day for each festival. Of course, nowadays we have a standard calendar, but the custom of an added day for the different festivals in communities outside the Land of Israel has remained in effect to this day.

Question Why then is there no difference between the number of days Rosh Hashanah and Yom Kippur are observed in Israel and elsewhere?

Answer According to the Torah, Rosh Hashanah is only one day. As it occurs on the first day of the month of Tishrei, the day that the new moon was sighted, even the Jews in the Land of Israel were unable to find out in time when the new month had been proclaimed, so they too kept two days. As to Yom Kippur, where those outside Israel should in theory have kept two days, the rabbis felt it was too difficult to expect people to fast for two days in a row (although there have been cases of extremely pious Jews who would do so).

Question Why do Jewish holidays occur on different calendar dates each year?

Answer Unlike the standard calendar in use throughout the western world, which is bàsed purely on the solar cycle of a 365 day year, the Jewish calendar is based on both the solar and lunar (moon) cycles. The Jewish month begins with the new moon, and ends when the moon cycle terminates. The lunar cycle is about 29 1/2 days, so – with rare exceptions – the Jewish months alternate between 29 days and 30 days in length. A Jewish year consists of 12 months, but if we multiply this by the average of 29 1/2 days per month, we get 354 days, or 11 days less than a solar year of 365 days. In order to ensure that the solar and lunar years are synchronized, Judaism adds a full month every few years. In the 19 year cycle that is used, there are 7 leap months, so that leap years occur every two or three years, based on the year of the cycle. The extra month is added after the month of Adar, and is known as Adar II or Adar Bet. Now, as the Jewish year consists of either 353-355 days in a standard year and 383-385 days in a leap year, we can understand that any given Jewish date will come out on different calendar dates in any two consecutive years – either about 11 days earlier than the previous year, or about 20 days later (if it was a Jewish leap year). Every 19 years, the two dates will coincide (if there was a secular leap day – February 29 – the two may be one day apart). What is always true with the Jewish calendar is that festivals which occur on the 15th day of a Hebrew month will take place at full moon.

We should also point out that, had the Jewish calendar only been based on the lunar year of 12 lunar months, without the added leap months, the Jewish calendar would have been like the Muslim one, where there is a net difference of 11 days each year as compared to the solar year. Thus, in the Muslim calendar, a given festival may occur in any season of the year, and Ramadan, the month-long fast, may occur in the middle of the winter – or in the middle of the summer.

Question What system was used for leap years before the current Jewish calendar went into effect?

Answer As prescribed by Torah law, the highest court in the Land of Israel was the one to determine when each new month began. (As we pointed out in the previous answer, the lunar cycle is 29 1/2 days, so the new moon might appear on either the 30th or the 31st night after the last new moon.) Now, a 12 month lunar year would mean a loss of 11 days yearly. As the Torah specifies that Passover must occur in the spring, the Sages would go out into the fields each year, some time before the spring, and if the trees had not blossomed by a certain date they would declare the year a leap year, thus adding an extra month to the year and ensuring that Passover would occur in the spring.

Question What is Rosh Hodesh?

Answer The words Rosh Hodesh simply mean "the head (i.e., beginning) of the month," and refer to the beginning of each new month. Rosh Hodesh is considered to be a minor festival, with certain modifications in the daily prayer service and grace after meals to indicate this. As we noted above, a Jewish month may be either 29 or 30 days long. Whenever a month is 29 days long, the following day – the first of the new month – is celebrated as Rosh Hodesh. When a month is 30 days long, two consecutive days are celebrated as Rosh Hodesh: the last (30th) day of the previous month, and the first day of the present month.

Question What is a day by Jewish law?

Answer According to Judaism, the day begins when night falls and continues until the following night. Evidence for this division can be seen from the very beginning of the Bible: "It was evening and it was morning – the first day." This is the time schedule followed for such matters as the observance of the Sabbath and the festivals. As it is unclear whether twilight is part of the previous day or of the following night, Jewish law requires a person to adopt the more stringent approach either way. This means that one must begin observing the Sabbath or festival before twilight (i.e., before sunset), but must observe it until the end of the following sunset (i.e., after nightfall).

Question What is the smallest unit of time in the Jewish calendar?

Answer While the Jewish calendar also divides the day into 24 hours, with 60 minutes to each hour, the minute is not divided into 60 seconds but into 18 *halakim* ("parts"), with each *helek* the equivalent of 3 1/3 seconds. Practically speaking, this division is of almost no significance. In fact the only time it is used at all is in those synagogues which have the custom, on the Sabbath before Rosh Hodesh, of announcing the exact instant of the new moon. That time is always quoted in terms of hours, minutes and *halakim*.

Chapter Three

Prayer

Question What purpose do we serve when we pray? After all, does God need us to praise Him?

Answer This question implies a basic supposition – that one prays primarily because of the effect one's prayer has on God. Many Jewish thinkers, though, make it clear that prayer is meant to have an effect on man, rather than on God. By praying, a person must contend with the fact that there is a Supreme Being above him. That awareness should cause him to improve his ways, and that, in turn, will affect God's relationship to the person. A great 19th century Jewish thinker, Rabbi Samson Raphael Hirsch, noted that the word *tefillah*, the Hebrew for prayer, is derived from the root, *PLL*, which implies judgment. Thus, when a person prays, he must, as it were, step aside and look at himself objectively, to see where he has come from and where he is headed.

Question Pious Jews attend the synagogue twice daily. How many times a day is a Jew required to pray?

Answer In reality, on each weekday, there are three prayers, in the morning, afternoon and evening. For convenience, the prayer schedule is generally arranged so that the afternoon prayer is said toward the very end of the afternoon, and the evening prayer at the very beginning of the evening. This way, the latter two prayers are combined. On Sabbaths and festivals, an additional prayer is added, and this follows the morning service. On Yom Kippur, as the sun is about to set and the day to end, a fifth prayer is added, giving the person one last chance to pray to God on this solemn day.

Question What are the names of these prayers, and where are these names derived from?

Answer Of the five different kinds of services, three derive their names from the sacrifices which were brought in the Temple in Jerusalem, for, as the Sages tell us, once the Temple was destroyed, the prayers were instituted to replace the sacrifices. Thus the morning prayer is known as *Shaharit* and the afternoon prayer as *Minhah*, these being the names of the sacrifices brought in the morning and the evening. The additional prayer on Sabbaths and festivals is known as *Musaf*, which in Hebrew means "additional," and the prayer is meant to be the counterpart of the additional sacrifices which were brought on these special days. The evening prayer is known as *Ma'ariv* or *Aravit*, from the Hebrew root *ERV*, which means the evening. It is not the counterpart of any sacrifice, because sacrifices were not brought at night. Finally, the prayer added at the very end of Yom Kippur is called *Ne'ilah*, implying the locking of the gates, as the festival draws to a close, and the last chance to pray for the coming year comes to an end.

Question   How does one define "morning," "afternoon" and "evening" in terms of the prayers?

Answer   The Jewish "clock" is oriented entirely to the sun. It too has a 24 hour day, but its "hours" are radically different from the standard clock hour to which we are accustomed. For ritual purposes, each day – and the day begins at sunrise and ends at sunset – is divided up into what one may refer to as 12 "relative hours." Of course in the winter these "hours" may be 50 minutes each or less, while in the summer they may be more than 70 minutes long. The night – from sunset to sunrise – is also divided up into twelve "relative hours." Based on the above, the morning prayer may be said from sunrise until 4 "relative hours" (1/3 of the daylight) have passed, although one section of the service, the reading of the *Shema* portion, must be completed within the first three "relative hours." The afternoon service can be said no earlier than half an hour after mid-day (the mid-point between sunrise and sunset), and no later than sunset. As to the evening prayer, it should ideally not be said earlier than nightfall, and one should not pray it later than midnight (the halfway point between sunset and sunrise).

Question   The Jewish tradition requires a quorum of ten men, known as a *minyan* for communal prayers. What is the origin of that requirement?

Answer   The source for this number is a most unlikely one. When Moses sent twelve spies to the Land of Canaan to spy out the land, all but two – Joshua and Caleb – came back with a report which plunged the Israelites into gloom and depression. When the ten spies who had distorted the truth were to be punished for their actions, we are told that God exclaimed, "How long shall I bear with this evil congregation, which murmur against me?" (Num.

14:27). From this, we deduce that a "congregation" consists of ten men, just as was the case with the "congregation" of the ten spies.

Question Why do Jews face east when praying?

Answer Jewish law does not refer to east as such. Instead, it specifies that one should pray toward Jerusalem, the place where the holy Temple once stood. In actual fact, the majority of Jews, who lived in Europe, did indeed face east, but those in countries east of the Land of Israel, such as Iran or Turkey, faced west. Jewish law specifies further that a person praying in Jerusalem must face the place where the Temple once stood. Incidentally, as a simple rule of thumb, when flying to Israel one should face the front of the plane when praying; and when flying from Israel one should face the rear.

Question A person who visits the synagogue will notice that while most prayers are recited while sitting, some of them are said while standing. For some of the standing prayers, one must even stand at attention, with both feet together. Why these variations?

Answer Generally, one stands for the more important parts of the prayer, as a sign of respect. Thus, for example, whenever the ark with the Torah scrolls is open, or the Torah scrolls are being carried, one stands up. The rule regarding the *Kaddish* states that the congregation is not required to stand up for the prayer, but is forbidden to sit down once it has started. The person reciting the *Kaddish*, of course, stands while doing so. The *Amidah*, also known as the *Shemoneh esrei*, is the central prayer of each prayer service. For it, one stands with both feet together, facing the Land of Israel. As the Sages tell us, during this prayer one emulates the angels when they praise God, for as Ezekiel describes it: "Their feet were straight feet" (Ezek. 1:7).

Question It is quite a common sight to see Jews swaying as they recite their prayers. Is there any ritual significance in this action?

Answer There is nothing in Jewish law which mandates swaying during one's prayers. This practice, though, is very common, and it has been surmised that the origin of the custom lies in the verse, "All my bones shall say, Lord, who is like unto You" (Ps. 35:10). By swaying, then, the entire body is engaged in the worship of God.

Question What is the *Shema*?

Answer The *Shema* is a compilation of three passages in the Torah (Deut.

6:4-9; Deut. 11:13-21; Num. 15:37-41), which are recited in both the morning and evening prayer services. Properly speaking, the *Shema* is not a prayer, but a Biblical text which the Jew is commanded to read twice daily, "when you lie down and when you rise up." The word "*Shema*" is the first word of the first passage, and is the opening word of the most solemn declaration made by the Jew: "Hear O Israel, the Lord is our God; the Lord is One." No other passage sums up the creed of the Jew in such succinct fashion, for that one verse proclaims three basic truths: 1. The existence of God; 2. His special relationship with the Jewish people; 3. The uniqueness and unity of God – the foundation of all monotheism. It was with this verse on their lips that countless Jewish martyrs met their fate – down to and including the Jews murdered by the Nazis in the gas chambers.

Question   The third paragraph of the *Shema* prayer refers to the commandment to place *tzitzit* – fringes – on every four-cornered garment. What makes this particular commandment so important that it is mentioned twice daily – in the morning *Shema* and the evening *Shema*?

Answer   Actually, this paragraph is not recited because of the commandment relating to *tzitzit*. In fact, that commandment only applies in the day time, for the Torah states, "you shall see it," from which the Sages deduce that it applies "when you can see it." The reason this paragraph was chosen was because of its concluding verses, which state that "I am the Lord your God who brought you out of the Land of Egypt." And the Torah clearly imposes a duty on Jews to remember the Exodus from Egypt, as stated in the verse, "That you remember the day you left Egypt all the days of your life" (Deut. 16:3). As quoted in the Passover *Haggadah*, the seeming redundancy of the word "all" teaches us that one must remember the Exodus both during the day and during the night. In order to fulfill this requirement, the paragraph of *tzitzit* was made part of the *Shema*, which must also be recited during the day and at night. As to why the entire paragraph, rather than its concluding passage is recited, the Talmud tells us that it is improper to quote just part of a paragraph in isolation of the rest. Thus the entire paragraph was added to the liturgy.

Question   When the cantor repeats the *Amidah* prayer and reaches the passage of *modim* ("we thank You ..."), the congregation recites a parallel passage beginning with the same words but with a different content. What is the origin of this custom?

Answer   In a number of instances, there are disputes in the Talmud regarding the content of a certain prayer passage. Often, the problem is resolved by

✦ *Prayer at the Western Wall in Jerusalem.*

assigning the different versions to different times or occasions. *Modim* is such an example, where the one version was incorporated into the *Amidah* prayer and the other was left as a reading by the congregation. A similar instance is the wording of the last blessing of the *Amidah*, where the resolution of the two versions saw one version, "*Sim shalom*," incorporated into the morning prayer service, and the other version, "*Shalom rav*," incorporated into the afternoon and evening services (according to many prayer rites). Again, there is a dispute as to the formulation of the beginning of the blessing which precedes the *Shema*, which was resolved by using "*Ahavah rabbah*" in the morning and "*Ahavat olam*" in the evening (again according to a number of rites, but not all).

Question What are the three parts into which the Jewish people is divided?

Answer The three consists of the *kohanim* – the priests, the *levi'im* – the Levites, and the *yisraelim*, or "Israelites." At the time of the formation of the Jewish people in the desert after the Exodus from Egypt, there were thirteen tribes, in that Joseph's children were divided into two tribes, Menasseh and Ephraim. After the sin of the Golden Calf, in which the *levi'im* – the Levites – were the only ones who did not participate, the Levites were assigned to work in the Sanctuary and, later, in the Temple in Jerusalem. Moses and his brother, Aaron, were of the tribe of Levi, and Aaron was appointed the High Priest, and all his male descendants are *kohanim*, or priests. For hundreds of years Jews were identified by their tribe, the identity being based on one's father rather than one's mother. In 722 B.C.E. the Kingdom of Israel fell, and with its fall the ten tribes living in it disappeared off the map, assimilated into the surrounding nations. The Kingdom of Judea, with the tribes of Judah and Benjamin, retained its Jewish identity, even after its fall in 586 B.C.E. In the turmoil following the destruction and exile, the lines between the two tribes were lost. Today, then, the *kohanim* are male descendants of Aaron, the *levi'im* are members of the Levite tribe, and the *yisraelim* are descendants of the tribes of Judah or Benjamin. Converts to Judaism are also considered to be *yisraelim*.

Question Why and when do the *kohanim* – the priests – bless the people?

Answer The Torah specifies, "They [the *kohanim*] shall place My name upon the Israelites, and I will bless them" (Num. 6:27). The exact text of this blessing is recorded in the Torah (Num. 6:24-26). Outside Israel, this blessing is given only at the additional – *musaf* – service of the three pilgrimage festivals and the High Holidays. In Israel, the *kohanim* bless the people at each morning service.

In theory, the *kohanim* should bless the people daily, as they did in the Temple in Jerusalem. For the *kohanim* to do so, there are a number of requirements, one of these being that the *kohanim* be joyful and not depressed. The rabbis reasoned that only when in living in the Land of Israel is a Jew truly happy. Outside the Land of Israel, the only true happiness a Jew has is on the festivals. Thus, in synagogues outside Israel the *kohanim* only bless the people on the festivals. This, as countless other laws and customs, points to the centrality of the Land of Israel and its idealization in Jewish thought and belief.

Question When the *kohanim* – the priests – bless the people, they customarily cover their heads and hands with a *tallit*. Why?

Answer By Jewish tradition, when the *kohanim* bless the people, God's Divine Presence, the *Shekhinah*, rests on their hands. In order to "shield" the congregation from this splendor, the *kohanim* cover their hands with a *tallit*. Incidentally, by Jewish law the *kohanim* are required to keep their eyes closed throughout the priestly blessing, for the same reason.

Question Have the censorship laws of various countries ever affected the classical Jewish texts?

Answer Surprising at it may appear to us living in a free society, for hundreds of years all Jewish writings, including the Talmud, had to be approved by the local censors before they could be printed. The local censor was often a Jew who had converted to Christianity, because he would be the only one with sufficient knowledge of the classic Jewish texts to be able to check the material. On the whole, the censors made a point of either removing or modifying any text which could be taken as a reference to Christianity. One example is a passage in the Talmud which – seemingly out of the blue – refers to an Egyptian. The passage seemed completely out of place, until it was noticed that the Hebrew word for "Egyptian" is *Mitzri*, and the Hebrew word *Notzri* means "Nazarene." Reading the text as *Notzri* – as it must have been before the censor modified it – placed the entire paragraph in perfectly logical context. The use of censorship, though, may have been self-defeating. There is a little volume which contains all the expurgated parts of the Talmud, entitled *Hesronot Ha'shas*, or "The Missing Parts of the Talmud." Apocryphally, this little book survived because a certain person who had converted to Christianity, for the material benefits rather than ideologically, wanted to preserve the texts for future generation, so he compiled the list and had it circulated to other censors, thus ensuring that the expurgated parts would not be lost or forgotten!

Question How about the prayers? Were they affected by censorship?

Answer Indeed they were. The *Alenu* prayer, which is said at the conclusion of each synagogue service, had a line cut out, one that to this day most printed editions omit. The passage involved, including the omission in italics, reads as follows: "... who has not made our portion as theirs, and our fate as all of their multitudes, *for they bow down to nothingness and emptiness, and prostrate themselves before a god who cannot help*, while we bow down and prostate ourselves before the King, King of kings ..." The fact that this was written as a reference to the pagans and not Christians did not, however, prevent the Christian censors from removing it from the prayer book.

Question In Judaism, the prayers are generally recited by each person individually, rather than in unison. Why then are the prayers couched in plural form?

Answer One of the basic principles of Judaism is that "all Jews are responsible for one another." The individual Jew cannot ignore the sins of another Jew, just as one's hand cannot ignore gangrene that has set in on one's foot. Thus, when praying, Jews beseech God for all of their brethren. By the same token, when the alphabetical confession prayer is recited, it is couched in the plural: *Ashamnu, bagadnu, gazalnu* – "We have sinned, we have deceived, we have stolen." This also allows for the individual Jew to confess to sins he has not committed, for he bears a certain responsibility for the sins of his fellow Jews who did commit those sins. There are a few prayers that are phrased in the singular, such as the supplication at the end of the *Amidah* prayer, *Elohai, netzor*, "God, guard my tongue from evil ...," that particular formula having been the prayer of one of the Talmudic Sages.

Question What is the origin of the popular hymn *Yigdal*, recited at the end of the Friday night or Saturday morning service in many congregations?

Answer *Yigdal*, while seemingly a hymn of praise and no more, consists of thirteen lines, each of which is a poetic rendition of one of the Thirteen Principles of the Faith that Moses Maimonides (1135-1204) laid down as a basic credo for all Jews. The principles may be found in Chapter 1, above.

Question Why do men recite a special blessing in the morning, thanking God for "not having created me a woman"?

Answer Various answers to this question have been given by different thinkers. It has been suggested that the blessing is based on the fact that women are exempt from many of the commandments which men are required to fulfill. Thus men have greater opportunities to perform commandments. Another view is that this may be a reflection of the fact that, until comparatively recently, women had a high risk of dying of the complications of childbirth. Thus men generally lived longer than women. Interestingly, in the 13th century, a blessing was devised to be said by women, the text being "Blessed are You, O Lord, King of the universe, who has created me in accordance with His will."

Various non-Orthodox bodies have instituted changes in the basic text of the blessing for men, adopting wording which was sexually neutral, so that both men and women can recite the same blessings.

Question In the above blessing, "Blessed are You, O Lord, King of the universe, who has created me in accordance with His will," the first words are addressed in the second person ("Blessed are You"), whereas the last words are in the third person ("in accordance with His will"). Is this not strange?

Answer If one examines all the blessings, one will find that this pattern, of beginning with the second person and ending with the third, is standard. It has been suggested that the reason for this is that when the person begins to recite the blessing he feels a certain closeness to God ("You"), then, as he ponders on God's greatness, the person must pull himself back in awe, and switches to the third person as a humble sign of respect.

Question Why are the prayers in Hebrew rather than in a language the synagogue-goer can understand?

Answer Of course, when the prayers were composed, Hebrew was the language spoken by Jews. In reality, Jewish law permits one to pray in any language. Two factors, though, have militated against the use of other languages in prayer; first, because the best translation is only an approximation of the original (an Italian proverb, based on a play of words, states that "the translator is a traitor"); and second, because this enables the Jew, wherever he is throughout the entire world, to feel at home in the synagogue.

Question Catholicism lays great stress on confession of one's sins to a priest. Is there a Jewish equivalent?

Answer Judaism certainly believes in confession, but with one major difference – to the Jew, the confession is directed to God rather than to a human intermediary. In fact, rabbinic authorities are highly critical of those who confess their sins aloud. To the Jew, confession is a necessary and integral part of repentance, for repentance consists of: 1. acknowledging that one has sinned (i.e., confession); 2. rectifying the wrong-doing if the sin was against one's fellow-man; 3. regretting one's actions; and, finally, 4. resolving not to commit that sin again. Confession is an integral part of the High Holiday ritual, especially on Yom Kippur. Various prayer rites, in fact, include confession in the morning prayer each Monday and Thursday. Furthermore, the weekday *Amidah*, recited three times every weekday, contains a blessing which begins "Forgive us... for we have sinned...," which is also a form of confession.

Question Jewish prayer includes a plea for rain between Passover (March-April) and Sukkot (September-October). Why should a Jew living in a country in which this may be the dry season pray for rain at that time?

Answer Throughout Jewish history, the Land of Israel has been the focus of all Jewish hopes and aspirations. Thus, when the Jew prays for rain, he prays for it in the Land of Israel. And indeed, in Israel rain is almost unknown in the summer. On the other hand, if a Jew lives in a country which is suffering from drought, there are special communal prayers for that misfortune. In fact, if the drought is severe enough, the entire community might even be called upon to fast and pray to God for rain.

Question Does the Bible play any part in the prayer service?

Answer In addition to the numerous quotes and paraphrases of Biblical texts in the prayers themselves, especially from Psalms, there are specific times when Biblical passages are read.

Question What is read, and when?

Answer The primary source for Biblical readings is the Torah or the Pentateuch. Already in the Torah do we find references of Moses instituting such a reading. Portions of the Torah are read at the Sabbath morning and afternoon services, the Monday and Thursday morning services, the morning service of all Biblically ordained festivals (the pilgrimage festivals, the High Holydays, the New Moon), fast days, Purim and Hanukkah. On fast days, there is an additional reading at the afternoon service.

Question Could you be a little more specific as to what is read each time?

Answer On the Biblically ordained festivals, the passages that are read from the Torah all deal with the festivals themselves. On fast days, the passage deals with Moses smashing the first tablets and his subsequent pleas to God to forgive the Jewish people. On Purim, the Torah reading concerns Amalek, the king who attacked the Jewish people as they left Egypt, for he is considered to have been the ancestor of Haman, the arch-villain of Purim. On Hanukkah, which is the festival which celebrates the Jews' victory over Antiochus and their rededication of the Temple, the passages chosen relate to Moses' dedication of the Sanctuary in the desert. Each day the Hanukkah Torah reading describes the gifts brought by the leader of one of the tribes. In other words, the reading on the first day of Hanukkah is that of the first day of the consecration of the Sanctuary, and so on, until the last day, which describes the last five days of the consecration. There are minor differences in the Hanukkah Torah reading between Israel and elsewhere.

Question Haven't you left out the reading on the Sabbaths, Mondays and Thursdays?

Answer Indeed I have, because these readings require a certain amount of introductory material. Unlike all the readings listed above, where each specific day has its own reading, the reading at the Sabbath morning service is sequential. Beginning with the Sabbath after Simhat Torah (the very last day of the Sukkot festive season), at which the very first chapters of Genesis are read, each subsequent Sabbath another portion is read, so that by the time the following Simhat Torah comes around the entire Torah has been read from the beginning to the end. Each weekly portion is known as a *sidrah* (or, alternately, a *parashah*). As to the Sabbath afternoon service and the Monday and Thursday morning services, a small section of the following week's *sidrah* is read, a "coming attraction," as it were of the next Sabbath morning's reading.

Question How many *sidrot* (plural of *sidrah*) are there?

Answer Based on a cycle which completes the reading of the entire Torah in a year, there are 54 *sidrot*. The Jewish year can have as few as 50 Sabbaths or as many as 54 (the latter in a leap year, where a month is added). In order to complete the cycle within the year, there are certain Sabbaths where two *sidrot* are read. The actual reading on each individual Sabbath is based on a comprehensive overall calendar.

We should also note here that the practice of reading the entire Torah over a year, which is the universal practice among Orthodox congregations today, is based on the custom that was prevalent in Babylon. In Eretz Israel, the custom was to complete the entire Torah reading over a three year or even a three and a half year period. The individual weekly readings were known as *sedarim*.

Question I can understand all the Torah readings on the festivals, Sabbaths and fast days, for these are all special days. But why the Torah reading on Mondays and Thursdays?

Answer Firstly, we should note that in ancient times these two were the market days, when farmers from the surrounding area would come to the nearest town with their wares. Thus it was on these days that everyone was able to attend the synagogue morning prayer service. It was for this reason that Ezra the Scribe instituted the Torah reading at the morning services of these days.

A beautiful *aggadah* gives us a remarkable explanation for the Torah reading in the middle of the week. The Torah, the *aggadah* tells us, is often compared to water – the "water of life," as it were. Now, we are told, just like a person cannot survive physically for three days without water, he cannot survive spiritually if he goes for three days without hearing the Torah. Thus, by having a Torah reading on Monday and Thursday in addition to that on the Sabbath, a person who attends the synagogue regularly will never go for three days without hearing the Torah.

Question What is an *aliyah*?

Answer Each Torah reading is divided into a number of portions, ranging from three (on a weekday morning, for example) to seven at the Sabbath morning service. For each portion, which is read by the *ba'al kriyah* – reader – a member of the congregation is honored by being called to recite blessings both before and after the reading of that particular section. A person who is so honored is said to have received an *aliyah*. The word itself means an "ascent," in that the person has ascended to the Torah reading. Actually, until the Middle Ages, it was the custom for every person who was called up to read his Torah portion himself. Those unable to do so would have the portion read for them by another person. In order not to shame those people who are unable to read the Torah portion themselves, the custom gradually evolved that a single reader reads the Torah for all those called up. One exception to this custom is the Yemenite Jewish community, in which, to this day, the person called up reads his own portion.

Question Who may be called up for an *aliyah*?

Answer Jewish law endows the *kohanim* – the priests, or those descended from Aaron, the first high priest – with a certain sanctity. Accordingly, the first person called up is a *kohen*. The second *aliyah* is reserved for a Levite – a member of the tribe of Levi. The other *aliyot* (plural of *aliyah*) are given out to members of the congregation who are neither *kohanim* nor Levites. (One should note that the way a person knows if he is a *kohen* or a Levite is by family tradition, the descent always following patrilineal lines, from father to son. People whose family tradition does not list them as belonging to either of these groups, are by default in the third category, "Israelites." The vast majority of Jews belong to this third category.)

Question Are there any limitations as to who may receive an *aliyah*?

Answer In general, *aliyot* are only given to male Jews who are thirteen years or older. While Jewish law as such does not prohibit a woman from receiving an *aliyah*, it has been standard practice for centuries for the *aliyot* to be given only to men. The reason why women are not given *aliyot*, according to the sources, is that such an action would be "unseemly." Indeed, if we consider that by Jewish law men and women are required to sit separately during prayers with a clear physical barrier between them, and that the reading of the Torah must take place in the men's section, we may be able to understand that it would be unseemly for a woman to be called up into the men's section in such circumstances. While it is true that the Reform movement and many Conservative congregations have accepted the principle of giving women *aliyot*, Orthodoxy cannot, on purely religious grounds, condone the practice.

Question What criteria are used in deciding who is called up for an *aliyah*?

Answer In the final analysis, those in charge make their decision based on whatever criteria they think are applicable. There are, nevertheless, specific individuals who are entitled to receive an *aliyah*, and those in charge of allocating *aliyot* must take these people into account. For example, a boy who has just turned thirteen is entitled to an *aliyah*, as is a groom (in the Ashkenazic rite on the Sabbath before his wedding and in the Sephardic rite on the Sabbath after the wedding). Of course, who is given which *aliyah* is discretionary (except for the first two, which, as we mentioned, are reserved for a *kohen* and a Levite respectively). Some *aliyot*, though, have traditionally been considered more "honored" than others. The third aliyah, known as *shlishi*, is one of these, and is generally reserved for one of the more important members of the congregation. The sixth *aliyah* – *shishi* – is also in that category, especially among the *hasidim*. The *aliyah* that completes the reading of one of the five books of the Torah is considered to be an especially important one. Of course, we should stress that such considerations are all artificial, for Jewish law considers all verses as equally holy. Thus, one has no right to even differentiate between "You must love your neighbor as yourself" (Lev. 19:18) and "The sister of Tubal Cain was Na'amah" (Gen. 4:22).

Question Are there any special requirements for the Torah reading?

Answer There are indeed two basic requirements: 1. There must be a quorum of ten adult males present, and 2. the reading must take place from a totally accurate hand-written Torah scroll. (If only a single error is found in a single letter, the scroll cannot be used until the error is corrected.)

Question Does one require any special skill to read the Torah?

Answer A great deal of skill and practice is indeed required, because the Torah scroll lacks much of what one might consider the "amenities" of a printed text, such as vowel points, punctuation, or cantillation signs. The reader, in essence, has to supply all of these himself, which means that he has to memorize all three elements. As the average *sidrah* contains about 100 verses, the reader has to spend quite a few hours preparing himself before the Sabbath Torah reading. (The other Torah readings are generally considerably shorter; the Sabbath afternoon and Monday and Thursday morning readings, for example, consist of only the first portion of the seven that will be read the following Sabbath, divided up among a *kohen*, a Levite and an Israelite.)

Question After each person's *aliyah*, the *gabbai* – synagogue warden – seems to offer some type of blessing. What is this all about?

Answer Here we are referring to what is known as the *mi she-berakh* – literally "He who blessed," called thus because they are the first two words of the text. In this blessing, the *gabbai* asks that God, who blessed our forefathers, should also bless the person who just received the *aliyah*. In many synagogues, this blessing is linked to a further one, in which God's blessing is invoked because "the person who just received the *aliyah* has pledged a certain amount – sometimes specified, sometimes unspecified (such as, "a gift") to the synagogue." In this second blessing, the person will often ask for specific people, whose Hebrew names he mentions, to be included. This means the *gabbai* has to list all these names as well. If this is carried to absurd lengths, the duration of the synagogue service can become seriously extended, to the annoyance of all those who did not receive *aliyot*. I well remember visiting a synagogue in my youth where an ordinance announced that "*Mi she-berakhs* will be limited to five names." The background for this rule was simple: before that, each person called up had asked to have every member of the synagogue included by name. Incidentally, the notice was only partially successful. The Sabbath I was there, I found one man including no less than fourteen names!

Question Are there any rules regarding the congregation's behavior during the Torah reading?

Answer Indeed there are. The Torah reading is no less than the word of God. As such, one is forbidden to do anything else while the Torah is being read. Conversation is, of course, utterly forbidden, for it implies nothing less than a showing of disdain for God's word. In fact one is even forbidden to study the Torah or any other holy work during the Torah reading. Some people have the custom of standing throughout the Torah reading, as a sign of respect. They usually sit down between *aliyot*. We should also mention another law in this regard, that where a person has been wronged and has been unable to obtain redress, he has the right to stop the Torah reading from taking place until he has obtained satisfaction or at least a guarantee that he will obtain satisfaction.

Question But isn't there any reading from the Prophets and the Hagiographa, the other two parts of the Bible?

Answer Indeed there are such readings, but not in the same way as the Torah reading, which encompasses the entire book over the course of the year. For example, after the Torah reading on Sabbath morning, those Biblically ordained festive days when work is forbidden, and the afternoon of fast days, a special portion, the *haftarah*, is read.

Question The *haftarah*? What is that?

Answer The *haftarah* is an extract from one of the Books of the Prophets, most commonly but by far not exclusively the Latter Prophets, which is read after the Torah reading on the above-mentioned days. After the prescribed number of people have been called up for *aliyot*, another person is called up for whom a generally small portion of the Torah is read (on Sabbaths, this is simply a repetition of the last few verses of the *sidrah*). This *aliyah* is known as the *maftir* – "the one who concludes" the reading, as it were. The Torah scroll is then raised for all to see and is rolled and tied up, ready to be returned to the Ark. The person who is the *maftir* recites the prescribed passage of the Prophets for that particular Sabbath. The passage is known as the *haftarah*, which, as can be seen, is related to the word *maftir*, and means "the conclusion." The origin of this additional reading from the Prophets is quite ancient, and may hark back to a time when Jews were forbidden to read the Torah in public under pain of death. The *haftarah*, then, was a passage chosen to reflect to some extent the content of what would otherwise have been the week's Torah reading.

Question Does there have to be a special reader for the *haftarah* as there is for the Torah reading?

Answer In most synagogues, the *haftarah* is read from a printed text, and all the elements missing from the Torah scroll – the vowel points, punctuation and cantillation signs – are printed in the text itself. Thus any person who knows how to read Hebrew and is familiar with the cantillation should be able to recite the *haftarah*. There are, though, certain synagogues where the *haftarah* is read from a hand-written parchment scroll, and in those cases the reader of the Torah will also read the *haftarah*.

Question In the ranking of *aliyot*, where does the maftir stand?

Answer Nowadays, the *maftir* is considered to be one of the major *aliyot*. Historically, though, the opposite was true. The *haftarah* was considered to be the least of the honors given out, and as "compensation," the *maftir* was introduced, so that even the person with the *haftarah* would have a Torah reading for himself. It just goes to show that even such a matter as the "importance" of *aliyot* is a matter of fashion.

Question Earlier, you mentioned that the Torah scroll is held up. What is the purpose of this?

Answer The purpose of this action is so that all may see the writing inside the scroll. When the Torah scroll is raised, all exclaim (using the Hebrew text, of course), "This is the Torah which Moses placed before the Children of Israel." Incidentally, the person who raises the Torah is known as the *magbi'ah* (the action is known as *hagbahah*) and the person who wraps, ties and covers the scroll is known as the *golel* (the action is known as *gelilah*). In many synagogues, *gelilah* is often given to a child. The Sephardic rite has the *hagbahah* before the Torah reading and the Ashkenazic rite has it after it.

Question Are any parts of the Hagiographa read in the synagogue service?

Answer As we mentioned, many Psalms appear in the prayers. In fact it has been estimated that a good third of the Psalms are recited on one occasion or another, such as in the daily prayers, when praying for a sick person, or at a funeral. In addition the five Books known collectively as the *megillot* – Ecclesiastes, Esther, Lamentations, Ruth, Song of Songs – are recited in many congregations on (respectively) Sukkot, Purim, Tisha be-Av, Shavuot and Passover. Now, though, I think we should move on to the question of general blessings, besides those said as part of the prayers.

Question Is it true that there is a blessing that is recited after excretion of waste?

Answer Indeed there is. After the above, Jewish law requires one to wash his hands, and then to recite the following blessing: "Blessed are You, O Lord, King of the universe, who formed man in wisdom and created within him various openings and orifices. Should one of these [that should be closed] open or should one of these [that should be open] close, one could not remain alive before You for even an instant. "Blessed are You, O Lord, who heals all flesh and performs wonders."

In essence, this remarkable blessing thanks God for enabling the most marvelous and complex of all organisms, the human body, to function without mishap. It was the existence of this blessing, in fact, that led a clergyman of another faith to convert to Judaism, as he was so taken by the fact that the Jew thanks God even for so mundane an activity.

One may also mention that the ritual washing of the hands after using the toilet, coupled with the required washing of the hands before eating a meal, resulted in Jews in the Middle Ages being less susceptible to various diseases, such as the Black Plague. Unfortunately, their neighbors, who noticed the difference in mortality between the Jews and non-Jews, often concluded that the Jews must have poisoned the wells, and that was grounds enough for many pogroms, in which Jews were killed or robbed of all their possessions.

Question Anyone visiting the vicinity of the Temple area in the Old City of Jerusalem will find there self-appointed Jewish "guards" who advise Jews not to enter the Temple Mount compound, even to pray. Why do the "guards" object to Jews setting foot on the Temple Mount?

Answer After the Jews returned from exile in the 4th century B.C.E., Ezra and Nehemiah rebuilt the Temple, which had been destroyed by Nebuchadnezzar in 586 B.C.E. At that time they consecrated the site to God. The Sages in the Talmud debate whether that consecration was for all time, or whether it lapsed when the Temple was destroyed. Their conclusion is that the consecration of the land was for all time. As such, they rule that no Jew who is ritually impure – and in our days everyone is presumed to be in this category – may set foot on the Temple Mount. While the Israeli government, as a secular body, does not forbid Jews from entering the Temple Mount, there are devout Jews that regard such an action as a grave violation, and who have taken upon themselves the duty to warn Jews against entering the Mount.

Chapter Four

Ritual Objects

Question   What are *tzitzit* and when are they worn?

Answer   The word *tzitzit* means a fringe. The word refers to a four-cornered garment with fringes in each of the four corners.

The Torah commands, "Speak unto the children of Israel, and bid them make fringes on the corners of their garments throughout their generations" (Num. 15:38). As interpreted by the Oral Law, any garment which has four corners or more must have a fringe in each of its four outermost corners. A small hole is made at the corner, and four strings, made specially for the purpose, are passed through. These are then doubled over and tied together, giving eight strings at each corner. As *tzitzit* are only worn during the daytime (for the Torah stresses, "you shall see them," implying the *tzitzit* are to be worn when it is light), women are exempt. Strictly speaking, this is one of the discretionary commandments. The Torah requirement is that if a man wishes to wear a four-cornered garment, he must ensure that he has fringes in the corners, but there is nothing forcing him to wear such a garment. Jewish custom, though, dating back hundreds of years, is that men make a point of wearing a special four-cornered garment with fringes in each corner, usually under their shirt. This way, they can observe an additional commandment each day. The *tallit* which is worn in the synagogue, a rectangular piece of cloth with fringes in each corner, is also worn in fulfillment of the commandment to wear *tzitzit*.

Generally speaking, nowadays there are no men's clothes that would have four corners, but there is one exception. Many rabbis wear a long black jacket (a Prince Albert), and the split at the back of the coat, which goes up more than half the length of the fabric, might result in four corners – with all the consequences that entails. As a result, these jackets – which nowadays are custom-made – are deliberately cut with one of the two flaps at the back rounded off rather than square, so that there are only three corners to the jacket, and it thus does not require *tzitzit*.

Question What are the different ways that *tzitzit* may be worn?

Answer As we pointed out above, it has been generally accepted that all males should wear *tzitzit*, even though this is a discretionary commandment. After all, why should one forgo the opportunity of being able to observe another commandment? While there was a time when four-cornered garments were common, this has not been the case for many centuries. As a result, a special garment was designed. It consists of a large cloth rectangle in which a section is cut out, so that the rectangle may be slipped over the neck. Each corner of the rectangle then has one of the four fringes inserted. This garment is generally referred to as either *tzitzit*, *tallit katan* ("small *tallit*" – as opposed to the *tallit gadol*, the "large *tallit*," which will be described below) or *arba kanfot* (literally "four corners").

The most common way that the *tallit kattan* is worn is under the shirt, where it is generally not visible. Some men, especially those who have studied in yeshivot, will so arrange it so that at least the four fringes dangle outside the shirt. Others, particularly *hasidim*, will wear the *tallit kattan* over their shirts and under their jackets. The latter two practices are based on their interpretation of the need to "see them" (i.e., the *tzitzit*), where they take this to be a literal rather than figurative requirement.

Question What is a *tallit gadol*?

Answer While observant men generally wear a *tallit kattan*, it is also customary to wear a larger, special four-cornered garment during certain of the prayer services. The *tallit gadol* or – as it is generally known – the *tallit*, is a large cloth rectangle, into which *tzitzit* have been inserted in the corners. The cloth generally has stripes woven into it. In most instances, the stripes are either black or blue, but recent times have seen the emergence of individual, hand-woven *tallitot* (the plural of *tallit*) with stripes of numerous colors and shades. The latter have not yet gained acceptance among the general community, and are on the whole worn by those willing to act in a somewhat unconventional manner.

Who wears the *tallit* is a matter of custom among the various communities. As a general rule, the cantor wears a *tallit* for every service at which he officiates, except for the evening service, as a sign of respect for the community. There is no such requirement to wear a *tallit* for the evening service, for there is no obligation to wear *tzitzit* at night, as pointed out above.

In addition, the *tallit* is worn by the congregants for the morning service (and additional service, when there is one), but there are differences in custom as to who wears it, with three different customs: 1. All males wear it (the Sephardic custom); 2. All males of *bar mitzvah* age wear it (the German custom); 3. All married males wear it (the custom of those *Ashkenazim* not of German ancestry).

We should note that there are two types of *tallitot*: those made of wool and generally worn full-length with most of the fabric over one's back and the two front corners draped over the shoulders; and those made of silk, which are most often folded over into a narrow band and worn as a type of shawl around the neck.

We should also note that while women are exempt from placing *tzitzit* in any four-cornered garment, the relatively recent decision by the Conservative movement to accept women as rabbis laid down the proviso that those women who wish to study for the rabbinate must observe all the commandments incumbent upon males, and that includes wearing a *tallit*. Among those women who do wear *tallitot*, multi-colored ones are quite popular.

Question   The Bible (Num. 15:38) makes reference to a "blue string" within the *tzitzit* or fringes. To what does this allude?

Answer   At the time of the Torah,one of the strings of the *tzitzit* was indeed a shade of blue referred to in the Torah as *tekhelet*. This blue color, as the Talmud tells us, was meant to remind the wearer of the sky, and hence of God. The color itself was derived from a mollusc of some kind. Unfortunately, the identity of the exact mollusc involved was forgotten, and the use of the blue thread lapsed. In our days, there are hasidic sects which claim to have deduced, from the Talmudic literature, the correct source of the blue dye, and they wear *tzitzit* with such a blue thread. Most Torah scholars, though, question the authenticity of the source of this dye.

Question   What are *tefillin* and when are they worn?

Answer   The word *tefillin* is usually translated as "phylacteries," but it is doubtful that the translation will be very helpful to a person not familiar with *tefillin*. Based on the verse, "You shall bind them as a sign on your hand and as frontlets between your eyes" (Deut. 6:8), the Oral Law tells us that this refers to two small black leather boxes with leather straps through an opening in each box. The straps enable one to attach one box to the hand (generally whichever hand one does not write with) and one box to sit on the forehead. Each leather box contains parchments on which are written four paragraphs of the Torah, including the first two paragraphs of the *Shema*, a passage which is said at both the morning and evening services.

The *tefillin* are worn only on weekdays, but not on Sabbaths and festivals. The explanation for this is that the *tefillin* are a sign acknowledging our relationship with God, as stated in the Torah verse above. As the Sabbaths and festivals are signs in their own right, there is no need for an additional sign on these days.

Only males aged 13 and up must wear the *tefillin*. Women are exempt, as this law is a "time-related" one, applying only to the daytime, and as such women are exempt. There have been cases throughout history of women wearing *tefillin*, and in our times some members of feminist groups, especially among the non-Orthodox ranks, have taken to wearing *tefillin*. As is the case with the *tallit*, all women candidates studying to be rabbis at the (Conservative) Jewish Theological Seminary must obligate themselves to fulfill all "time-related" commandments, and that includes wearing *tefillin*.

Question What is the *mezuzah*?

Answer One of the external signs of a Jewish home is the small generally metal or wooden case attached to the right side of the front door. Colloquially, this case is known as a *mezuzah*, but that is incorrect. Inside the case there is a small rectangular piece of parchment, on which are hand-written two paragraphs from the Torah: Deuteronomy 6:4-9 and 11:13-21, which are also the first two paragraphs of the *Shema* passage. On the other side of the parchment are the three Hebrew letters *Shin*, *Daled* and *Yod*, which spell out one of God's names. When the parchment is rolled up, this name of God remains visible on the outside of the parchment.

Question What does the word *mezuzah* mean?

Answer In both the paragraphs contained on the scroll, there is a reference to writing "them" (which the Sages understood to mean these paragraphs) on "the doorposts of your homes and of your gates." Now, the word for doorpost is *mezuzah*, and as the two passages have to be placed on the doorpost, over the course of time the word came to represent the scroll that is placed on the doorpost.

Question What is the significance of the *mezuzah*?

Answer Although the Torah does not give a specific reason for placing the *mezuzah* on one's door, the different commentators have offered reasons for it. One, for example, sees this as a reminder of God's presence everywhere, just as the *tzitzit* serve this purpose. Another regards it as a device to keep evil from the home. This view deduces a modicum of support from God's name (made up of the three Hebrew letters *Shin*, *Daled* and *Yod*) on the outside of the parchment, which it takes as an acronym of *Shomer Daltot Yisrael* – "He who guards Israel's doors."

Question Which doors require a *mezuzah*?

Answer In general, every door in the house needs a *mezuzah*, except if a) it leads to an area less than 6 ft. by 6 ft. in size, or b) it leads to a bathroom. In addition, if one has a gate consisting of two posts and a lintel over the top, it too requires a *mezuzah*.

Question Where is the *mezuzah* to be affixed?

Answer It is affixed on the right doorpost (based on going into the room in question), and must be within the top third of the post. There is a difference of opinion among the rabbis as to whether it should be affixed in a horizontal or vertical position. As a compromise, Ashkenazic Jews affix it slanted.

Question What precautions are needed in buying a *mezuzah*?

Answer As the parchment scroll is hand-written, a decent scroll cannot be cheap. Unfortunately, there have been those who – through ignorance or avarice – have "cut corners," by selling the outer case (which, as we mentioned, is not the *mezuzah* proper) with a photostated copy of the original text, or even with any other type of printed material. In some cases, when these *mezuzah* cases are made in certain countries – often Asian – the error is inadvertent, based on ignorance of the requirements of Jewish law. Regardless of what the reason, unless the case contains a properly hand-written parchment scroll (and one often needs a rabbi to determine if the text was written accurately), it cannot be considered a proper *mezuzah*, and the placing of such a case on one's door in no way fulfills one's obligation under Jewish law.

Question What is the Torah?

Answer As mentioned in the first chapter, the word "Torah" has many meanings, and can refer, for example, to all branches of Jewish religious learning, as in the phrase "to study Torah." When referring to an object, though, the word refers to a scroll, hand-written in Hebrew on parchment, of the entire Five Books of Moses. The Torah scroll is made up of pieces of parchment obtained from a kosher species of animal sewn together to form a single long scroll. The Torah scroll is without a doubt the most venerated of all Jewish ceremonial objects, and there are various laws which reflect this. Thus, for example, if a Torah scroll is being carried from one place to another, all present must rise and remain standing until the scroll has been put down. It is customary not to touch the naked parchment with one's hand;

✦ *A silver* mezuzah *case; Russia, 1873.*

✦ *The "breastplate" which often adorns the Torah scroll; Germany, 1826.*

instead one handles it through the fabric of one's *tallit*. Another sign of this veneration is that if, Heaven forbid, a Torah scroll is burned in a fire, it must be buried in Jewish cemetery, just as if it had been the remains of a person.

Question How is the scroll kept?

Answer First, it is mounted on two generally wooden rollers, known as *atzei hayyim* ("trees of life"), so that it can be rolled back and forth to the appropriate place. It is then covered. In the Ashkenazic synagogue, the cover is generally made of cloth (most often velvet), and this slips over the *atzei hayyim*. When the Torah scroll is to be read, the cover is removed. In the Sephardic synagogue, on the other hand, the cover is solid and is made of wood or metal, with a base on which the Torah stands. With Sephardic Torah scrolls, the cover is permanently in place and swings open to reveal the text for the Torah reading. Whereas the Ashkenazic scroll is laid down horizontally on the *bimah* (see below) during the Torah reading, the Sephardic scroll stands vertically on its base throughout the Torah reading.

Question Are there any differences between the two types of scrolls beyond those mentioned above?

Answer Although there are over 300,000 letters in the Torah scroll, all Torah scrolls in the world are identical – well, almost identical. There is exactly *one letter* where there is a disagreement between the Ashkenazic and Sephardic versions, where the Ashkenazic version has the letter *alef* at the end of a certain word and the Sephardic version has the letter *heh*. As the letter is silent, there is no difference in prônunciation between the two versions.

Great care is taken in ensuring the absolute accuracy of a Torah scroll, and if an error is found, the scroll can no longer be used for the public Torah reading until the error has been corrected. In fact, if a total of three errors were found in a Torah scroll, it cannot be used any more until the *entire text* has been checked by a scribe for accuracy.

Question In the modern era, can't any of this process be mechanized?

Answer Indeed it can, and in the last few years a computer program was developed to do just that. The Torah scroll is scanned by an optical scanner, using special software which recognizes Torah script, and the text is then matched with the complete Torah text stored in the computer's memory. If there are discrepancies, such as missing letters or superfluous letters, the computer printout will reveal this.

Question If the computer is so accurate, why not have all Torah scrolls checked this way, rather than by scribes?

Answer Many years ago, when Israel built its first computer, it was dubbed "the *golem*," the *golem* being a mythical creature said to have been created by a medieval rabbi, who molded it out of clay and placed the Divine Name in its forehead. The *golem* is reputed to have carried out all types of actions for its master, but what it lacked, of course, was independent reasoning power. Thus the Israeli *golem*-computer was given that name because it was able to carry out various tasks, but only after having been instructed precisely what to do. The same problem arises with the computer which examines the Torah text. It can scan the letters and notice any discrepancies between the correct text and that of a given scroll – and in this it is definitely superior to any human being – but it cannot, for example, tell whether a given letter meets the halakhic requirements for that particular letter. Only a person who knows the rules involved can make such decisions. (In fact, we should point out, even an expert in the field cannot always decide if a given letter is "kosher" or not. Thus, *halakhah* dictates that in certain cases of doubt, one must call in a child who has just begun to read and ask what he thinks the letter is. The child's statement is then accepted as authoritative.) We may also mention, in passing, that the original *golem* was the source of a great deal of discussion among rabbis, and there are even learned responsa about whether it could be included in the required quorum of ten for prayer.

Question What are the different silver objects which are placed on Torah scrolls?

Answer Not all the objects are made of silver; other metals, wood or ivory are sometimes used. The Torah scroll that is used generally has what is called a *yad* ("hand"), or pointer hung on a chain and draped over the *atzei hayyim*. The *yad* is used to point to the text as it is read, so that the reader will not touch the parchment itself. Often, there will be a breastplate hanging over the front of the scroll, reminiscent of the *Urim ve-Tumim* breastplate that was worn by the high priest in the Temple. Finally, above the *atzei hayyim* there is often a *keter* ("crown") which covers both, or two separate *rimonim* ("pomegranates"), which are meant to adorn the Torah scroll and show our veneration of it.

Question What is a *megillah*?

Answer The word *megillah* simply means a scroll. In general use, though, it has attained a specific meaning, namely a parchment scroll containing a

handwritten Book of Esther. The *megillah* is read on Purim, the day celebrating the Jews' deliverance at the time of Mordecai and Esther. The *megillah* is the only reading – beside the Torah, of course – that must take place from a handwritten scroll.

An examination of the cross-pollination of languages is the quite frequent use in the United States today of the word, such as in the phrase, "the whole *megillah*," which simply means the whole story.

Question What is the *bimah*?

Answer The *bimah* is a raised platform, in most cases in the middle of the synagogue, which is set aside for the reading of the Torah scroll, although it is sometimes also used as a stand for the cantor when he leads the prayers. The *bimah* is also known as the *almemar*.

Question What is the *aron kodesh*?

Answer The translation of the term, "holy ark," tells it all. The *aron kodesh*, situated at the very front of the synagogue, is the place where the Torah scrolls are stored when not in use. Traditionally, it has an embroidered velvet curtain hanging in front of its facade, but nowadays various other materials and methods have been used to ornament it.

Question What is the *ner tamid*?

Answer Synagogues generally have a *ner tamid* ("eternal light") burning just in front of the *aron kodesh*. This commemorates the oil lamps which were lit daily on the *menorah* in the Temple, and which burned for 24 hours. This continuously burning lamp symbolized, among others, God's constant care for His people.

Question What is the *mehitzah*?

Answer The word *mehitzah* simply means a partition, and is the term used for the dividing barrier separating the men and women in Orthodox synagogues. The separation of the sexes was already a feature in the Temple, where there was a separate *ezrat nashim*, or "women's courtyard." According to Jewish law, the sexes must be separated during worship, thus enabling people to concentrate on the prayers rather than on the members of the other sex. In Europe, it was often the practice to have a separate balcony for women, although Jewish law only requires some type of barrier (according to Rabbi Moses Feinstein, one of the foremost halakhic decisors of our times,

✤ *A keter ("crown") for the Torah scroll; Poland.*

this must be at least 60 inches high, although others have ruled that 40 inches is sufficient), even if the sexes are on the same level.

We may point out that it was the question of "family pews," i.e., of families sitting together, that marked one of the first breaks from Orthodoxy in the other Jewish religious movements.

Question What is the *shofar*, and when is it used?

Answer The *shofar* is a horn, generally that of a ram where available. This is hollowed out and produces a type of musical instrument. The Torah requires that the *shofar* be blown on Rosh Ha-Shanah, but it is also blown after the daily morning service during the month preceding Rosh Ha-Shanah and at the conclusion of the Yom Kippur fast day.

In ancient times, the *shofar* was used to signal groups of people, as, for example, to summon troops to battle, much as a bugle was used in previous centuries.

Chapter Five

The Sabbath

Question We are told that Jewish law forbids a person to drive a car or turn on electricity on the Sabbath. How can these possibly be forbidden when the Torah was given over 3,000 years ago?

Answer We Jews believe that the Torah was given by God. As such, God gave us a document that would be equally valid in all places and at all times. Whereas a man-made legislative code can become archaic, the same is not true for the Torah.

As to the different questions regarding work on the Sabbath, nowhere does the Torah tell us what work is permitted and what is forbidden. All it tells us is that one may not work on the Sabbath. The oral law then goes on to explain that, as the verses in the Torah describing the work to be performed in the building of the Sanctuary are interrupted by an exhortation to keep the Sabbath – an exhortation which seems out of place – this must be teaching us that one is not permitted to work on the construction of the Sanctuary on the Sabbath. By extension, all those categories of work needed in constructing the Sanctuary (the Mishnah lists 39 of them) are forbidden on the Sabbath.

This is the key to answering our question. The Torah (and here we include the oral law as well) never specifies which action is forbidden as such. It merely gives us *categories* of work. For example, one of the categories of work forbidden on the Sabbath is kneading, for they had to bake loaves for the Sanctuary. The category of kneading, though, does not only include dough, but putty as well. Similarly, each other category includes a broad class of actions. In fact, each category is referred to in Hebrew as an *av* – a "father" – and includes various sub-categories known as *toladot* – "descendants." An example of a category of forbidden work would be reaping. That is the *av*. Reaping implies using an instrument, but plucking anything growing from the ground or a tree is also forbidden, in this case as a *toladah* – a "descendant."

It follows that when a rabbi today is asked a question about the use of a car on the Sabbath, for example, he must examine what the process involves, and whether that process involves any one of the "categories" of work. In this case, the category is making or stoking a fire, and that is what happens every time a person puts his foot on the gas pedal. By the same token, another category of work is damping a fire – and that happens every time one presses the brake pedal. Thus, driving a car on the Sabbath is forbidden by Torah law.

Question Does that mean that every action forbidden on the Sabbath is forbidden by the Torah law?

Answer Not necessarily. Some of the actions forbidden on the Sabbath are forbidden by rabbinic rather than Torah law. The rabbis, realizing that the legal penalty for desecrating the Sabbath is death, wished to ensure that people keep as far away as possible from any action which might conceivably involve Sabbath desecration. In order to ensure that this was the case, they enacted decrees of their own, whose sole purpose was to "fence off," as it were, the Sabbath prohibition. In fact, such rabbinic laws are often referred to as being a *geder* – a fence, although the official name is a *gezeirah*, or (rabbinic) decree.

A few examples may explain the concept better. As we mentioned in the previous question, one may not pluck anything off a tree. As a *gezeirah*, the rabbis forbade anyone from smelling fruit still growing a tree, because if one smells it and likes the odor, he may decide to pick the fruit. Another example relates to cooking, which is forbidden on the Sabbath by Torah law. As a *gezeirah*, the rabbis forbade a person from leaving a pot on the fire before the Sabbath, because he may come to adjust the fire. If, however, the fire is covered by a tin sheet or some other device which serves as a clear reminder that it is the Sabbath, one may leave his pot on the stove before the Sabbath.

Question I can understand why the Torah forbade one to light a fire on the Sabbath, because at that time the Torah was given this required a great deal of work. But why is one not permitted to turn on a light switch today, where there is almost no effort involved?

Answer There is a basic error in this question: it confuses the actions forbidden on the Sabbath, included in the verse, "You shall not do any work" (Ex. 20:10), with what we today consider to be work. The Torah definition of work, as a modern-day commentator explains it, is an action which is creative, where a change is made in reality. This is in keeping with the idea of the six days of Creation, where God's actions were all of a creative nature. Moving a heavy set of furniture from one room in one's house to another room in it would not be forbidden, even though it would involve strenuous work, but that is not considered to be a creative act. Turning on a switch, though, is considered to be a creative act, and is thus forbidden. Incidentally, the prohibition against lighting a fire on the Sabbath includes lighting a fire from one which is already burning. Even at the time that the Torah was given, that action hardly required any effort.

Question What is the law of *muktzeh*?

Answer One of the regulations instituted by the rabbis was the law of *muktzeh*, a word which, translated literally, means "cut off" or "set aside." In order to ensure that people would not accidentally perform one of the forbidden categories of work on the Sabbath, the rabbis forbade one from even handling any object the use of which is prohibited on the Sabbath. For example, one is not allowed to handle either a pen or a hammer on the Sabbath. There are also other categories of items which are considered to be *muktzeh* for a variety of other reasons, but this is not the place to enter into that.

Question It is customary to light candles in the Jewish home on Friday afternoon, before sunset. What is the origin and purpose of this law?

Answer As the Sabbath is meant to be a joyful day, the Sages instituted the requirement to light candles before the Sabbath, to ensure that there will be light on Friday evening. There is a view that this law was introduced by the rabbis (the so-called Pharisees) to counter the ruling by the Sadducees, who held that the verse, "You shall not light a fire in all your habitations on the Sabbath day" (Ex. 35:3), meant that no fire was allowed to be burning during the Sabbath, whether for light, heat or to keep food warm. Thus, unlike the Sadducees, we sit in a bright, well-lit home.

Question How many candles are lit?

Answer The law requires the woman of the house to light two candles. We find that the Torah lists the Ten Commandments twice, once in Exodus and once in Deuteronomy. In one case, the commandment about the Sabbath states, "Remember the Sabbath day to keep it holy" (Ex. 20:8), while in the other, it states, "Observe the Sabbath day to keep it holy" (Deut. 5:12). The two candles are thus symbolic of "Remember" and "Observe."

There is another custom, whereby a woman lights a candle for each member of her household. In addition, if a woman ever forgot to light candles for the Sabbath, there is a custom that from the following Sabbath on, for the rest of her life she lights one more candle than she used to light previously, as a reminder for the future.

Question At what age do women begin lighting Sabbath candles?

Answer Generally, a woman must begin lighting two candles when she is married. The Habad (Lubavich) *hasidim* have had a campaign underway for a number of years to have every girl from the age of three and up light a single candle each week, but this is not required by Jewish law.

Question What happens when the wife is not present on Friday?

Answer As the purpose of the candles is to have light on the house on the Sabbath, the candles must be lit whether a woman is present or not. Where the wife is not present, the husband should light the candles.

Question When must the candles be lit?

Answer As lighting candles is forbidden on the Sabbath itself, the candles must be lit before sunset. Traditionally, women light the candles no later than 18 minutes before sunset, thereby ensuring that they do not accidentally wait until it is too late. The custom in Jerusalem is for women to light candles 40 minutes before sunset. In Jerusalem and in many other Israeli towns, special sirens are sounded at candle-lighting time, to inform everyone that the time has come.

Question How are the candles lit?

Answer Although this seems to demand a straightforward answer, the matter is not as simple as it seems. The question actually involves a conflict of two Jewish laws: on the one hand, it would appear logical that the woman should recite the blessing ("...who has commanded us to light the Sabbath candles") and then light the candles, just as in the case of every other blessing, which precedes the action which is about to be taken. After all, one recites a blessing *before* eating food. On the other hand, if a person states that the Sabbath has begun for him, *even before sunset*, that person is no longer permitted to perform any work: the Sabbath has begun for him or her. By reciting the blessing, the woman is in effect stating that the Sabbath has begun for her. Here we seem to have hit a Catch 22 situation: the blessing must be said before the lighting – but once the blessing has been pronounced, the woman is no longer permitted to light the candles! To get over this hurdle, the rule in this particular case is that the woman lights the candles *before* the blessing, then, with her eyes closed, she recites the blessing, and only afterwards looks at the candles burning, as if she had just lit them. After that, it is customary for the woman to recite a short prayer for the welfare of her family.

✦ *The blessing over the Sabbath candles; drawing, Russia.*

✦ *Various wine goblets for the* Kiddush; *19th century.*

Question As you mentioned, the reason two candles are lit is in order to commemorate the two versions in the Ten Commandments, "remember" and "observe" the Sabbath. Why are there two different versions?

Answer Various explanations have been offered of the difference between the two. Probably the most common explanation is that "remembering" the Sabbath refers to taking certain positive steps, as, for example, making *Kiddush* on the Sabbath. "Observing" the Sabbath, on the other hand, means refraining from doing anything which violates the Sabbath. Thus the two references include all those positive and negative actions which together add up to perfect Sabbath observance.

Question What is the procedure for the traditional Friday night meal?

Answer We will first give a general description of the meal. The next few questions and answers will serve to elaborate on various aspects of our answer here.

After the family members come home from the synagogue – whether women attend the synagogue on Friday evening is a matter of local custom – all sing *Shalom Aleikhem*, a song welcoming the two angels who, by tradition, accompany people home from the synagogue on Friday evening. The table is set, and a goblet, often of silver, is ready with wine for *Kiddush* (see below) and two *hallot* (plaited bread loaves) covered with a cloth lie on the table. The family head recites *Kiddush*, the text of which is to be found in any *siddur*. There are different customs as to whether other men present also recite the *Kiddush* after the family head has done so.

All members of the family now wash their hands, as is done whenever one is about to eat bread, using a glass or cup to pour water on their hands – twice on each hand. They recite the blessing on washing the hands: "... *al netilat yadayim* – who has commanded us concerning the washing of the hands." The family head then places one *hallah* loaf on top of the other, makes a slight incision with a knife in the bottom *hallah*, and then recites the blessing on bread, "... *Ha-motzi* – who brings forth bread from the earth." All respond Amen. The family head then cuts up the bottom *hallah*, and gives every person present a slice. At that point, the festive meal begins.

The meal itself is different both qualitatively and quantitatively from the meals during the rest of the week. First, no one is rushed. The entire family remains together for the entire meal. There are no distractions such as television programs or telephone calls. The meal, which a festive one, is accompanied by the singing of *zemirot* – the Sabbath table hymns – and by family members offering Torah thoughts, generally on the weekly Torah reading. Finally, the meal concludes with the Grace after Meals.

Question What is *Kiddush*, and why is it said?

Answer The word *Kiddush* means "sanctification." *Kiddush* itself is an extended blessing said while holding a goblet of wine. After it is said, everyone is given a little of the wine to drink.

By reciting the *Kiddush* over wine before the meal, we are in essence "elevating" the meal from being merely a way to satisfy our hunger to part of our service of God. The *Kiddush* text itself thanks God for sanctifying us with His commandments and granting us the Sabbath, which commemorates both the creation and the Exodus.

In general, the *Kiddush* is a good example of one of the basic concepts of Judaism: It is the goal of the Jew – through the practice of the commandments – to try to raise up every action of his life to be part of his service of God. Thus, we are told that when the meal is conducted properly, the table is considered to be an altar before God.

Question Can you elaborate on the two angels?

Answer According to a *midrash*, there are two angels that accompany every person home from the synagogue, one a "good" angel, and the other, a "bad" one. When the angels see everything set out as it should be, with the table laid and the house spic-and-span, the good angel exclaims: "May your house be like this next week as well." The bad angel is forced to respond, "Amen." If, however, things are not as they should be, the positions are reversed: the bad angel exclaims: "May your house be like this next week as well." The good angel is now forced to respond, "Amen." The song *Shalom Aleikhem* was composed in honor of these angels. Its four verses respectively first greet, welcome in, ask blessings of, and finally bid farewell to the angels. Incidentally, the third verse has been a cause of rabbinic controversy: some rabbis have objected to the idea of asking an angel for blessings, for Judaism – unlike many other religions – does not believe in using intermediaries in the relationship between man and God.

Question What purpose is served by washing the hands before reciting the blessing on bread? Is this a hygienic rule?

Answer The law requiring the washing of hands goes back to the Second Temple era, at the least. At that time, there were extensive rules regarding ritual purity and ritual impurity. A person coming into contact with something which was ritually impure (such as a dead body) had to perform various actions to remove the ritual impurity. (A ritually impure person was not allowed to enter the Temple precincts and was limited in various other activities.) After the Temple was destroyed, most of these rules lapsed. Washing the hands before a meal is nevertheless a holdover from that era, and serves to remind us of the time that the Temple existed.

Of course, the fact that Jews wash their hands when getting up in the morning, before eating and after using the toilet serves as a hygienic measure, and during the Middle Ages Jews were often less susceptible to various diseases which were rampant.

Question Why are two *hallot* used when reciting the blessing for bread on Friday night?

Answer As with many other rituals, the use of two *hallot* rather than one is symbolic. When the Israelites were in the desert, they would collect a measure of manna each morning for that day's food supply. Any manna left overnight would spoil. On Friday, though, they would collect a double portion, for both Friday and the Sabbath, and here the manna would remain unspoiled overnight. In commemoration of that double portion, two *hallot* are used at each of the Sabbath meals. In cutting the *hallah*, on Friday night the bottom one is cut, this time symbolizing the fact that after the manna fell each day, a coating of dew fell to protect it. During the day, though, the top *hallah* is cut.

Question Why are the *hallot* covered with a cloth during *Kiddush*?

Answer Jewish law has a rigorous classification of which blessing one is to say first when he has more than one blessing to pronounce. Here, we have a choice of reciting the blessing on the wine or the blessing on the *hallah*. Under normal conditions, a person should recite the blessing on bread before that on wine. On the other hand, one must recite *Kiddush*, which includes the blessing on wine, before the meal. Thus, two contradictory factors come into play, and this poses a problem. The rabbis solved the problem with typical ingenuity. In order to avoid the dilemma, we have the *hallah* present on the table, but not visible. This way, we are able to recite the blessing on the wine first, as if there is no *hallah* present.

Question Are there any specifications for the *hallot*?

Answer Traditionally, *hallah* loaves are braided, but this is not a halakhic requirement. All that the *halakhah* requires is that both loaves be complete, rather than partial or sliced up loaves. As far as the recipe – well, that depends on the individual family, and recent years have shown the growth of such special *hallot* as whole wheat loaves.

Question Does Jewish law have anything to say on what dishes are served on the Sabbath?

Answer Beyond a call to have fish and meat at Sabbath meals, there is no halakhic rule as to what should or should not be eaten – of course within the limits of the laws governing kosher foods. There are nevertheless two specifically typical Sabbath dishes, very popular among Ashkenazic Jews, which owe their presence in the menu to halakhic concerns.

The first of these is *gefilte fish* – patties made of ground fish. As we mentioned, there are 39 categories of work which are forbidden on the Sabbath. One of these is separating the bad (or inedible) from the good. You can imagine the problem involved in eating fish if you are not allowed to separate the bones as you go! Thus, the theory goes, *gefilte fish* was adopted for Sabbath use, for this way all the bones are removed before the Sabbath.

The other dish with a halakhic basis is the *cholent*, a stew made of meat, potatoes, and possibly – depending on custom – barley, beans, and, especially among Sephardic families, whole eggs in their shells. This dish is placed on the fire before the Sabbath and is allowed to remain on the fire until lunch the next day. (The newly popular electric crock pots are said to do wonders for *cholent*!) Now, as we mentioned earlier, the Sadducees would not leave any fire on in their homes on the Sabbath. The Talmudic Sages (the "Pharisees"), from whom normative Judaism is directly descended, ruled that one cannot light or adjust a fire, but one is certainly permitted to leave anything on the fire over the Sabbath. In order to accentuate the difference, the Rabbis insisted that one must have warm food on the Sabbath day itself – specifically to prove that we are not Sadducees. While even a cup of hot coffee meets the bill, the *cholent* is a direct – and far more tasty – response to that requirement.

We should also note that, according to a common Yiddish saying, *cholent* is proof of the ultimate revival of the dead, because if anyone can eat a hearty dish of *cholent*, go to sleep on Sabbath afternoon and still wake up afterwards, that is clear proof that there is such a thing as life after death!

Question In an earlier answer, we noted that carrying even something light from one's house is forbidden. Is there any way this action may be permitted?

Answer We have to start here with a short description of the prohibition involved. This will help us understand under what circumstances one is permitted to carry things outside the home.

As a general rule, there are three different types of domains in regard to the Sabbath: private domains (i.e., belonging to individuals), public domains (and the definition of "public" is any place where 600,000 people pass through in any given 24 hour period), and the *karmelit*, which is neither private nor public (e.g., roads where less than that number of people pass through). By Torah law, one is permitted to carry from a private domain to a *karmelit*, but not to a public one or within a public one. By rabbinic law, one is not permitted to carry between a private domain and a *karmelit* either, lest he carry between a private and a public domain.

Enter the *eruv*. The word *eruv* means "mixing," in this case referring to mixing or merging various domains. This is a rabbinic device meant to circumvent an action which is prohibited by rabbinic law. By surrounding an area – in Israel this may include an entire city – with a "partition" made of posts at least 10 handbreadths (40 inches) high, linked by string or wire going over the top of each post, the entire area is considered to be a single domain, and once certain other provisions have been met, one may carry within the entire area on the Sabbath. The reason this is permitted is that no street in the entire city in which the *eruv* is made has the status of a public domain by Torah law, so that carrying in the streets is only prohibited by rabbinic law. And, as mentioned above, an *eruv* is a device enabling one to do something which would otherwise be forbidden by rabbinic law. Thus if one lives in a town with an *eruv*, he may carry there even on the Sabbath.

Nowadays, every city in Israel has an *eruv*, as do many localities in other cities, especially in North America. These often use telephone poles as the basis for the *eruv*.

Question In the prayers of the Sabbath, the blessing concludes, "who sanctifies the Sabbath." In the prayers of festivals, the blessing concludes, "who sanctifies Israel and the seasons." If a festival is on the Sabbath, the blessing concludes, "who sanctifies the Sabbath and Israel and the seasons." Why this convoluted form, and why is "Israel" listed between "the Sabbath" and "the seasons"?

Answer The Sabbath, as we know, occurs on every seventh day, tracing back to the creation. The festivals, though, are not preordained on a specific day. Until the Temple was destroyed in 70 C.E., the date depended on when the New Moon was proclaimed by the Sanhedrin, the high court of the Jewish people, as it were, that sat in Jerusalem. Depending on when the new moon appeared – and this could appear on one of two specific days each month – the Sanhedrin declared the New Moon on that day, and the festival or festivals of that month occurred on the date assigned by the Torah for that festival, as, for example, Passover on the 15th of the month of Nissan. (Today, we work on a calendar prepared almost 2,000 years ago.) Thus we see that the Sabbath was sanctified by God at the creation, while the festivals, on the other hand, are sanctified by Israel – by the day that the Jewish people determines them to be. The Jewish people, unlike the festivals, receive their sanctity directly from God. Thus it is as if the blessing stated, "[God] who sanctifies the Sabbath and Israel, [who in turn] sanctify the seasons."

This is a remarkable example of God delegating to man decisions regarding the Torah law. On the verse, "These are the feasts of the Lord, the holy convocations, which you shall proclaim them [*otam* in Hebrew] in their seasons" (Lev. 23:4), the Talmud understands the word as *atem* – "you" – rather than *otam*. The implication is that *you*, the people of Israel, are to proclaim the dates of the festivals.

An even more remarkable story of man's freedom in legislating Torah law is a story recorded in the Talmud, about a dispute between Rabbi Eliezer and the other Sages, as to whether a certain utensil was considered ritually pure or impure. To bolster his case, Rabbi Eliezer ordered that a stream which ran nearby should reverse the direction in which it flowed. The other Sages were unimpressed by this divine intervention. Streams do not establish the law, they proclaimed. Rabbi Eliezer then ordered a tree to move, which it did. Again, the other Sages were unmoved. Rabbi Eliezer appealed to the wall of the study hall to fall down. It began to do so, but was ordered by the Sages to remain standing. Out of respect for Rabbi Eliezer and the Sages, the wall remained at an angle. Even that did not move the Sages. Finally, Rabbi Eliezer called upon Heaven to witness that he was correct. Immediately a voice came from Heaven, and corroborated that the law was indeed in accordance with Rabbi Eliezer. Upon hearing this, one of the other Sages, Rabbi Joshua, exclaimed, "[The law] is not in heaven!" Once the Torah was given to mankind, it is only subject to human interpretation, and even God cannot intervene. The Talmud then goes on to mention that a certain Sage met the Prophet Elijah and asked him how God had reacted when he heard this statement by the Sages. Elijah told him that God, as it were, chuckled, and exclaimed, "My sons have defeated me; My sons have defeated me."

Question What does Jewish law say about violating the Sabbath for a person who is ill?

Answer One of the major principles of Judaism is based on a phrase in a verse in Leviticus, "You shall live by them" (18:5). On this, the Sages comment, "You shall live by the commandments, and shall not die by them." Whenever there is a case of conceivable danger to human life, all necessary steps must be taken. Thus, if a person is seriously ill, one may take whatever steps are necessary to effect his recovery. As the Talmud puts it, "It is better that he violate one Sabbath, so as to enable him to observe many Sabbaths thereafter."

There is a story told about a certain Torah scholar who was always very lenient when anyone asked him about violating the Sabbath for anyone who was ill. One of his students finally mustered up enough courage and asked him, "Rabbi, could you possibly explain why you are so lenient in regard to the Sabbath laws?" "I am not, my son," the rabbi answered, "I am merely very stringent in regard to what is considered to be serious illness."

This need to remain alive is indeed paramount. Thus there is a story of some young men who came to the saintly Hafetz Hayyim. They had been drafted into the Czar's army, and wanted to ask the rabbi what they were permitted to eat and what they were forbidden to. In those days, soldiers were sent to the most isolated places to serve for years on end. The food supply was meager at best, and the Hafetz Hayyim told the young men that they were permitted to eat whatever was served. The alternative was starvation, possibly even to death. But the rabbi added only one proviso: "My sons, although you may eat everything served, don't smack your lips at the non-kosher food." Eating everything might be a necessity, but one must still keep in perspective that certain things are forbidden under normal circumstances.

Question Is there a rule as to how many meals one must eat over the Sabbath?

Answer According to *halakhah*, one must eat three meals, at each of which one recites the blessing over two *hallah* loaves. The three meals should ideally be eaten after the prayer services on Friday night, Saturday morning, and before sunset on Saturday.

Question What is *shalosh se'udot*?

Answer Literally, the words mean "three meals," but the term has taken on the meaning of the third Sabbath meal. You may hear this meal referred to as *sholeshudes*. All that is, is a Yiddish corruption of the original Hebrew expression. This meal, generally begun just before sunset and continuing until night, is usually marked by slow, soulful melodies, as it gets darker and darker outside. (Before electricity, the meal no doubt ended in complete darkness.)

Question What is *Havdalah*?

Answer *Havdalah* is the ceremony held after it gets dark on Saturday night, and marks the transition from the Sabbath back into the weekday. *Havdalah*, which means separation, uses three key elements: a goblet of wine, spices, and a candle with more than one wick. Each has its own symbolism. The wine is used to see out the Sabbath, just as wine was used in *Kiddush* on Friday night to see the Sabbath in. Kabbalistically, we are told that during the

Sabbath the Jew receives a second, additional soul, which in Hebrew is referred to as the *neshamah yeteirah*. As we feel sad at the departure of the "second soul" after the Sabbath, we comfort the remaining soul with the spiritual pleasure of the spices we smell. Finally, we are told in the Aggadah that after the first Sabbath of the creation, Adam struck two rocks together and produced a spark. This symbolized the fact that from then on he could work and produce. The candle thus symbolizes the fact that we can once again perform creative work. As the additional soul only applies to the Sabbath, and as one is permitted to light a fire from another on festivals, the *Havdalah* ceremony after a festival consists only of the wine.

Question Why is the song *Eliyahu Hanavi* – "the Prophet Elijah" – sung after the *Havdalah* ceremony?

Answer By Jewish tradition, the Prophet Elijah will come before the advent of the Messiah and will announce the Messiah's coming. As we are told that Elijah cannot arrive on the Sabbath, now that the Sabbath has ended we again await his coming, bearing the glorious announcement that the Messiah has finally arrived.

Question What is the Jewish view of the Messiah?

Answer Judaism, basing itself on the prophecies of its prophets, sees the advent of the Messiah as bringing with it an eternal era of peace, with men "beating their swords into plowshares." No person can be accepted as the Messiah unless he personally fulfills that mission. As to what life will be like when the Messiah arrives, Maimonides (1135-1204), quoting the Talmud, states that life will continue as it does at present, except for the fact that Israel will not be subjugated in any way by any other nation. Beyond that, as Maimonides points out, all speculation is pointless.

Question What are the often-quoted references to the *status quo* regarding religious matters in Israel?

Answer When the State of Israel was established in 1948, David Ben-Gurion, in order to avoid friction between the religious and non-religious citizens of the new state, reached an agreement with the religious political parties whereby questions of public religious observance would remain as they were at the time, thus maintaining the "*status quo.*" Thus, for example, as Haifa, then known as "the Red Haifa" because of the high proportion of socialist and anti-religious people in the city, had public bus transportation on the Sabbath, the public busses were permitted to operate on the Sabbath. All

other cities, where there had been no public transportation on the Sabbath, were not permitted to institute this after the establishment of the state.

Since that agreement forty years ago, there have been claims by both the religious and the non-religious that the *status quo* has been tampered with, each side – understandably – claiming that the other side has made "gains" at its expense. In truth, there have been changes. As a result there have been calls by members of both sides for a redefinition of the *status quo*. The government, on the other hand, knowing a hornet's nest when it sees one, has had enough sense to leave things as they are.

Question Given all the different restrictions on working on the Sabbath, how does the Israeli army function on that day?

Answer The Israeli army does indeed observe the Sabbath. That does not mean that non-religious soldiers are forced to refrain from smoking, etc. It does, however, mean that the Friday night and Saturday morning meals are begun with the recitation of the *Kiddush* by one of the religious soldiers present. The army chaplaincy, in fact, supplies wine for *Kiddush*. Soldiers may not smoke in the dining room during the Sabbath meals, and any soldier doing so may face a court-martial. Given the fact that there are many functions that are absolutely essential to Israel's safety and that cannot be suspended on the Sabbath, these functions come under the category of *pikuah nefesh* – potential danger to life. As such, the army sends out patrol cars to sweep the borders, mans intercoms that link the different bases, and performs other such essential functions. Generally, though, no practice ma- neuvers will be held on the Sabbath, as these are not considered to be essential to protecting life.

Many years ago, the then chief chaplain of the Israeli army, Rabbi Shlomo Goren, who later became the Ashkenazic chief rabbi of Israel, was asked by a religious soldier if the soldier was permitted to trade a job which he had been assigned to perform on the Sabbath, which involved violating the Sabbath law, with a non-religious soldier, who did not object to perform this particular job on the Sabbath. In return, the religious soldier would take a midweek assignment on behalf of the non-religious soldier. In his reply, Rabbi Goren ruled according to the accepted *halakhah*, but the form of his reply has since become a minor classic. According to Rabbi Goren, there were two possibilities: either the particular function was permitted, given the circumstances of the danger in which Israel finds itself, on the Sabbath, or it was forbidden as being unnecessary. If it was permitted, the religious soldier should make a point of carrying out the function itself, and if it was forbidden, it could not be delegated to a non-religious soldier. This ruling in essence corroborates the basic principle of Judaism, that "all Jews are responsible for

✴ *A silver spice-box for the* Havdalah *ceremony; 18th century.*

one another," and a religious Jew cannot ask one who is not religious to perform a forbidden action. In fact if a non-religious Jew performs such a function on the Sabbath, *halakhah* forbids anyone to benefit from it.

Question How about electricity in Israel on the Sabbath? Isn't that produced by Jewish labor? If, as pointed out in the previous answer one cannot benefit from the work performed by a Jew on the Sabbath, what do religious Jews do about electricity?

Answer There are two streams of thought among religious Jews on this question. The vast majority of religious Jews accept the view that the work performed in supplying electricity on the Sabbath is essential, because hospitals and other such essential services must be kept operating. Thus they do not regard the work carried out in supplying electricity as being a violation of the Sabbath as such. Others, who adopt a more stringent ruling, believe that one may not use electricity in Israel on the Sabbath, because the workers are Jewish. Many of them have installed separate lighting systems run off 12-volt car batteries. During the week these batteries are charged up by electricity. Before the Sabbath, a switch is thrown and the electricity turned off. This way, the electric power on the Sabbath comes from the batteries.

Question How does the State of Israel deal with the Sabbath laws?

Answer By law, Saturday is the day of rest for all Jews in Israel. That means that all government offices, except those deemed essential, are closed. For example, there is no mail delivery. Generally, all manufacturing plants must close down, with special exemptions being given to those production processes which cannot be turned off without extensive (and often expensive) delays in restarting. Such plants generally pay a substantial premium to those willing to work on Saturday. By law, no person may be denied a job on the grounds of his or her refusal to work on the Sabbath. Individual municipalities may enact by-laws regarding Sabbath observance, and most cities permit restaurants wishing to do so to remain open on Saturday. (As a matter of principle, no restaurant open on Saturday will be granted a kashrut certificate). Generally, all stores must be closed. Most cities do, however, permit places of entertainment, such as movies, to remain open on Saturday.

Chapter Six

The High Holidays

Question When and what are the Ten Days of Repentance?

Answer Beginning with Rosh Ha-Shanah, on the first two days of the Hebrew month of Tishrei and the Hebrew year, until and including Yom Kippur, the tenth day of the month, ten days are set aside annually for everyone to take stock of his actions over the previous year. On Rosh Ha-Shanah, we are told, God judges every human being. Those who are totally righteous are immediately sentenced to life, while those who are totally evil are immediately sentenced to death (the sentence here does not refer to this world, but rather to the World to Come). All those in neither category, i.e., most of mankind, are given a grace period until Yom Kippur in order to improve their ways, and the people in this category only have their decree decided finally on Yom Kippur. Between Rosh Ha-Shanah and Yom Kippur there is exactly a week. The Sages mention that proper behavior and repentance on each day of that week can atone for all one's sins on the corresponding day of the week throughout the year, so that during that week a person can atone for his sins during all the weeks of the year.

Question Why does the Torah refer to Rosh Ha-Shanah, which is the beginning of the year, as "the seventh month" rather than the first?

Answer While by Jewish tradition Rosh Ha-Shanah is indeed the beginning of the year, marking the anniversary of man's creation (i.e., the sixth day of the creation was on 1 Tishrei), pride of place is nevertheless given to Nissan, the month during which the Jews left Egypt. In fact the Torah tells us quite clearly, "This month [i.e., Nissan] shall be unto you the beginning of months: it shall be the first month of the year to you" (Ex. 12:2). As the Exodus from Egypt marked the formation of the Jewish people as a nation, it is considered preeminent, and the references to months in the Torah take Nissan as the first month.

Question The Hebrew year beginning at the end of September 1989 and ending in September 1990 is the Hebrew year 5750. What is the basis for this figure?

Answer The Hebrew year is calculated in terms of the creation of the world, *anno mundi*, as recorded in Genesis. Using the ages of the different individuals mentioned in the Book of Genesis when they gave birth to their sons, the year of the creation of the world was calculated millenia ago. As a rough guide, adding 3760 to the secular year gives one the Hebrew year equivalent (at least for that portion of the Hebrew year from January to Rosh Ha-Shanah in September or October).

We should note that the idea of dating years based on the creation is a relatively (in terms of Jewish history) recent phenomenon, going back less than 2,000 years. During the monarchy, all contracts were dated according to the year of the king's reign. In order to keep matters easy, the rule was that regardless of which month the king took office, the second year of his reign began on the 1st day of Nissan, and each 1st of Nissan would mark the beginning of another year of his reign. This, of course, was far easier than having to use the specific date the king took office, and allowed for a degree of uniformity. Events in the prophets are often listed as occurring in a specific year of a particular king's reign.

Incidentally, the same system is used to this day in at least Great Britain, and various official royal proclamations refer to both the calendar year and the year of Queen Elizabeth's reign.

Question One of the customs at the evening meal on Rosh Ha-Shanah is to eat an apple dipped into honey. What is the basis for this custom?

Answer As with many such customs, the apple dipped in honey is symbolic: in this case, it symbolizes our wish that the year which is now beginning will be a sweet one.

But that is not the only symbolic custom of the evening. For example, it is customary to eat the head of a fish, and to exclaim before eating it: "Let us be the head rather than the tail." A number of fruits and vegetables are also eaten, all of their names having some (usually pun-like) association with good fortune. The customs in this regard depend on the place and the language spoken. For example, some people eat dates (*tamar* in Hebrew), *she-yitamu son'einu* – "that our enemies cease." Two items are specifically Yiddish: carrots (*mern*), "so that we will multiply" (also *mern*); *farfel* – "for a full year" (*far a fuln yor*). It has been suggested that the same technique can be applied in English. A prime candidate for inclusion will no doubt be lettuce: "let us ..." You may fill whatever you want in to that particular statement.

We should also note here that while the custom throughout the year is to dip one's bread into salt before eating the first bite, the custom from Rosh Ha-Shanah until the end of Sukkot is to dip it into honey instead, again as a symbolic gesture of our desire for a sweet year.

Question Do all of these symbolic customs apply to the second night of Rosh Ha-Shanah as well?

Answer Indeed they do, and in fact there is one additional observance on that night. On the second night of Rosh Ha-Shanah, one should either eat a new fruit (one that one has not eaten yet that season) or wear new clothes that have not been worn before. The reason for this is not custom, but Jewish law. The reason for it also gives us an insight into the way the rabbis sometimes solve the insoluble.

To start with, as we noted in an earlier chapter, the reason we keep two days of Rosh Ha-Shanah even though the Torah only calls for one day, goes back to the time when Rosh Ha-Shanah was determined by seeing the new moon appear. At that time, the Sanhedrin in Jerusalem would proclaim that Rosh Hashanah had begun, and would send out messengers after Rosh Hashanah to inform people on which of the two possible days the holiday had been declared. Of course, only the people in Jerusalem knew for a fact which day was actually Rosh Ha-Shanah. Everyone else had to keep two days because of the uncertainty involved. In regard to Rosh Ha-Shanah, there is a rabbinic debate as to whether both days of Rosh Ha-Shanah must be considered as possible candidates for the real one-day festival, or whether the second day is merely an extension of the first. Now, whenever a holiday begins, one says the *She-heheyanu* ("who has kept us alive ...") blessing, women when lighting the candles and men during the *Kiddush*. Here we have a quandary: If the two days are distinct from one another, we must say *She-heheyanu* on both, whereas if the second is only an extension of the first, no blessing is needed. As we have no way of clarifying which of the two views is right, the rabbis came up with a simple device: by having everyone eat a new fruit or wear new clothing – either of which requires the recital of the *She-heheyanu* regardless, the woman in lighting the candles and the man in *Kiddush* recite the blessing, having in mind that they want the blessing also to apply to the fruit or clothing. Case solved!

Question What changes are made in the synagogue in preparation for the High Holidays?

Answer The different covers used throughout the year – on the *bimah*, on the ark and on the cantor's lectern – are all replaced with white ones. White is traditionally associated with purity, as early as the prophets, as we can see in, "Though your sins be as scarlet, they shall be as white as snow" (Isa. 1:18). By the same token the cantor wears a white gown, known as a *kittel*. Some individuals also have a custom of wearing a *kittel* for the High Holiday prayer services, especially on Yom Kippur.

Question What does the blowing of the *shofar* – the ram's horn – on Rosh Ha-Shanah signify?

Answer The Torah, which calls for the blowing of the *shofar* on Rosh Ha-Shanah, does not give any reason for the commandment. All it states is, "The seventh month, on the first day of the month... is a day of blowing the *shofar* unto you" (Num. 29:1). The Sages, though, give a kabbalistic (mystical) type of explanation, that on Rosh Ha-Shanah, when everyone is judged in the light of his actions of the previous year, the sound of the *shofar* converts God's attribute of strict justice into that of mercy, thus ensuring that God's judgment will be tempered with mercy, rather than solely with the justice of the case against each person. Symbolic of this are the six verses from the Bible which are chanted before the blowing of the *shofar*. The first letters of the verses spell out the phrase *kera satan* or "Tear up Satan," thereby, as it were, asking the Almighty to destroy all the evil that has accumulated within us over the course of time.

Question If the Torah specifically commands us to blow the *shofar* on Rosh Ha-Shanah, why do we not blow it when Rosh Ha-Shanah occurs on the Sabbath?

Answer In the Temple in Jerusalem, the *shofar* was indeed blown on Rosh Ha-Shanah, regardless of what day of the week that was. The rabbis, though, fearing that people might carry the *shofar* to the synagogue on the Sabbath if there was *shofar* blowing on that day – carrying in the public domain is a violation of the Sabbath which in theory carries a death penalty – decreed that there should be no *shofar* blowing on the Sabbath. Here we see the tremendous power of the rabbis, who can actually issue a decree which nullifies a command of the Torah. This power, though, may only be used to have a person *abstain* from doing something positive commanded by the Torah. The Sages, though, cannot issue a decree ordering or permitting a person to carry out an action which the Torah forbids.

One should point out that since Rosh Ha-Shanah is two days, even if the first day is the Sabbath, the *shofar* is at least blown on the second day. (The way the calendar was arranged, the second day of Rosh Ha-Shanah cannot occur on the Sabbath.)

✡ *A Yemenite* shofar; *19th century.*

יוצר ליום ראשון של ראש השנה

אור נבראה

✡ *Opening of the Rosh Ha-Shanah prayers from the* Leipzig Mahzor; *14th century.*

Question What are the different "sounds" of the *shofar*, and how many of each are blown?

Answer In reality, the Torah recognizes only two kinds of "sounds," which it refers to as the *tekiah* and the *teruah*. The general rule is that the *teruah* is preceded and followed by a *tekiah*. Now, as the Torah speaks three times of the blowing of the *shofar*, our Sages deduced that by Torah law one must blow the sequence *tekiah-teruah-tekiah* three times, thus giving a total of nine "sounds" that must be blown.

Enter the problem. *Tekiah* is accepted universally to mean a single uninterrupted tone. As far as *teruah* is concerned, though, there is a three way disagreement. One view regards *teruah* as being a staccato series of at least nine fast pulses (what we today refer to as *shevarim*, which means "broken"). Another view is that the *teruah* consists of three wailing cries, with the volume going up and down for each (what is referred to by us as *teruah*). Finally, the third view is that the *teruah* is a combination of the two above: nine pulses followed by three cries (what we call *shevarim-teruah*). In order to satisfy all three opinions, we have to blow the *shofar* using all three combinations (the description below uses the terms in the sense we use them today):

1. *Tekiah-teruah-tekiah*
2. *Tekiah-shevarim-tekiah*
3. *Tekiah-shevarim-teruah-tekiah.*

As *shevarim-teruah* are regarded as two distinct "sounds" for counting purposes, we can see that the above three sequences add up to a total of ten "sounds." Now, since, as we noted before, the Torah requires three sequences, we arrive at the figure of 30 "sounds" which must be blown on Rosh Ha-Shanah. By custom, though, a total of 100 "sounds" are blown, or 10 sequences of the above 10 "sounds," with these interspersed throughout the additional service on Rosh Ha-Shanah. While 100 "sounds" is almost a universal custom, there is a Yemenite custom of blowing only 71, the number representing the number of judges of the Sanhedrin, the religious high court which would convene in the Temple in Jerusalem.

Question May one fulfill the obligation to hear the *shofar* blown if one hears it on the radio?

Answer As hard as one may find it to believe, this general question is already asked in the Mishnah (ca. 200 C.E.). There the question is discussed about whether a person who blows the *shofar* into a pit has fulfilled the obligation. The conclusion reached is that if the person heard the *shofar* sound itself, he has fulfilled his obligation, whereas if he only hears the echo he has not fulfilled it. Using this analogy, modern-day rabbis have ruled that hearing the *shofar* over the radio is considered to be equivalent to hearing its "echo," rather than the sound of the *shofar* itself, and one has not fulfilled the obligation.

Question Before the *Kedushah* responsive reading in the additional service of the High Holidays, a very solemn prayer is recited. What is this prayer and what is its origin?

Answer The prayer, "*U-netaneh tokef*" – "Let us recite the awe of this holy day," is one that often moves people to tears. It describes how God judges each person during these days, determining who will live and who will die, who at the appointed time for his death and who prematurely, "who by water and who by fire, who by the sword and who by wild beasts, who by hunger and who by thirst..." The melody, too, lends awe to the occasion. The prayer ends on a triumphant note: "But repentance, prayer and giving charity avert the evil decree!"

Legend has it that the prayer was composed in the Middle Ages by a certain Rabbi Amnon. As was common during that time, tremendous pressure was placed on the Jews to "see the error of their ways" and to convert to Christianity. Of course, special pressure was exerted on the rabbis, as leaders of their congregations. Time after time the local bishop tried to persuade Rabbi Amnon to convert, but the rabbi rejected these overtures out of hand. Once, when the pressure was too great, Rabbi Amnon told the bishop that he wanted three days to consider conversion, and he would return with his answer after that time. As soon as he left the bishop, Rabbi Amnon was overwhelmed with remorse, because his request for time to reconsider implied that there was something to consider – and that is completely counter to Jewish belief. When the three days had elapsed, Rabbi Amnon simply did not show up. Finally, the bishop sent his men to bring Rabbi Amnon before him in chains. When the bishop asked him why he had not shown up at the appointed time, Rabbi Amnon replied that he had been so overcome with remorse for what he had said that he had simply been able to return to the bishop. The bishop then asked him what punishment he felt he deserved for not returning, and Rabbi Amnon replied that his tongue should be cut out for having dared utter the words he had uttered. The bishop did not take his suggestion, but ordered that his hands and legs be cut off instead. This was during the High Holiday period, the legend goes on, and the dying Rabbi Amnon was carried into the synagogue to pray. Just before the *Kedushah*, he stopped the prayers and asked for permission to praise God. He then uttered the *U-netaneh Tokef*, and died just as he ended it. Later, he appeared to one of his disciples in a dream and dictated the words of the prayer to him – and that, according to legend, is the text we use to this day.

Question Do Jews ever bow during their prayers?

Answer In general, during the *Amidah* prayer recited three times daily, there are four times when one bends the knees and then bows the head, but this is not a bow in the accepted sense of the word. On the other hand, there are six times a year that the Jew bows down with his head to the ground, once each on the two days of Rosh Ha-Shanah, and four times on Yom Kippur. The Rosh Ha-Shanah bows and one of those on Yom Kippur take place when the prayer entitled *Aleinu* is recited. *Aleinu* is a prayer describing how we are duty-bound to worship God and prays for the time when all will acknowledge God as King of the Universe. The bow takes place as the cantor recites the words, "we bend our knees, and bow down and pay homage to the King of Kings, the Holy One, blessed be He." The other three bows take place in the section of the additional service on Yom Kippur which describes the service which took place in the Temple, during which the High Priest uttered God's Ineffable Name – recited even by him only on that day – upon which everyone bowed to the ground. Generally, the men bow down, although there are a few women who also bow. If the floor is made of stone (as is the case in Israel) and there is no covering such as a carpet, care must be taken not to have the head touch the stone floor, because that is considered in Jewish law to be an idolatrous practice. Israelis who know the law therefore put down a newspaper to prevent their heads from touching the ground.

Question What is *tashlikh*?

Answer *Tashlikh* is a symbolic custom which goes back many centuries. On the first afternoon of Rosh Ha-Shanah (the second afternoon if the first day is the Sabbath), people go down to any source of water – the ocean, a river, even a well – and empty their pockets into the water, while symbolically emptying their sins in the process. While various great rabbis have endorsed the custom due to its hundreds of years of tradition, there have been others that denounced it sharply, seeing the practice as rank superstition.

Question What are *kapparot*?

Answer Before Yom Kippur, there is a custom for each person in a family to purchase a live fowl (a rooster for each male and a hen for each female). This fowl is kept until the day before Yom Kippur, and on the morning of that day it is held over the person's head as he or she recites the *kapparot* text. According to this text, the fowl should serve as a *kapparah* – an atonement – for the person's sins. The fowl is then slaughtered, and it or its value is donated to the poor. Many modern Jews substitute money for a fowl, and read a text where the money which is to be donated to charity should atone for one's sins. Here too there are those who are in favor of the custom, while others have expressed vehement opposition to it. After all, if a person wishes to donate money to charity, he should do so without the rigmarole of the *kapparot*.

Question Star baseball pitcher Sandy Koufax refused to pitch in a World Series game which was played on Yom Kippur. Yom Kippur, more than any other day, is considered to be sacred by all Jews. It is a fast day, and in Israel, for example, about 3/4 of all Jews – including many who do not classify themselves as religious – fast on that day. What is the significance of the fast on Yom Kippur?

Answer Yom Kippur, the last of the Ten Days of Repentance which begin with Rosh Ha-Shanah, is the most solemn day of the Jewish year. It is on this day that every human being is judged and his or her fate decreed. As the day on which we are all judged, it is a time for prayer and repentance. In regard to Yom Kippur, the Torah states, "On the seventh month, on the tenth day of the month, you shall afflict your souls" (Lev. 16:29). This "affliction," as explained by the Talmud, consists of five prohibitions (as we will discuss below), one of these being to fast. The fast begins just before sunset on the day before Yom Kippur, and extends to nightfall on the night following Yom Kippur, for a total of about 25 hours. Males of 13 and older and females of 12 and older are required to fast during this time. Yom Kippur is so much part of Jewish life that even avowedly non-religious Jews often fast and consider it as a day of introspection.

Question Of all the different special days of the Jewish year, which is the most important?

Answer Although most people would tend to answer Yom Kippur as the most important day, that is inaccurate. The most important day is the Sabbath – and there is definite proof of this: One who violates the Sabbath is, by Torah law, theoretically punishable by death after a trial before a Jewish court of law, while one who violates Yom Kippur is punishable by *karet*, literally "cutting off," a punishment only God Himself imposes. All Jewish authorities agree that the former is by far the more severe punishment. The number of people called up to the reading of the Torah has a direct relationship to the importance of the day: on weekdays three people are called up; on the New Moon and the intermediate days of festivals, four are called up; on the festivals themselves, including Rosh Ha-Shanah, the number is five; on Yom Kippur six are called up; and only on the Sabbath are there seven.

Question If the Sabbath is the most important day, why is Yom Kippur referred to as the "Sabbath of Sabbaths" in the Torah?

Answer As seen from numerous instances, the Torah refers to various festival days as "Sabbath." If we take the days which the Torah assigns to festivals during the year (excluding the extra days added by the Sages, primarily for those living outside the Land of Israel), during which one may not work, we find these are Rosh Ha-Shanah – 1 day, Yom Kippur – 1, Sukkot – 1, Shemini Atzeret – 1, Pesah (first and last days) – 2, Shavuot – 1, giving a total of seven days. Of this "week" of seven festival days, the most important is undoubtedly Yom Kippur, hence "the Sabbath of Sabbaths," where the word "Sabbaths" refers to all the festival days.

Question In which way is the *minhah* (afternoon) prayer which precedes Yom Kippur different from the normal *minhah* prayer?

Answer The *minhah* prayer before Yom Kippur has an extensive addition in the *Amidah* – the *vidui*, which is the confession recited as part of all the *Amidah* prayers of Yom Kippur. Although Yom Kippur has not yet started, our Sages tell us, we recite the *vidui* just in case we might choke at the final meal before Yom Kippur, thus dying without confessing.

The idea of worrying about eventualities is actually discussed in the Talmud, although in a somewhat different context. Jewish law requires the High Priest, who offers the Yom Kippur sacrifices in the Temple, to be married. Here the Talmud raises an interesting question: what happens if the High Priest's wife dies before he brings the sacrifices? He is then no longer married, and cannot bring the sacrifices. The solution that the Talmud offers is that he should marry a second woman, just as a " backup" in case his wife should die. One of the Sages, though, feels that this is an impractical suggestion. After all, he argues, if we must worry about one wife dying, should we not worry about both? That being the case, why draw the line at two, or three or four? The other Sages, though, answer that we base ourselves on probability. Thus, although the chance is remote, the High Priest's wife may indeed die just at that time, but the chances of two women dying are infinitesimal. By the same token, we worry about the possibility of a person choking at the last meal before Yom Kippur, and not about the possibility of that occurring at an earlier meal.

We can also note that ideally the cantor in the synagogue too, especially one who officiates on the High Holidays, must be married. The reason for this is evidently that only a person who has to contend with all the myriad problems of supporting a wife and family can really pour out his heart with conviction.

Question   Why do Jews fast on Yom Kippur?

Answer   The source for this law is the verse which states, "On the tenth day of this seventh month there shall be a day of atonement: it shall be an holy convocation unto you; and you shall afflict your souls" (Lev. 23:27). As we see, the Torah does not specify what form this affliction is to take. The oral law, which by Jewish tradition was handed down together with the written Torah, and without which, indeed, much of the Torah would be unintelligible, states that this affliction includes five elements. These prohibit: 1. eating or drinking; 2. washing (except for the bare needed for ritual requirements); 3. anointing oneself with a lotion; 4. wearing footwear which contains leather; and 5. sexual relations.

A hasidic rabbi once exclaimed: "I don't understand why the law forbids us to eat on Yom Kippur and on Tisha be-Av. On Yom Kippur, when we spend the whole day in the synagogue praying to God for forgiveness, who wants to eat? And on Tisha be-Av, when we remember how the glorious Temple was destroyed, who can possibly eat?"

Question   The evening service at the beginning of Yom Kippur begins with the haunting *Kol Nidre*. What is the significance of *Kol Nidre* at the beginning of the most solemn day of the Jewish year?

Answer   Properly speaking *Kol Nidre* is not really part of the prayers on Yom Kippur, and, in fact, is said before the prayers begin. In it, the cantor, assisted by two other members of the congregation, annuls the vows of all the members of the congregation. This prayer has been one of the most misunderstood in the liturgy, and anti-Semites have cited it as evidence that the Jewish religion does not require Jews to fulfill their vows and promises. The truth, though, is that the *Kol Nidre* only annuls vows made between man and God, such as a vow to fast on a specific day. It has no effect on vows made by one individual in regard to another, such as an oath in court.

Before the cantor begins the *Kol Nidre*, he recites: "With the permission of the court below [i.e., the two congregation members and himself] and the permission of the Heavenly court, we grant permission to pray with the sinners." This section, we are told, was instituted during the Spanish inquisition, when thousands of Spanish Jews, under threat of death, had converted to Christianity. The "sinners," then, were those who outwardly protested that they were Christians, but inwardly remained Jews. It was the vows of these so-called Christians, in which they had renounced their own faith and adopted Christianity, that were annulled. As the prayers of these Jews had to be held secretly, in constant fear of informers, we may understand the hauntingly beautiful melody of the *Kol Nidre*.

Franz Rosenzweig, one of the great Jewish thinkers of the 20th century, relates how he had decided to leave Judaism for Christianity, but then he realized he did not know what he was leaving, so he decided to at least visit a synagogue once. It so happened that he wandered into a synagogue at the *Kol Nidre* prayer, and he was so taken by the melody that he went on to explore his religion further. Rosenzweig later became one of the leaders of a Jewish revival in Germany. Tragically, this great man was afflicted with a disease which made him lose all motor ability, including even the power of speech. All he could move was a single finger. Yet, simply by pointing at a board of the alphabet, he dictated some of his greatest works to his wife, as she sat by him and transcribed his thoughts.

Question Can true repentance on Yom Kippur result in having all one's sins forgiven?

Answer Before we answer this question, we have to note that among the various ways that all the commandments can be divided into groups, one is to differentiate between those which involve only the person and God, such as keeping the Sabbath and laying *tefillin*; and those which affect one's fellow man, such as giving charity or visiting the sick. The same division holds true for sins. Certain sins are only against God, such as eating non-kosher food, while others are against one's fellow-man, such as stealing from or harming another person. As a general rule, with some exceptions for extremely grave sins, a person who has committed a sin against God may repent and be forgiven. If he has sinned against another person, all the repentance in the world does nothing, *unless* the sinner has undone whatever sin he committed: he has returned what he stole, paid for the damages he caused, etc. Generally – and against popular belief – Judaism believes that sins between man and his fellow-man are worse than those between man and God, because the former really contain two elements: a sin against man *and* a sin against God.

Question How about sins against one's fellow man that cannot be rectified, as, for example, where the person sinned against has died?

Answer In such circumstances, some people visit the grave of person who was sinned against, and broken-heartedly request his forgiveness.

The story is told of a man who came to the Hafetz Hayyim, who was known for his stress on not slandering any other person (in fact he wrote a number of volumes on the laws pertaining to slander), and begged the rabbi's advice. It seemed that he had slandered a certain person and as a result the person had suffered very great damage, which could not be rectified. What could he do to undo the damage he had done?

The rabbi told him to take a feather pillow, walk down the road, and scatter the feathers as he went. After scattering all the feathers, he was to retrace his steps and collect up all the feathers. Then he was to return to the rabbi. Well, in those days, and especially with a great sage such as the Hafetz Hayyim, one did not question the decision, even if one could not understand why he had been told to act in this fashion. The man left and did exactly as he had been told. A number of hours later he came back to the Hafetz Hayyim, frantic. There was no way he could fulfill the rabbi's orders. Most of the feathers had been carried away by the wind, and he only had a handful to show for the entire pillow full he had started out with. The Hafetz Hayyim then explained what this mission had all been about. Slander is one of the easiest sins in the world to commit, but once a person has slandered another, almost nothing he can do can serve to rectify the loss. One must, therefore, be very careful when one speaks about another person.

Question The classic Hebrew confession, the *vidui*, is worded in the plural and is arranged alphabetically in the Hebrew. Why?

Answer If we look through the list of sins recorded in the confession, we will find that very few people could have committed every sin listed there. On the other hand, as a basic principle of Judaism is that all Jews are responsible for one another, if any Jew sins it is considered as if the Jewish people had sinned. Thus, even though we ourselves may not have committed a specific sin, we know that some Jews somewhere must have committed them – and we are thus morally responsible. The plural form of the *vidui*, then, indicates that the confession is one on behalf of all of Israel. As to the alphabetical form, part of the reason for this may lie in the fact that this was a mnemonic device. After all, before the printing press, prayer books were hand-written and very scarce, and people often had to pray by heart. Another reason for this alphabetical listing may lie in a story which is brought in the Mishnah. A certain man acted as cantor in the presence of a number of the great rabbis. Instead of relying on the ordained text, which describes God as "great, mighty, and revered," he added numerous other adjectives in praise of God. Rather than being impressed with the man's piety, the Sages were angry at the man. Their logic was impeccable: if we stick to the text, we know that we are limiting our praise of God because that is the way the prayer was formulated. Once we decide to add our own adjectives, we are implying that only the adjectives we have used refer to God, and no more. We are, as it were, circumscribing God, and that is forbidden. Similarly, the use of the alphabet may imply that we are fully aware that there is no way we could possibly confess all our sins. Thus we restrict ourselves to the sins listed in the *vidui* as it stands.

Question   What is the origin of the *yizkor* – the memorial prayer for the dead? Why is it said and when?

Answer   The prayer as we have it, probably dates to the Middle Ages. At first, this was a prayer recited by each individual congregation, in which mention was made by name of all those members of the congregation who had been martyred for their faith. Later, the custom arose for each individual to recall all the departed members of his or her family. The purpose of the prayer is to pray that God grant perfect repose to the departed. An integral part of the prayer is to pledge to give charity on behalf of the departed, with the hope that the merit of this good deed will reflect upon the departed. *Yizkor* is said on the last day of the three pilgrimage festivals, as well as on Yom Kippur. The Sephardic ritual also includes a *yizkor* service just before the Yom Kippur evening service.

Question   What is *seder ha-avodah*?

Answer   *Seder ha-avodah* is a sizable part of the cantor's repetition of the *musaf* prayer on Yom Kippur. The name itself may be translated literally as "the order of the service," the reference being to the sacrificial service in the Temple on Yom Kippur by the High Priest. As was mentioned earlier, Judaism sees prayer as substituting for the sacrifices which were terminated by the destruction of the Temple. As the different sacrifices lay at the heart of the service on Yom Kippur, our own prayer service carries a "blow by blow" description of the Temple service. It is during this portion of the prayer that there is a custom to bow down to the ground on three separate occasions, each time when the prayer describes one of the three occasions that the High Priest and all those in the Temple courtyard would bow down as the High Priest pronounced God's ineffable name.

Question   Why is the Torah read at the afternoon service on Yom Kippur? What is read?

Question   While it is true that most Torah readings are in the morning service, Yom Kippur is far from the only occasion that there is a Torah reading at the afternoon service. In fact there is a Torah reading at each Sabbath afternoon service, where the portion read consists of the first of the seven portions that will be read on the following Sabbath morning. In addition, there is a Torah reading at the afternoon service of each fast day. The Yom Kippur reading, though, has a very specific message. The reading, from Leviticus 18, describes the different prohibitions in regard to sexual relations, such as incest, adultery and homosexuality. We are told that this passage was

"The Day of Atonement"; painting by Maurycy Gottleib, Poland.

chosen deliberately for the Torah reading at this time because of the vital importance of the message and the fact that most people are in the synagogue to hear the reading. The *haftarah* – the prophetic reading which follows the Torah reading – is the Book of Jonah. This reading is singularly appropriate, relating how the entire city of Nineveh had been under threat of destruction by God because of its evil ways, and how everyone from the king down repented, as a result of which the city was saved. The message, of course, is that full repentance brings salvation.

Question   What is the *ne'ilah* service?

Answer   The word *ne'ilah* means "sealing" or "concluding," and refers to the last prayer service of Yom Kippur, as the day is drawing to a close. This is the fifth prayer service of Yom Kippur. Yom Kippur, in fact, is the only day of the entire year in which there is a fifth prayer service. The prayer service itself recognizes the finality of the hour. For example, whereas throughout the Ten Days of Repentance we ask God to "write us" into the Book of Life, at *ne'ilah* we beg Him to "seal us" into that book, this marking the final decision by God for the coming year. The service itself ends with a clarion call of "acceptance of the Yoke of the Kingdom of Heaven." It includes the cantor reading the first verse of the *Shema* aloud, this then being repeated by the congregation; the sentence "Blessed be the name of His glorious kingdom forever" three times responsively; and then "The Lord is God" seven times. Finally, the service concludes with *Le-shanah ha-ba'ah bi-yerushalayim* – "This coming year [not, as is mistakenly translated, 'next year'] in Jerusalem." Many congregations break into joyful song or even dance to these words. As our Sages tell us, once Yom Kippur is over, all should go home happy, confident that the merciful God has forgiven them their sins.

Chapter Seven

Sukkot

Question What is Sukkot and why is it celebrated?

Answer The word Sukkot itself means "booths." Sukkot is the festival in which Jews live in booths, as a reminder of the 40 years the Israelites lived in booths in the desert, until finally arriving in the Promised Land. This is in fulfillment of the verses, "You shall dwell in booths seven days ... that your generations may know that I [God] made the children of Israel to dwell booths, when I brought them out of the land of Egypt" (Lev. 23:42-43).

Question When is Sukkot celebrated?

Answer Sukkot is celebrated from the 15th day of Tishrei, exactly two weeks after Rosh Ha-Shanah and on the fifth day after Yom Kippur.

Question If Sukkot commemorates leaving Egypt and living in booths, why is it held in Tishrei (September or October), at the beginning of the fall (at least in the northern hemisphere), rather than in the spring, when the Exodus actually took place?

Answer Jacob ben Asher (1270?-1340; one of the great codifiers of the *halakhah* and the author of the code called *Tur*) discusses this very question. Although his answer seems to be "second-guessing" God, in that the date was set by the Torah, his comment is most perceptive. Imagine, he tells us, if Sukkot was scheduled for the spring. At that time of the year, after everyone has been cooped up at home for the entire winter, there is a tendency for people to want to be outdoors and enjoy the warming sun. If Sukkot had been in the spring, there would be nothing in our actions indicating that we were doing anything in fulfillment of a divine command. By placing Sukkot in the fall – in fact six months to the day after Passover – at a time when the weather begins to get chilly, it becomes obvious to anyone that sees us that our motivation in going into the *sukkah* is not our own enjoyment, but rather in fulfillment of the commandment.

Question How long is the Sukkot festival?

Answer By Torah law, Sukkot itself is celebrated for seven days. The eighth day, Shemini Atzeret, is considered by our rabbis to be a separate holiday. By Torah law, one is not permitted to work on the first day of the festival and on Shemini Atzeret, and that is the pattern in which the holiday is celebrated in Israel. Outside Israel, because of the original difficulties in ascertaining the correct date of the festival, one is not permitted to work for the first two days. By the same token, Shemini Atzeret is observed for two days (even though we refer to the second day by a different name, as Simhat Torah). Thus outside Israel, nine days are celebrated.

Question What is the purpose of Shemini Atzeret?

Answer Unlike Sukkot, which has a clear theme celebrating the Exodus and the agricultural season (as we will see below), Shemini Atzeret is not listed in the Torah as having either national or agricultural significance. Instead, a charming *midrash* tells us, God was reluctant to have Israel part from Him after the seven days of Sukkot, much as a parent does not want to part from a child. He therefore added a day, to have Israel spend one more day with Him.

Question Is there any special way that the temporary *sukkah* booth must be constructed?

Answer As far as Jewish law is concerned, the walls of the *sukkah* may be made of any substance provided that "it can withstand a normal wind." What determines the temporary nature of the *sukkah* is its "roof," which is made up of what is referred to in Hebrew as *sekhakh* – literally "a covering." The *sekhakh* must be made of something from the plant world, such as bamboo poles, palm branches, thin planks, etc. It cannot, however, be a solid piece of wood. Jewish law requires that the *sekhakh* be thick enough that there be more shade than sunlight in the *sukkah*, and it must be thin enough that the stars can be visible at night. Furthermore, the *sukkah* cannot be situated underneath a roof or even a tree, but must be open to the sky. Because of this requirement, many apartment buildings in religious neighborhoods in Israel are built with larger porches on the lower floors, and the porch on each subsequent floor somewhat smaller, thus ensuring that each apartment has at least a part of its porch open to the sky for *sukkah* purposes.

✦ Sukkot *in a courtyard in Me'ah She'arim, Jerusalem.*

✦ *With the* arba minim *on Sukkot at the Western Wall in Jerusalem.*

Question For what must the *sukkah* be used, and who is required to use it?

Answer Throughout the festival, the *sukkah* is meant to replace one's home. At the least, all meals should be eaten in it. Ideally, one should sleep in it as well. As the commandment to remain in the *sukkah* is time-related, women are exempt from either eating or sleeping in the *sukkah*. The Sages laid great store in observing the commandment of remaining in the *sukkah*. After all, they reason, it is one of only two commandments in the Torah that is performed with every single part of one's body (immersing oneself in a ritual bath at the appropriate time is the other). Every other commandment, such as *tefillin*, involves only certain parts of the body, but not the whole.

Question What are the *arba minim*?

Answer The *arba minim*, or the Four Species as translated, are four species of plants that are held during certain parts of the morning service during Sukkot. As the Torah tells us, "You shall take for yourselves on the first day the fruit of a goodly tree, a branch of palm trees, and the boughs of a thick tree, and willows of the brook; and you shall rejoice before the Lord your God seven days" (Lev. 23:40). Now, if one examines this verse objectively, only two of the four species are stated clearly: palm and willow branches. But what are "the fruit of a goodly tree" and "the boughs of a thick tree"? Obviously, unless there is some type of supplementary information available, these phrases are meaningless. Enter the oral law, which, according to Jewish tradition, was given together with the Written Law – the Torah. (In fact, verses such as the above are considered to be clear indications of the fact that the Torah *had* to have some type of parallel interpretation.) According to the oral law, "the fruit of a goodly tree" is the citron, while "the boughs of a thick tree" refers to the myrtle. The oral law also informs us how many of each are required. Thus we have the Four Species: a citron, a palm branch, three sprigs of myrtle and two of willow, or, respectively in Hebrew, the *etrog*, *lulav*, *hadasim* and *aravot*.

Question Is there any symbolism in the choice of these particular species?

Answer The Torah does not mention any such symbolism, but our Sages in the Midrash do. They note that the citron has a pleasant smell and taste, the myrtle a pleasant smell but no taste, the palm (at least the date which grows on the palm) has a pleasant taste but no smell, and the willow has neither taste nor smell. These four, our Sages tell us, symbolize the four kinds of Jews: the citron represents the Jew who has "both a pleasant taste and smell" – who has both Torah knowledge and does good deeds. By the same token, the myrtle represents the Jew who does good deeds but does not have Torah knowledge, the palm represents the Jew who has Torah knowledge but does not perform good deeds, and finally the willow represents the Jew who has neither Torah knowledge nor performs good deeds. And the *midrash* concludes: "What does God do with them all? He has them all bound together into one unit, and this way one will atone for the other."

Question When are the Four Species taken up?

Answer Just before the *Hallel* prayer, the Four Species are picked up, and are held throughout that prayer. Toward the end of the prayer, as certain specific verses are recited, the Four Species are shaken in six directions. A common (but not the only) custom is to shake the Species to the north, west, south, east, up and down. The Four Species are also carried during the *Hoshanot* prayer, which we will describe later in this chapter.

Question Where are the Four Species obtainable?

Answer In the United States and most other countries except for Israel, sets of the Four Species are generally sold by Jewish book and gift stores. Synagogues too often do the ordering for their congregants. In Israel, things are not that simple – after all, who said living in Israel is simple? There, one has to buy each of the four species separately. Before Sukkot, various impromptu centers spring up, consisting of individual tables where one or more of the species are sold. As there are various standards for each of the species, those who wish to be ultra-scrupulous may spend hours on end searching for three perfect myrtle branches or for a totally unmarked citron. The price of each item, especially of the citron, depends on the degree of its perfection. There have been cases of individual citrons that sold for hundreds of dollars. In order to try to keep the prices in check, there have been communities which clamped a maximum price on each item. Thus the rabbinate in Baltimore recently set a limit of $35 on any individual citron, and no seller may exceed that price. One of the great hasidic dynasties went a step further, by decreeing that only one set of the Four Species be bought for each of its synagogues, with that set being used by all the congregants.

The idea of setting an upper limit on prices is not new. The Talmud, in fact reports that there was a shortage of fish, and the merchants in a certain town raised the price exorbitantly. To counteract this, the rabbi simply forbade anyone from buying fish for the Sabbath. Only when the fish merchants agreed to bring the prices down to the normal level did the rabbi remove his ban.

As we all know, Bar Mitzvahs and weddings have had a tendency of growing ever more lavish, as "keeping up with the Cohens" has become the rule. This often results in the family going deeply into debt to pay for the reception. In order to eliminate this problem, the present-day hasidic Rabbi of Gur has decreed – and when the rabbi decrees, his *hasidim* obey! – that the number of guests at any wedding of his *hasidim* cannot exceed 150. The rabbi also decreed that newlyweds in Jerusalem cannot buy anything larger than a three room apartment. (They may buy four room apartments in other areas, where the prices are cheaper. This has resulted in communities of Gur *hasidim* springing up all over Israel, in places where *hasidim* had not been seen before.) This takes the pressures off the parents to purchase ever larger apartments for their children. An apocryphal story is told of a leading *hasid* who was very wealthy, and who came to the Rabbi of Gur to ask him to lift the 150 person limit. After all, he told the rabbi, he was certainly able to afford a much bigger wedding. "If you're that wealthy," the rabbi is reported to have told him, "maybe you should buy yourself another rabbi!"

Question In what way does the taking of the Four Species on the first day of Sukkot differ from this action on the other days of the festival?

Answer The Torah commands, "You shall take for yourselves on the first day..." (Lev. 23:40), and then goes on to enumerate the Four Species. From this verse, it is clear that only on the first day of the festival must one take up the Four Species. On the other days, the requirement to take up the Four Species is by rabbinic decree. If we read the words of the verse carefully, we will see that there is another requirement, "You shall take *for yourselves*," which, as interpreted by the oral law, means that – at least on the first day of the festival – the Four Species have to belong to the person. (On the other days, where the requirement is only rabbinic, there is no such limitation.) This requirement, though, presents problems, because not everyone has his own set of the Four Species. Our Sages, however, came up with a simple solution: on the first day, rather than *lending* one's friend the Four Species, one must *give* them to him as a gift. This way, when the other person recites the blessing over the Four Species, he is doing so over a set which belongs to him. But this, too, can present a problem. What happens if the friend decides he does not want to return the set? If his ownership is absolute, what is to prevent him from keeping the set? The rabbis have a solution for this problem as well, and this is the method that is universally used to our day: the gift is given *conditionally* – provided that the recipient returns it to the original owner after use. In synagogues, where a few sets of the Four Species are laid out for the congregants, it is tacitly understood on the first day of the festival that whoever picks up the Four Species to recite the blessing becomes their owner for that time period.

Question What changes occur on the Saturday of Sukkot?

Answer As one is generally not permitted to carry anything outside one's house on Saturday, our Sages decreed that the Four Species are not to be used on that day. Thus, when the first day of the festival is a Saturday, the Four Species are only taken up from the second day of the festival and thereafter.

In every country but Israel, the second day of the festival is also a holiday, with all the restrictions involved. In Israel, on the other hand, where there is only one day when work is forbidden, should the first day of the festival be Saturday, adventurous souls do not buy the Four Species at all until Saturday night, in preparation for use on Sunday morning. Depending on the year and the crop, this can result in incredible bargains or incredibly poor quality!

Obviously, once the holiday is over, the value of citrons declines drastically – almost like yesterday's paper – and one can sometimes see citrons on sale in the markets after Sukkot at a price "per kilo."

Question What are *hoshanot*?

Answer The word *hoshanot* is taken from two Hebrew words, *hosha na* ("Please save [us]"), and refers to a prayer which is said every morning of Sukkot. The two words are pronounced as one (*hoshana*) when referring to this prayer. On each day of Sukkot except the Sabbath, a Torah scroll is taken out of the Ark after the *shaharit* or *musaf* service, depending on custom, and is brought to the *bimah* in the middle of the synagogue. All those who have the Four Species make a single circuit of the *bimah*, while reciting the prayer, whose refrain is *hosha na*. The basic theme of this prayer is that God grant us freedom from want in the coming year, through an abundant rainfall. On the Sabbath, the Torah scroll is taken out and a *hoshana* prayer is said, but no circuit is made of the *bimah*. On Hoshana Rabbah (The Great Hoshana), the seventh day of Sukkot, seven circuits are made, each accompanied by its own prayer stanza with the *hoshana* refrain. After the seven circuits, the Four Species are laid down and everyone in the synagogue picks up a bunch of five willow sprigs and beats it the on the ground until at least some leaves fall off. These prayers are collectively known as the *hoshanot*. The five willow sprigs are also known colloquially as *hoshanot*, because of their use as part of the *hoshana* prayers.

Question What are the dimensions of the *sukkah*, and how many walls must it have?

Answer The Talmud specifies that the minimum size of a *sukkah* is one which will hold a person's head, the majority of his body, and a corner of a

✿ *Simhat Torah in the Leghorn Synagogue; Solomon Hart, 19th century.*

table to eat from. Translated into numbers, the dimensions the Talmud gives are 7 handbreadths by 7 handbreadths, or about 28 inches by 28 inches, with a minimum height of 40 inches. There is no maximum size, but the maximum height is about 30 feet, for, as the Talmud tells us, once the *sekhakh* is higher than that, the eye does not discern the *sekhakh* – and what good is being in the *sukkah* if one does not realize he is in it? As to the walls, the absolute minimum requirement is two and the beginning (at least 4 inches) of a third wall.

Question You mentioned earlier that the extra day celebrated outside Eretz Israel following Shemini Atzeret is known as Simhat Torah. Why are the two days given different names?

Answer This question is a most pertinent, because, unlike all the other festivals, where the first day and the added day are referred to by the same name, this is an exception, with the second day having its own distinct name. In order to answer our question, we must first examine how Shemini Atzeret is celebrated in Eretz Israel.

In addition to the standard holiday prayers, Shemini Atzeret has a number of unique components:

a) *Hakafot* (literally: "circuits"), where during both the evening and the morning services all the Torah scrolls, after having been taken out of the Ark, are carried around the synagogue interior seven times. The path that the Torah scrolls takes is usually lined by all the male congregants, who reverently kiss each Torah scroll each time it passes them. In many synagogues, each circuit is followed by an extended period of dancing to the words of various religious songs, the entire *hakafot* sometimes going on for hours.

b) The reading of the Torah. In most synagogues, the Torah is read at night – the only time during the entire year that there is a Torah reading at night. In the morning, the Torah reading, which is the last section of the Book of Deuteronomy, is repeated time after time until every single adult male has been called up to the Torah. Indeed, all the children are also called to the Torah in a group, and they recite the blessings in unison with an adult who has been honored with the privilege of accompanying them. This honor is known as *kol ha-ne'arim* (literally: "all the children").

c) After the *haftarah* reading there is *hazkarat neshamot* or *yizkor*, during which those who have lost close relatives recite a special prayer in memory of their departed relatives. In many synagogues, it is the custom for those who have not lost any relatives to leave the synagogue during this time.

d) *Tefillat Tal*, the prayer for dew. This is a very solemn prayer, and the cantor wears a special white robe, the *kittel*, during the prayer and thereafter until the end of the service. This is the same type of robe worn by the cantor on the

High Holydays, and, in fact, the melody used for the *Tal* prayer is that used during the High Holyday services. If we realize that dew is the only source of water for the crops in Eretz Israel throughout the entire summer season, a period of four or five months during which there is no rain, we can understand why this prayer is so solemn.

As we can see from the above, Shemini Atzeret in Eretz Israel is a mixture of joyous parts of the prayer (the *hakafot* and the Torah reading in which everyone is called up), and solemn parts (*yizkor* and the prayer for dew).

With this as background, we are finally able to answer the question we posed earlier, as to why the two days are given different names, Shemini Atzeret and Simhat Torah. Whereas in Eretz Israel all four parts are recited on the one day, Shemini Atzeret, outside Eretz Israel they are divided between the two days. On Shemini Atzeret only *yizkor* and the prayer for dew are added (although in hasidic communities there are also *hakafot* on that day), while on Simhat Torah there are the *hakafot* and the special reading of the Torah. Thus, the two days are basically celebrated differently.

If I may be so bold as to add my own personal thought here, I once remarked that the observance of this day/these days is symbolic of Jewish life. For the Jew living in Israel, life is a mixture of the joyous and the sad, for that is the way life normally is. For the Jew living outside Israel, there is a certain built-in artificiality of life, where he, in a way, has to "compartmentalize" himself. This is symbolized by the separate days, one for the serious aspects of the festival and the other for the joyous aspects.

Question Doesn't dancing in a synagogue seem a little unusual?

Answer A story – probably apocryphal – is told of Emperor Franz-Joseph of Austria-Hungary, who once asked to see how the Jews celebrated Simhat Torah. His advisers then took him to all the prim and decorous synagogues in Vienna, and he saw how in each case the Torah scrolls were taken around by solemn-looking men, and how this was followed by a desultory minute or two of singing. Finally, as the Jews accompanying the emperor wished to bring him back to the palace, Franz-Josef turned to them and asked them: "Are you sure that those are all the synagogues in the city?" Hesitatingly, one of his escorts stammered, "N-n-n-o, your majesty, there is still one that we haven't shown you, but that is of the *hasidim*, and we didn't think you'd find it particularly to your liking." "I'll decide that," said the emperor, and they all set out for the hasidic synagogue. When they got there, they walked in and were ignored totally. The hasidim, in ecstasy, were dancing around the Torah completely oblivious of their distinguished visitors.

A few minutes later, the emperor and his escorts left, and Franz-Josef turned to them. "I admire you Jews," he said, and before anyone had a chance to say a word he went on: "By us, the madmen are together with everyone else. With you, all the madmen are confined to a single place."

To an outsider, indeed, the joyous, even what may be called unruly, dancing might appear to be inappropriate, indeed even "mad," but this, too, is a way of worshipping God, one in which a person can let himself go and, in the words of David, "all my bones shall say, Lord, who is like unto You." (Psalms 35:10)

Question What is the meaning of the name Simhat Torah?

Answer The words Simhat Torah mean "the celebration of the Torah," and we saw above that the two unique observances of the day, the *hakafot* and the Torah reading for every male present, are indeed celebrations of the Torah.

Question Why is the Torah "celebrated" just on this day?

Answer As we pointed out earlier in this chapter, the Torah reading cycle for the year begins on the Sabbath following Simhat Torah. The 54 *sidrot* of the cycle continue throughout the year, until the entire Torah has been read by the end of the year. It is on Simhat Torah (in Eretz Israel on Shemini Atzeret) that the Torah reading, with the reading of the last section of Deuteronomy, concludes. This is then followed by a preliminary reading of the first chapter of Genesis, symbolic of the fact that the Torah has no end. It is the celebration of the completion of the Torah reading cycle and the beginning of the new cycle that is celebrated on this day.

Question Elsewhere, you mention that originally the custom of reading the entire Torah over the course of a year was only one of the customs (although the one that has been universally accepted for many centuries), and that there were places where the cycle took three years or even three and a half years. How did the people with the latter customs celebrate Simhat Torah?

Answer The answer is a simple one: they didn't – at least not on the day that we do, and possibly not in the same form we do. In fact, the entire day of Simhat Torah as we know it was devised in geonic times (some between the 6th and 10th centuries C.E.). This also probably accounts for the fact that this is the only "added day" in the calendar that has a special name of its own.

Chapter Eight

Passover

Question   Where is the name "Passover" derived from?

Answer   We are told in the Torah that when God smote all the firstborn of Egypt, he "passed over" the houses of the Israelites. The latter had smeared the doorposts of their homes with the blood of a lamb they had slaughtered as a sacrifice. This served as a sign that the house was one of Israelites. The Hebrew word for "passed over" is *pasah*, and hence the Hebrew name by which the festival is known is Pesah. Later, the sacrifice offered on the first evening of Passover was also referred to as the *pesah* (= paschal; the English word is obviously derived from the Hebrew) sacrifice.

Question   By what other names is Passover known?

Answer   There are three other Hebrew names for the festival: *Hag he-Aviv* – the Spring Festival – based on the time of the year the festival must occur; *Hag ha-Matzot* – the Festival of *Matzot*, as the Torah refers to it throughout; and *Zeman Herutenu* – the Festival of our Freedom, although the last name is only found in the prayers. It is interesting that the Torah refers to the festival as *Hag ha-Matzot*, while the common everyday use is *Hag ha-Pesah* (the Festival of Pesah). A beautiful commentary points out that when God, as it were, refers to the festival, He refers to it in terms of what the Jews do for Him, namely baking the *matzot* for the festival, while the Jews refer to the festival in terms of what God did for them, in that He passed over the Israelite homes and slew the Egyptian firstborn.

Question   As the Jewish calendar is based on 12 lunar months of 29 1/2 days, that adds up to 354 days. Does that not mean that the Hebrew calendar slips back 11 days each year? What ensures that Passover is indeed the Spring Festival, as the Torah states it is to be?

Answer   The Sages were very much aware of this problem, and would therefore add a month (Adar II) after the month of Adar if they felt that the wheat and the fruit on the trees were insufficiently ripe. (Adar is the month preceding the one in which Passover occurs.) Later, when the calendar was formalized, it was determined that seven leap months were to be added in every 19-year cycle, thus ensuring that Passover is always in the Spring.

Question   When is Passover, and how long is the festival?

Answer   Passover begins on the 15th day of Nissan, and by Torah law lasts for seven days. Outside Israel, as we will see below, it lasts for eight days.

Question   What general laws apply to Passover?

Answer   Passover involves one major change, which requires a complete restructuring of the home for Passover. This is the requirement to remove all leavened goods and those products which contain leaven (e.g., bread, cake or cookies, yeast, pasta, etc.) from one's home before Passover, and to use only unleavened products throughout Passover. The law requires not only disposing of all such foods, but also not using dishes which were used to prepare such foods. Thus the observant Jew must get rid of all leaven and replace all his dishes, pots and silverware with others that are only used for Passover. Of course as the Jewish home requires two sets of dishes – one for meat and one for dairy products – this means that each home must have four sets of dishes. No wonder that storage space is so vital to the observant Jew!

Question   Why is *matzah* eaten during Passover, and why is bread forbidden during this time?

Answer   In regard to Passover, the Torah states, "Seven days shall you eat unleavened bread; on the first day you shall put away leaven out of your houses" (Ex. 12:15). The Torah tells us that following the smiting of the Egyptian firstborn the Jews were driven out of Egypt, and they left in such a hurry that their dough did not have time to rise. To commemorate the momentous event of the Exodus from Egypt, which marked the founding of the Jewish people as a nation, Jews are required to eat *matzah* – a mixture of flour and water which is baked immediately, in order not to give the mixture time to ferment or rise – throughout Passover. Certain rabbis also imparted a symbolic meaning to this law: leavened bread, which has been allowed to rise, symbolizes pride and haughtiness, whereas *matzah* is a symbol of humility and modesty. During the Passover holiday, the Jew must not only remove all traces of leaven from his house, but must remove all traces of spiritual leaven – pride – from his heart, and must be humble before his God.

Question What is *hametz*?

Answer Any product made of any of five specific grains which has been allowed to ferment or any leavening agent is generally referred to as *hametz*. Thus, we speak of *hametz* being forbidden on Passover.

Question How must one dispose of his *hametz*?

Answer Obviously, one uses up as much as possible before Passover. In the weeks before Passover, the Jewish housewife (hopefully working with her husband) will completely scour the home from top to bottom, to ensure that no crumbs of bread are left in some unsuspecting place (as underneath couch cushions, for example). Thus, by the night before the Passover *seder*, the house will be completely free of any leavened products, except for the amount needed for the last meals. In order to ensure that there is no *hametz* lying around anywhere, as soon as possible after nightfall the husband – usually accompanied by the children – makes a thorough search of the entire home (one should even include the family's car/s in the search). It is customary for the children to hide 10 small pieces of bread throughout the home, and woe befall the father who only finds nine! (A hint: wrapping the *hametz* in plastic or aluminum foil in advance will prevent crumbs from falling all over the place.) The search is conducted by candle light, although various authorities permit the use of a flashlight. The electric lights are all extinguished before each room is searched, because a candle would be valueless in illuminating dark corners if the electric lights were on. By custom, any *hametz* foun is picked up by sweeping it into a wooden spoon with a feather. (A "*hametz* search kit" is often sold by Jewish bookstores.) Whatever *hametz* is found is put aside, to be burned the next day.

After the search is complete, the father makes a declaration, in which he states that in case there is still *hametz* lying around of which he is not aware, he renounces his ownership of it. That way, even if there is some undetected *hametz* in the home, it no longer belongs to the family. The next day, after breakfast, all the *hametz* is burned, together with the feather and the spoon used in the search. The father then makes a final declaration, renouncing ownership of any *hametz* of which he may be aware or is not aware. The law gives specific times for these actions: one is only permitted to eat *hametz* for the first quarter of the day (as defined from sunrise to sunset), and all *hametz* must be burned by the end of the first third of the day.

A story is told of how a famous rabbi's wife was working hard at scrubbing down all the chairs in her home before Passover. The rabbi, feeling for his wife's hard work, told her that the *Shulkhan Arukh* – the standard code of Jewish law – certainly does not require anyone to go to such lengths. Upon hearing this, she exclaimed: "If I left things to you and your *Shulkhan Arukh*, we'd be eating bread on Passover!" While the story may be apocryphal, the lengths to which Jewish women went – and still go – in preparing the house before Passover, is mind-boggling. And after all the weeks of work by the wife are finished and the husband spends the hour or two required to check the house for *hametz*, he can announce smugly to all that the house is clean of any leaven!

Question   What happens if one has a large quantity of *hametz* which must be disposed of?

Answer   The *halakhah* offers a solution for such possibilities, and it is a solution of which most people avail themselves. When we consider that whiskey is considered *hametz* (it is fermented from wheat), as are various other liquors, the requirement to get rid of all *hametz* can cause a considerable financial loss. What one may do is sell all his *hametz* to a non-Jew for the duration of Passover. This way, the person does not, indeed, own any *hametz* during the festival. Generally, one appoints the local rabbi to be one's representative, and it is he who sells *hametz* belonging to the individual members of the congregation to a single non-Jew. It is important to stress that this is not a legal fiction – if it was, it would not be a valid sale, and then everyone would own his own *hametz* throughout Passover! Firstly, the *hametz* must be locked away in a specific place within the home, and that place must be rented to the non-Jew for the duration of Passover. Secondly, the non-Jew must give a nominal deposit to buy the *hametz*, with the understanding that he has the right to obtain it all if he later pays the full market price for it. Every person who sells *hametz* must then be willing to part with his *hametz* should the non-Jew be willing to exercise his option. That is the key and the crux of the sale. Of course, the non-Jew generally does not exercise his option, and the rabbi then terminates the sale after Passover.

Question   What is the "Fast of the Firstborn?"

Answer   On the morning before Passover, it is customary for all the male firstborn to fast, to commemorate the fact that during the Exodus God killed all the Egyptian firstborn, while saving the Jewish ones. The custom is for the fast to start at dawn and to end at nightfall. But there is another custom which comes to the rescue of the firstborn. Thus, there is a custom, after the morning service, for the rabbi or some other member of the synagogue to complete a tractate of the Talmud he has been studying for some time before this day. The person who is completing the tractate recites the last few lines aloud, while everyone present listens to him. As the conclusion of the study of a Talmudic tractate is a cause for rejoicing, all those present join in the festivities and refreshments – including the firstborn, who may break their fast in honor of the occasion. Once they have broken their fast, the firstborn may eat normally for the rest of the day. This is surely the shortest fast of the year! We should note that it is customary for the father of a male firstborn who is under *Bar Mitzvah* age to fast instead of his son until the boy reaches Jewish adulthood. Of course, here too the fast only lasts until the Talmudic tractate has been completed.

Question When is one forbidden to work and when is one permitted to do so during Passover?

Answer By Torah law, one is forbidden to work on the first day and on the last day of the seven-day festival, and that, indeed, is the situation in Israel to this day. Outside of Israel, because of the original doubts there were about the occurrence of the New Moon, the festival is eight days long and one is forbidden to work on the first two and the last two days. Unlikely the Sabbath, on festival days one is permitted to carry from one domain to another, and is permitted to cook food or perform those actions generally needed for cooking food.

The days between the first and last days of the festival are referred to as *hol ha-mo'ed*, a term generally referred to as "the intermediate days of the festival." The literal translation of the term, though, is "the weekday of the festival" – and that is exactly what these days are: a combination of weekday and festival days. Jewish law restricts a person to only performing those types of work where the failure to work would result in a financial loss to the individual. One is not, however, permitted to carry out those types of work which will result in a financial profit.

In Israel, the days of *hol ha-mo'ed* are indeed treated as "weekdays of the festival," and all stores and government office are only open in the morning, giving everyone employed in them half a day off. In the ultra-Orthodox Me'ah She'arim quarter they go further, and all stores except those which sell food are closed completely throughout Passover.

Question What is the Passover *seder*?

Answer The *seder* is the traditional meal eaten on the first night of Passover (first two nights outside Israel), and which commemorates the Exodus from Egypt. The word *seder* means "order," in that the lengthy family service and meal have a definite order of procedures, beginning with the *Kiddush* at the beginning of the meal and ending with the recital of various prayers of praise to God. The entire ritual is found in the *Haggadah*.

Question   What is the *Haggadah*?

Answer   The *Haggadah* is a volume containing the entire service to be recited at the Passover *seder* . We may note that it is the most popular of all Jewish religious book, with more than 3,000 known editions having been published to date. The editions range from simple ones on newsprint (Israeli newspapers often include a copy of the *Haggadah* in their pre-Passover editions) to elaborate creations illustrated by some of the world's leading artists.

Question   What are some of the distinctive parts of the *seder*?

Answer   The *seder* as a whole may be divided into two broad areas – the ritual and the recital. If we may refer to them as such, the "highlights" of the *seder* include:

1. *Kiddush* – sanctification over wine – which marks the beginning of every evening and morning meal on the Sabbath and festivals. This will be the first of four cups of wine drunk throughout the *seder*.
2. *Mah Nishtanah* – the recital by the youngest participant at the *seder* of the "Four Questions," which point out the differences between this night and all other nights.
3. The recitation of the "Four Sons" passage, describing four types of sons, how they behave and how they should be treated (we will deal with this topic in some detail a little later in this chapter).
4. The telling of the story of the Exodus from Egypt.
5. The recital of the Ten Plagues, accompanied by spilling a drop of wine at the mention of each plague.
6. The recital of the first part of the *Hallel* prayer.
7. The Passover meal itself, with two essential ingredients: the *matzah* and the *maror* (bitter herbs).
8. The *Afikomen*. Each participant eats a piece of the special *matzah* which was set aside for the purpose before the meal began. This is symbolic of the Paschal Lamb which was eaten in Temple times. In order to keep the young children awake until the end of the *seder*, it is customary for the father to hide the *Afikomen*. The child who finds it usually refuses to return it so that the meal can be concluded until a suitable "ransom" has been paid or promised.
9. Grace after meals followed by the completion of *Hallel*.
10. *Shefokh Hamatekha* – a prayer recited with the front door open as a sign of our trust in God. In it, we ask God to punish those who refuse to acknowledge Him. We should realize that the Passover *seder* night was often the occasion for attacks by the Gentiles on the defenseless Jews, and

it often took a great deal of courage to open the front door, if only for a minute or two.

11. Various prayers which praise God and celebrate the miracle of the Exodus, with the official conclusion of the *seder* marked by the words, *Le-shanah ha-ba'ah bi-Yerushalayim* – "This coming year in Jerusalem."

12. Concluding songs. It is customary after this to sing various songs with responsive refrains, concluding with *Had gadya – One little kid.*

Question Why this emphasis on four – four cups of wine, four questions, four sons?

Answer The number four has profound significance in the Exodus from Egypt, in that God's promise to deliver the Israelites is couched in four separate terms, as seen in the verse, "*I will bring you out* from under the burdens of the Egyptians; *I will free* you from their bondage; *I will redeem* you with a outstretched arm, and with great judgments; *I will take* you to Me for a people" (Ex. 6:6-7). The number four in the *seder*, especially the four cups of wine, is symbolic of these verses. Rabbi Ovadyah Yosef, former Sephardic chief rabbi of Israel, once remarked jokingly that it would have been quite sufficient had God visited *four* (rather than ten) plagues on the Egyptians, and then have had *ten* (rather than four) cups of wine at the *seder*.

Question How about the four sons? Is there any other significance in that number?

Answer Repeatedly, the Torah stresses the need for the father to instruct his children about the Exodus. In fact there are four distinct references to this responsibility. Based on the verses in the Torah, the *Haggadah* describes four possible reactions to the Exodus and the commemorative Passover celebration: the "wise son," who wishes to know more of what is involved; the "wicked son," who mocks the festival; the "simple son," who sees what is going on, is surprised, but cannot really phrase any but the most general of questions: "What is this?" Finally, there is "the son who does not know how to ask" at all. As has been said, the lesson of the "four sons" is that each son must be treated individually, and one cannot offer the same education to everyone alike.

A great rabbi noted how the "four sons" may parallel what happened in the United States: the "wise son" was the great-grandfather who came from Europe. He still knew all the traditions. His son, though, the "wicked son," threw out the traditions, seeing them as outdated relics. *His* son, in turn, would still come to the grandfather for the *seder*, but could only look in amazement and ask "what is this?", because it was all so strange to him. Finally, the fourth generation could not even go to his own grandfather,

✣ *A page from the illuminated* Darmstadt Haggadah.

because his grandfather was the "wicked son," and thus he was "the son who does not know what to ask."

Question What is one required to eat at the Passover *seder*?

Answer While there are many foods which are traditional at the *seder* meal – *gefilte fish*, chicken soup with *matzah* balls, for example – there are only two foods that are required by Jewish law within the meal. These are *matzah* – which reminds us of the fact that the Jews were forced to leave Egypt in a hurry and were therefore forced to bake their bread before the dough fermented – and the bitter herb, symbol of the bitterness of Egyptian slavery. These are both eaten at the beginning of the meal. In order to mitigate somewhat the bitterness, the bitter herb is dipped in *haroset* – a paste, or "dip" usually made of apples, nuts, cinnamon and wine – which is symbolic of the mortar with which the Israelites had to work. In Temple times, when the Paschal Lamb was sacrificed, one was also required to partake of the meat of the lamb at the *seder*.

Question What must be mentioned at the *seder* table?

Answer Rabban Gamaliel stated that "Whoever has not mentioned the following three items has not fulfilled his obligation, and these are they: the paschal sacrifice, *matzah* and *maror* [the bitter herb]." As part of the *seder*, each is mentioned, and the reason for its inclusion is described. While we no longer have the Paschal Lamb (which needed to be sacrificed in the Temple in Jerusalem), we do have the other two, and it is the custom to point to each as one recites the passage about its importance. One of the first printed *Haggadot*, the Prague Haggadah of 1526, has a marginal note that when mentioning the *maror*, the husband should point at his wife, in accordance with Ecclesiastes 7:26, "I find more bitter than death the woman." In fact, an illustration in a famous illuminated *Haggadah* of the Middle Ages actually shows the husband pointing at his wife as he makes the required recitation. Women's lib had a long way to go in those days!

Question There are those who claim that Jews invented the sandwich with the "Hillel sandwich" eaten at the *seder*. What is the "Hillel sandwich" and what is its significance?

Answer At the beginning of the *seder*, one first eats the *matzah*, after reciting the appropriate blessing. One then recites the blessing on the bitter herb and eats it. Later, just before the meal, one makes a "sandwich" of two pieces of *matzah* with the bitter herb (the latter having been dipped in *haroset* first) between them. That is the "Hillel sandwich." The origin of this custom, as of many other Jewish customs, has a basis in Jewish law. While Jewish law has accepted the fact that we eat the *matzah* and bitter herb separately, Hillel ruled that the *matzah*, the bitter herb and the flesh of the Paschal sacrifice had to be eaten together. He based himself on the verse, "They shall eat it [the Paschal Lamb] together with *matzah* and bitter herbs" (Num. 9:11). Of course, we no longer have the Paschal sacrifice, but the *matzah* and bitter herb are still eaten together as the "Hillel sandwich," out of respect for that great authority's view.

Question What must be used for the bitter herbs?

Answer Many people believe that one needs ground horseradish for the bitter herb. The Talmud, though, lists a number of vegetables in descending order of preference. The most preferable of all vegetables for use as the bitter herb is, according to the Talmud, romaine lettuce, which has a slightly bitter taste. Romaine lettuce is definitely preferable for a number of reasons: a) the amount one must eat is a fluid ounce within the space of a few minutes, an unbelievably large amount in the case of horseradish, considering its pungency; b) that quantity of ground horseradish can present a real health hazard (although it will do wonders for the sinuses!). In fact, any person who is in poor health who plans to use horseradish in order to observe this *mitzvah* should first check with his doctor.

Question Are there any limitations on the type of *matzah* to be used at the *seder*?

Answer In order to answer this question, we first have to understand what *matzah* is. Simply put, *matzah* is a mixture of flour and water which is baked before the dough has time to rise. (The *halakhah* gives 18 minutes as the maximum time within which the dough must be baked.) It is accepted as axiomatic that flour mixed with water will ferment, so the flour ground for baking *matzah* must be stored in a way as to ensure that it will not come into contact with water before it is kneaded for dough. In general, the precautions taken to keep the flour separate from water commence from the time the wheat is ground into flour, and the *matzah* eaten on Passover is made in accordance with these precautions. For the Passover *seder*, though, a higher standard is required: the *matzah* must be made from wheat which has been kept from contact with water *from the harvest on*. This is known as *matzah shemurah*, which, translated literally, means "guarded *matzah*." There are those who adopt a more stringent view, and eat only *matzah shemurah* throughout Passover.

Question Some people have the custom of not eating *gebrokht* throughout Passover. What is *gebrokht?*

Answer Again, we will need an introduction to understand the answer. Jewish law accepts as axiomatic that once dough has been baked into *matzah*, it can no longer ferment. There is therefore no prohibition against taking *matzah* and grinding it into flour to be used as *matzah* meal, or to soak this meal in water, for it cannot ferment. It is that rule which enables one, for example, to make *kneidlach* – *matzah* meal dumplings, which are served in chicken soup – on Passover, or to make Passover cakes out of *matzah* meal. Some communities, though, have a custom which forbids allowing *matzah* to come into contact with water, for fear that some of the dough was not baked through and the addition of water may make that dough ferment. Now we can finally answer what *gebrokht* is. The word itself simply means "broken," but it is a type of code name for *matzah* which has been "broken down" to be mixed with water. Thus, if we say that a person does not eat *gebrokht* on Passover, we mean that he will not eat anything made out of *matzah* meal or made by soaking *matzah* in water. We do stress, though, that this custom is a stringency above and beyond the requirements of Jewish law. Oh, in case you should ask: People who do not eat *gebrokht* on Passover use substitutes for making cakes, such as almond paste or potato flour (potato flour is permitted, as the potato is not one of the five species of grain which are deemed capable of fermenting).

Question What is egg *matzah?*

Answer This is *matzah* in which the flour is mixed with egg yolks (and often fruit juices) rather than with water. The Talmud refers to this class of *matzah* as *matzah ashirah* ("rich" or "enriched" *matzah*). While the Talmud permits the eating of such *matzah*, it is the Ashkenazic practice to limit its use to the very young, the old and the ill.

Question Who is required to eat *matzah* and bitter herbs at the *seder?*

Answer This law applies equally to all adult men (i.e., aged 13 and over) and women (aged 12 and over). As a general rule, women are exempt from those commandments which must be performed at a specific time (such as laying *tefillin* in the morning), and they should be exempt from eating *matzah* and bitter herbs as well under the same grounds. This case, though, is an exception, and women are obligated as well as men. The Talmud derives this from a verse in the Torah, which states, "You shall eat no leavened bread with it [i.e., the paschal sacrifice]; seven days shall you eat unleavened bread with it"

(Deut. 16:3). From this, our Sages deduced that whoever is forbidden to eat leavened bread during Passover (and this, of course, includes women) is also required to eat *matzah* on the festival.

Question   What is the Passover *seder* plate?

Answer   It is customary to have a large plate in the center of the festive table (among some communities the custom is to have such a plate in front of each adult male participant), on which various items are displayed symbolically.

Question   What are the different items, and what do they symbolize?

Answer   The items include a roasted egg, the *zero'a* (a roasted shankbone or other bone), *maror* (some of the bitter herb), the *karpas* (a vegetable, generally celery or a boiled potato, but it can be another vegetable), some of the *haroset* (a paste, as described earlier), and the *hazeret* (also a vegetable). The symbolism involved follows:
1. The egg – commemorates the *hagigah* ("festive") sacrifice that was brought to the Temple on each pilgrimage festival.
2. The *zero'a* – commemorates the paschal sacrifice which had to be brought specifically on the first night of Passover.
3. The *maror* – as mentioned earlier, this symbolizes the bitterness of the Jews' slavery in Egypt.
4. The *karpas* – a vegetable eaten before the meal proper, for the sole purpose of arousing the curiosity of the children present, due to the change in the order of eating.
5. The *haroset* – the paste made to look like mortar, again symbolizing the hard labor of the Israelites in Egypt.
6. The *hazeret* – The Talmud states that Rabbi Judah the Patriarch's (ca. 200 C.E.) table was always graced with abundant vegetables, this being one of the symbols of his status as the recognized leader of world Jewry. On Passover, then, when every Jew must feel himself a prince, the *hazeret* symbolizes grandeur and royalty.

Question   Why are there three *matzot* at the *seder* table, unlike the two loaves (of bread) required for every Sabbath or festival meal?

Answer   Symbolically, the three *matzot* have been related to the forefathers of the Jewish people (Abraham, Isaac, Jacob) or to the three groups into which Jews are divided (priests, Levites, Israelites). The real reason, though, is probably because two of the three *matzot* are meant to serve the same purpose as the two loaves that one is required to have on every Sabbath and festival, while the third *matzah*, which is broken into two (as some *Haggadot* put it, not paying much attention to their arithmetic, "two uneven halves"), is added for the Passover *seder* specifically. It is this third *matzah* which symbolizes the festival.

Question   Why is the third (actually the middle) *matzah* broken?

Answer   The reason given is that the broken *matzah* symbolizes the poverty of the slaves in Egypt, who could not afford to buy a whole loaf. The broken "larger half" also serves another purpose, because it is the mission of the children to "steal" this piece of *matzah* from their father, and to hide it from him. As this piece, known as the *afikomen* (in Greek the word means "dessert"), must be the last thing eaten at the *seder*, the children use their leverage to obtain promises of various gifts to return it. In reality, though, the prime purpose of the hiding of the *afikomen* is in order to keep the children wide awake until the end of the *seder*.

Question   What is the "half-*Hallel*," and when is it recited on Passover?

Answer   The *Hallel* (literally "Praise") proper consists of Psalms 113-118, which all praise God. The *Hallel* is recited on all three pilgrimage festivals, as well as on Hanukkah. On Rosh Hodesh – the day/s of the New Moon, two short passages are left out, and the *Hallel* minus these passages is known as "half-*Hallel*" (this is *not* an arithmetical half!). On Passover, the full *Hallel* is recited on the first day (first two days outside Israel), and thereafter the "half-*Hallel*" is recited for the remaining days. The reason for this, we are told, is that our joy at our deliverance cannot be complete, because it was acquired at the expense of the Egyptians who died in the Red Sea. This is an interesting insight, given the way the Israelites were treated by the Egyptians, with their male children thrown into the river, etc.

A *midrash* parallels this thought. We are told that when the Egyptians drowned in the red Sea, thus finally freeing the Israelites from the threat of their yoke, the Heavenly Hosts wished to recited praise of God for delivering Israel. God then rebuked them, saying: "My creatures are drowning in the sea, and you wish to recite praise?"

Question   What happens when an American Jew (or a Jew of any other land) visits Israel for Passover?

Answer   As we mentioned earlier, the Jews in Israel observe Passover for seven days, while those who live elsewhere must observe it for eight days. As Jewish law requires a person who visits another area to observe all those customs of his own domicile which are more stringent than those of the place he is visiting, many halakhic authorities rule that Jews from outside Israel must observe eight days of Passover, even though the eighth day is already the day after Passover for those Jews who live in Israel. Thus it is possible for guests in an Israeli's house to still be eating *matzah* on the eighth day, while everyone else in the house is already eating bread!

Question Why does the Passover *seder* have sad connotations in Jewish history?

Answer Beginning in the Middle Ages, the Jews were often accused of using the blood of Christians in the baking of their *matzot*. The irony of the accusation is that it probably traced back to the Catholic belief that the wafers used in the Mass are transubstantiated into the flesh of Jesus. All the Jewish (and often learned Christian) denials of the charge were often of no avail, and if any Christian child disappeared before the Passover season, the response was all too often wanton pogroms, which were an excuse for pillage, rape and murder. As late as this "enlightened" century, there was a blood libel in Russia, when a Jew, Mendel Beilis, was imprisoned for two years in Kiev (1911-1913) on the charge of having killed a 12-year old Russian lad. Only after this lengthy imprisonment and a world-wide outcry, was Beilis finally brought to trial and declared innocent by a jury of simple Russian peasants.

Chapter Nine

Shavuot

Question   What is the festival of Shavuot?

Answer   Shavuot, which in Hebrew means "weeks," is the festival which celebrates the giving of the Torah at Mount Sinai. It was on this day that God gave the Torah to Israel. During the Temple period, it was also the occasion when the first fruits were brought to Jerusalem to celebrate the new crop.

Question   What other names does the festival have?

Answer   Shavuot is also known as *Hag Matan Torateinu* – the "Festival of the Giving of our Torah," and as *Hag ha-Bikkurim* – the "Festival of the First Fruits."

Question   When does the festival occur?

Answer   Nowadays, the festival occurs on the 6th day of Sivan (outside Israel on the 7th as well), which is either in May or June.

Question   When you say "nowadays," does that mean that there were times when the festival did not necessarily occur on that date?

Answer   That is the exact implication. Unlike all the other Torah-ordained festivals, where the Torah gives an exact date for the festival, the date of Shavuot is not specified as such. Instead we are told, "You shall count unto you from the morrow after the Sabbath, from the day that you bring the sheaf of the heave offering; seven complete Sabbaths shall there be... And you shall proclaim on the selfsame day, that it may be an holy convocation unto you" (Lev. 23:15, 21). The preceding verses of the chapter are all about the festival of Passover, and the oral tradition tells us that the reference to "the Sabbath" in this verse is not a reference to the Sabbath as such, but to the first day of the festival of Passover. (There are numerous places in the Bible where festivals are referred to as "the Sabbath.") Thus, we see that the day of "holy convocation" comes seven full weeks after the second day of Passover. Now at that time, as we have mentioned earlier, the months were determined by the appearance of the new moon, which might come either 29 or 30 days after the previous new moon. And as there are two new moons in the 49 days separating the two festivals, one always knew that the festival would occur in the month of Sivan, but not on which day. For example, on some years it might be the 5th of the month of the month. It is only after the Jewish calendar was standardized and the months given specified numbers of days that we are guaranteed that Shavuot will always occur on the 6th of Sivan.

Question   Why is the festival called Shavuot – "Weeks"?

Answer   Although the Torah uses only the name, "The Festival of the First Fruits," it has been known throughout history as Shavuot because of the seven full weeks that must be counted between the second day of Passover and this festival.

Question   How is this "counting" accomplished?

Answer   Starting from the second night of Passover, toward the conclusion of the evening service, the cantor recites a blessing which ends, "...who has commanded us concerning the counting of the *Omer*." During the entire seven weeks, each day is counted, for example, "Today is 33 days, which are 4 weeks and 5 days of the *Omer*." The blessing and the count are repeated by the congregation. Even when a person prays alone, he must still count the days.

The period of the counting of the *Omer* is one of semi-mourning; according to tradition, many disciples of Rabbi Akiva, of Talmudic fame, died in a plague between Passover and Shavuot. No marriages are performed during this period and shaving or having a haircut is forbidden. The example given above, the thirty-third day of the *Omer*, is actually a minor festival, which commemorates a break in the plague. The day is known as Lag ba-Omer (the numerical value of *lag* is 33) and it is a popular date for weddings, particularly in Israel.

Question   What purpose does the counting accomplish?

Answer   It serves as a tangible link between the two festivals. Furthermore, it is meant to show how eager the Jew is for the advent of Shavuot, representing as it does the giving of the Torah.

Question What is the *omer* mentioned in the counting?

Answer The word *omer* itself is nothing more than a measurement of dry volume. The Torah commands the Jews, at the time of the existence of the Sanctuary or Temple, to cut down an *omer* of barley on the second day of Passover, this being the "heave offering." It is this act which initiates the counting period which will culminate in Shavuot. Nowadays, although the Temple no longer exists, the counting nevertheless begins on the second evening of Passover.

Question Why is it that the date of Shavuot is dependent on the date of Passover?

Answer Our Sages tell us that the two festivals are complementary, and that each is incomplete without the other. On Passover, the Jews were granted their physical freedom, but this still left them, "enslaved," as it were to their passions. On Shavuot the Jews received the Torah and thus got the tools to master their passions and drives. Then they achieved the ultimate freedom. Thus the two festivals are intimately bound together.

Question Are there any other views of the date of the Shavuot festival?

Answer Unlike the Sages, who tell us that by oral tradition the Torah's reference to "the Sabbath" is in reality a reference to the first day of Passover, there were deviant groups that interpreted the words literally. According to the view held, for example, by the Sadducees, the counting of the seven weeks begins on the evening after the first Sabbath following the first day of Passover. Thus the seven weeks always end on a Saturday and Shavuot is always on a Sunday. On the other hand, the festival may occur on any one of a number of different dates. To this day, the small Samaritan community celebrates Shavuot according to this calendar.

Question What special customs are there on Shavuot?

Answer The synagogue and the home are decorated with greenery. Numerous reasons are given for this particular custom: It is on Shavuot, for example, that the earth is judged for the coming year as to its fruit production, and one should pray for a good year; the greenery reminds us of Mount Sinai in the middle of the desert, yet which had grass for the flocks to graze; it reminds us of the first fruits that were brought to the Temple on that day with great pomp and ceremony.

Many religious people spend the entire night (the first night outside Israel) of Shavuot studying Torah, and then pray the morning service at the earliest possible time – just in time to reach the *Amidah* prayer at exactly sunrise. In Jerusalem, many institutions whose students stay up the whole night have the custom to bring all of them to the Western Wall for the morning prayer. It is a splendid sight to see thousands of young men and young women descending on the Old City of Jerusalem in the early hours of Shavuot morning, in order to pray at the Wall.

The origin of the custom of studying Torah the whole night goes back to a midrashic story. We are told that on the night before God was going to give the Torah to Israel, many of the Israelites, rather than remaining awake in anticipation of the most momentous event in history, went to sleep instead, and Moses had to wake them to receive the Torah. In a way, then, by staying up all night now and studying Torah, we, as it were, "atone" for the sin of the people of that generation.

It is customary to eat dairy food during some of the meals of Shavuot. Many reasons abound for this tradition. We are told, for example, that before the first Shavuot, the Jews ate all kinds of foods because they had not yet received the Torah and the laws of Kashrut. Once they received the Torah, they had to make all their non-kosher dishes kosher. As a result of the problems involved with meat, they ate only dairy foods. Others see the origin of the custom in the verse, "Honey and milk are under your tongue" (Song 4:11), which is taken to refer to the giving of the Torah, and of course, if one consumes milk products he cannot eat meat at the same time. Another explanation for this is that the Torah was given on a Sabbath, and thus, even though the Jews had learned what they had to do with their dishes and pots, they were unable to do so because of the laws of the Sabbath. As a result they were only able to eat dairy products.

The Book of Ruth is read before the reading of the Torah, telling as it does the loyalty of the Moabite Ruth to her Jewish mother-in-law, Naomi, after both their husbands had died. Eventually Ruth was married to Naomi's kinsman, Boaz, and from their union began the dynasty which led to David, King of Israel. Here too, there are various explanations for this custom. Among these are: Ruth was the symbol *par excellence* of lovingkindness for her mother-in-law, forsaking her own country and people to go with her. It is appropriate to read this glowing account of lovingkindness on the anniversary of the day the Torah was given, for the Torah is a Torah of lovingkindness.

Another explanation for the reading of the Book of Ruth on Shavuot is that the story of Ruth takes place at the time of the wheat harvest, and that is when Shavuot occurs.

Yet another reason is a masterpiece of logical thought. According to it, the book is read to show us that the written Torah as received by Moses at Sinai and the oral law, as eventually encapsulated in the Mishnah, Talmud, etc., are all a single organic whole, and that one cannot separate one from the other. The proof of this is the story of Ruth. After all, if we take the verses in the Torah as written, we are told, "An Ammonite or Moabite shall not enter into the congregation of the Lord" (Deut. 23:4). Using that as the basis, we would assume that Ruth, as a Moabite, was forbidden to marry Boaz, and there should be no Davidic dynasty. The oral law, though, stresses that the law applies to "a Moabite, but not a Moabitess," and that a Moabite woman may marry a Jew. Thus, we see that without the oral law, the Torah law as it stands would be construed in an entirely different fashion; the two are an organic whole, each incomplete without the other. Finally, another reason given for the reading of Ruth on Shavuot is that it was on that day that King David, her descendant, was both born and died.

Question What is *Tikkun Leil Shavuot*?

Answer This refers to the custom of staying up the entire night to study the Torah. By extension, it also refers to a collection of extracts from all the basic holy books – the Torah, Prophets, Hagiographa, Mishnah, Talmud, Midrash, etc. – which is to be recited while staying up on the night of Shavuot. This custom is observed by many, although yeshivah students will often simply continue studying whatever they have been studying during their regular study hours.

There is a story told of the Magid of Dubno, who, so the story goes, spent all of the night studying the Talmud passage he was engaged in at the time. Some people came over to him and asked him why he was not studying the *Tikkun Leil Shavuot*, as everyone else was doing.

The Magid had an immediate answer for his questioners. And, of course, as always his answer took the form of a parable.

"Once a poor man came to a large city," he said, "and found himself in a large department store. As he stood by amazed, he saw a salesman come into the store with a batch of cloth swatches, and the store owner put in a large order, paying the salesman a good percentage of the money immediately. 'That is a fantastic way to get rich quickly,' he thought to himself. 'All one needs is a few swatches of cloth, and one can make a fortune.' Taking whatever little money he had, he bought little swatches of different types of cloth and arranged them in a portfolio. He then came to the store keeper and asked him for an order. When the store keeper asked him how much stock he had of any given item and was told that the man had nothing but what he had in his portfolio, the store keeper understandably threw him out of the store. Dusting himself off, the poor man came back to the store keeper. He wanted to know why he had been treated so differently than the salesman. 'Fool,' the store keeper told him, 'Whatever the salesman shows me is but a minute fraction of what he has in stock. Whatever quantity I ask for can be delivered to me within days or even hours. Of course I am willing to put up money for his merchandise, but what are you selling? What do you have to back you?'"

"The same is true with me," went on the Magid. If a person knows all of the Torah and studies it throughout the year, he can afford to study the *Tikkun Leil Shavuot* on Shavuot night. After all, he is just giving a sample of all the wares that he has at his disposal. In my case, though, if I would study the *Tikkun*, it would be like displaying swatches without anything to back them up. Woe to the humiliation should I be asked to produce any more of the 'samples' that I had displayed. I therefore decided to study the same material that I am studying right now. That, at least, I may know, and I am not afraid that anyone will challenge me to see the rest of my 'samples'."

Chapter Ten

Purim

Question   What is Purim?

Answer   Purim is a holiday celebrated in the month of Adar (February or March), commemorating the salvation of the Jews and the downfall of the wicked Haman. The story took place in ancient Shushan, in Persia, under King Ahasuerus (Xerxes).

Question   What is the story of Purim?

Answer   If you were expecting miracles, guess again. It's really all a bunch of coincidences. After all, the book begins with King Ahasuerus asking his wife, Vashti, to appear before him. She refuses, and loses her head in the process. The throne is vacant, and Esther is chosen to fill it. Meanwhile, by coincidence, Esther's uncle, Mordecai, overhears two of the king's guards, Bigtan and Teresh, plotting against the king. Mordecai tells Esther, who tells the king, who gets rid of the two upstarts. Meanwhile, the wicked Haman, chief minister of the realm, incensed by Mordecai's failure to bow down to him, acts like any self-respecting anti-Semite: he resolves to get rid of Mordecai – and of every single Jew in the kingdom at the same time. He even offers the king 10,000 silver ducats for the privilege! The king agrees to the date set by Haman for the mass murder. Mordecai hears of the evil decree and in his despair puts on sackcloth. Esther is told of her uncle's "strange" behavior and sends to ask the reason. Mordecai informs her of Haman's dastardly plan and beseeches her to speak to the king. She requests that the Jews fast for three days and nights and pray for her success. After the fast ends, she approaches the king who receives her graciously. She invites him and Haman to join her in a dinner party. In the meantime, Haman decides he cannot wait – he wants to get rid of Mordecai immediately, on a gallows he had built especially for the purpose. Haman rushes over to the king with his new request. By another mere coincidence, the king is having an "off night," and cannot sleep. He calls to have the royal history read to him, and mention is made there of Mordecai's rescue of the king. On hearing that Mordecai was never rewarded, Ahasuerus decides he must rectify the situation. He asks who is waiting in the courtyard, and, by another mere coincidence, finds Haman there, waiting for an audience. The king has a simple question: What should be done for a person "whom the king wishes to honor?" Haman, sure the king is planning something to honor him, has the perfect answer: The king's horse should be sent for, the person should be dressed in the king's clothes and should ride the king's horse, with someone calling out in front of him, "Thus shall be done to the person the king wishes to honor." A perfect suggestion, agrees the king. "Now go and do that to Mordecai." Haman is forced to lead Mordecai around the city. By now, Haman realizes that things are not going entirely his way, but before he has time to think, he is whisked away to a feast that Esther has prepared for the king and him. At the dinner, Esther has but a single request: that the king and Haman should come back the next day. Finally, at the second supper, Esther reveals her true identity – she is a Jewish woman. Consternation! Confusion! Haman begs for mercy – but the noose he prepared for Mordecai fits him equally well – as he soon finds out! Instead of the Jews being killed, they are given permission to kill their enemies. Esther remains the queen, and Mordecai becomes the chief minister of the realm, where, as the Book of Esther tells us in most striking words, "he was accepted by the majority of his brothers." All we have are coincidences – no wonder the Book of Esther does not mention the name of God even once!

Question So why celebrate Purim?

Answer The Book of Esther is evidence of one of God's ways of working: not every miracle has to be a reversal of the laws of nature. The miraculous does not only consist of the splitting of the sea; "coincidence," too, is one of God's ways of affecting history. Miracles such as those in the Book of Esther are in the category of *nes nistar* – the "hidden miracle." (Note the similarity between the word *nistar* and the name Esther.) Nor are all such "hidden miracles" relics of ancient times. In a book entitled *Pipeline to Battle*, by Peter W. Rainer, the author tells of the a battle which occurred on July 4, 1942 in North Africa, between the British forces and Rommel's troops, over the last major fortress which defended Alexandria. The fall of the fortress would leave the road open to Alexandria and Egypt, and right on to Palestine. Yet something "miraculous" happened, and the Germans inexplicably surrendered. After their surrender, the British found out what had caused this sudden German turnabout. It seems that the Germans, fighting through the blazingly hot desert, had run out of water, and hoped to replenish their supply by cutting through the British water pipeline. But when they cut through the

✿ *An illuminated* Megillat Esther; *Ferrara, 1616.*

pipeline, they found it was carrying salt water rather than fresh water. It seems that the British were testing the pipeline – a new one – for leaks, and rather than risking the scarce fresh water they had, had decided to use sea water for this purpose. The Germans, left stranded without water, had no choice but to surrender. Of course it was purely coincidental that just at that critical juncture in the war the pipeline was carrying sea water, but one begins to wonder whether "coincidence" is not another way for expressing God's involvement in human history.

Question How is Purim celebrated?

Answer As far as Jewish law is concerned, there are four basic observances: The *megillah* – scroll – of the Book of Esther is read in the evening and morning (yes, that's where the phrase, "the whole *megillah*" comes from!) and the reading must be heard by every adult Jew. Gifts of at least two kinds of food must be sent to at least one person (*mishloah manot*). Every Jew must give alms to at least two poor people (*matanot le-evyonim*). And a festive meal must be eaten on Purim afternoon.

One must also add a passage which begins *Al ha–Nissim* – "for the miracles" – in the *Amidah* prayers and in the grace after meals throughout the day.

Jewish law also requires one to drink enough "not to know the difference between 'Blessed be Mordecai' and 'Cursed be Haman.'"

Question Who has to hear the *megillah* read?

Answer Rationally, we would say that women should be exempt from hearing the *megillah* read, because women are generally exempt from any law which applies only at a specific time. In this case, though, all adult men (i.e., 13 and older) and women (12 and older) must hear the *megillah* read, because, as we are told in the Talmud, "the women, too, were saved in that miracle."

Question There is a custom that every time Haman's name is mentioned in the reading of the *megillah*, all the children (and many adults) set up a clamor. What is the origin of this custom?

Answer The *megillah* mentions that Haman was "an Agagite," which, by tradition, means that he was a descendant of Amalek, the king who, taking advantage of the Israelites' weakness after having just left the slavery of Egypt, attacked them. The Torah thus commands us, "You shall blot out the remembrance of Amalek from under Heaven" (Deut. 25:19). By banging on the ground or using the Purim *gragger* (rattle), we are figuratively "blotting out" the name of Haman, Amalek's descendant. Interestingly, there used to be a custom that when a Jew bought a new pair of shoes he would write the word "Amalek" on the soles. This way, whenever he took a step he was busy "blotting out Amalek."

Question What is the purpose of *mishloah manot* – the sending of food to friends?

Answer Simply put, this is meant to increase feelings of friendship between individuals. The law itself requires the sending of at least two kinds of food (the word *manot* means "portions" in Hebrew, and obviously the minimum of "portions" – the plural – is two) to at least one person. Of course this is only the minimum, but in the spirit of the day, many people send *mishloah manot* to all their friends.

Question How about the *matanot le-evyonim* – the gifts to the poor?

Answer Here, as the verse in the *megillah* stresses "*le-evyonim*" – to the poor – as a plural noun, we understand that it means at least two poor people. For those of us living in affluent areas, this present a problem: Where can you find poor people on Purim? If no poor people are available, one can put the money in a charity box for the poor. The law, incidentally, is quite clear that the gifts to the poor are more important than the sending of gifts of food to one's neighbor.

Question How much must one drink in order not to know the difference between "Blessed be Mordecai" and "Cursed be Haman"?

Answer This Talmudic statement has been interpreted in many ways: some people take it literally – one should get drunk. Most authorities, though, are opposed to this, because a person who is drunk can hardly say the daily prayers in that state. A more moderate view points out that the exact words of the Talmud are that one should drink "until he cannot tell ..." It interprets the word "until" to mean "up to that point, but not including it," i.e., one must not drink enough to become drunk. A third view is based on the fact that by using *gematria* – the system which assigns each Hebrew letter a specific numerical value – one is able to work out a value for each of the two phrases, "Blessed be Mordecai" and "Cursed be Haman." They believe, therefore, that a person should drink just enough so as not to be able to make the *gematria* calculations involved – thus not knowing "between 'Blessed is Mordecai' and 'Cursed is Haman'." And then there is the "cop-out" view: that a person must take a drink and then, at some time of the day, take a nap.

A person who is napping obviously does not know the difference between the two phrases!

Question   If Purim marked such a great deliverance of the Jewish people, why does one not say *Hallel*, the prayer of praise for God, which is said on the Biblical Pilgrim festivals and on Hanukkah?

Answer   This question is discussed by our Sages, who explain that, unlike Hanukkah, which occurred in the Holy Land, Purim took place in Persia. Any miracle, our Sages tell us, which takes place outside of the Holy Land is by its nature an incomplete miracle, and as such not worthy of the *Hallel*.

Question   What other customs are there on Purim?

Answer   It is customary for children to wear disguises on Purim, especially when they come to hear the megillah read and when delivering *mishloah manot*. In Tel Aviv, there used to be an annual Purim parade (which was reintroduced in 1988 after a hiatus of decades), known as the Adloyada, a take-off on the words *ad delo yada* – "until he cannot tell" (i.e., between Blessed is Mordecai and Cursed is Haman). In many yeshivot and schools, a Purim play is enacted by the students, who use it as an annual opportunity to poke fun at all the foibles of their rabbis and teachers. Some yeshivot even appoint a "Purim rabbi," who "takes charge" of the activities for the day. A story is told of a brilliant young scholar who was appointed "Purim rabbi" in his yeshivah, and rather than leading all the frivolity, gave a long and complicated Torah discourse, with quote after quote from the rabbinic literature. The other students, in the spirit of the day, went to the real rabbi complaining that their "Purim rabbi" had broken the terms of his "contract." The rabbi listened to their complaint, and finally told them: "My dear students, in principle you would have a point, except for one thing: not a single quote used by the 'Purim rabbi' exists! Every single quote was made up by him!" Case dismissed.

Question   What is Shushan Purim?

Answer   The *megillah* tells us that the Jews throughout the Persian Empire were given the 13th of the month of Adar to oppose with force those who had planned to kill them. Later, when the Jews celebrated their deliverance, it was celebrated on the 14th of Adar, the day after the deliverance. By Esther's request, the Jews in Shushan were also given the following day, the 14th of Adar, to take revenge of their enemies. Thus these Jews celebrated their deliverance on the 15th of Adar. When the law was finally established, it was ruled that all cities that had a wall around them at the time of Joshua (just as Shushan), would celebrate on the 15th of the month, while all others would celebrate it on the 14th. In practice, the only city which we are sure had a wall around it in Joshua's time (an arbitrary date, to be sure) is Jerusalem. There are a number of Israeli cities which might have been walled at that time, but there is no definite proof. These cities, including Acre, generally celebrate Purim on the 14th, but may have the *megillah* read two days in a row (the 14th and 15th) in order to remove any possible doubts.

Question Does that mean that Jerusalem and Tel Aviv celebrate Purim on different days?

Answer That is exactly the case. In fact, there are people who spend the 14th of Adar outside Jerusalem, where they celebrate Purim, and then return to Jerusalem on the 15th, to celebrate it another day. An old Yiddish folk song wonders why " Purim cannot be more than a single day." Well, in Israel it *can* be! But that's nothing – it may even be *three* days, as we will see below.

Question How can Purim possibly last for *three* days?

Answer Granted, this is an uncommon event, and it only applies to Jerusalem (and theoretically Shushan, if Jews still live there). On rare occasions, the 15th of Adar – the day which Jerusalem celebrates as its Purim – occurs on a Saturday. Here there is a problem, because on Saturday one cannot give charity to the poor, send gifts to one's neighbor or read the *megillah* (the latter for fear that the *megillah* would be carried to the synagogue and/or back). The different laws of the day are therefore divided up: On Friday, the *megillah* is read and gifts are given to the poor (so that they will at least have money to buy food for the Sabbath). On Saturday, one only adds the *Al ha-Nissim* section to the *Amidah* prayers and to the grace after meals, for, after all, Saturday is the actual day of Purim. Finally, on Sunday one sends gifts of food to friends and holds the festive holiday meal. To give one an idea of how infrequent this event is, between now and the year 2019, a period of thirty years, it will only occur three times: in 1994, in 2001, and finally in 2011.

Question What is Ta'anit Esther?

Answer The Hebrew words mean "The Fast of Esther." In commemoration of Esther's fast before going to see Ahasuerus, Jews fast on the day before Purim. (If this falls on a Friday or Sabbath, the fast is observed on the previous Thursday.) Further details on this fast are to be found in the chapter on fast days.

Question   Are there any others Purims that are celebrated?

Answer   Just as all Jews celebrate Purim in commemoration of their ancestors having been saved from the wicked Haman, many individual Jewish communities ordained their own Purims to commemorate their deliverance from various troubles, each in its own way. Among the numerous examples, one finds the Padua Purim, celebrated on 11 Sivan, which commemorates the Jews' deliverance from a major fire in 1795; the Florence Purim, 27 Sivan, where, by the intercession of the local bishop the Jews were saved from a mob in 1790; the Baghdad Purim, 11 Av, which celebrates the conquest of the city by the Arabs and the defeat of the Persians who had mistreated the Jews; the "Purim of the Christians," 2 Elul, celebrating the defeat in Morocco of King Sebastian of Portugal, who had attempted in 1578 to restore to the throne a king that all despised (a special *megillah* was written in celebration); the "Snow Purim," 24 Tevet, celebrated by the Jews of Tunis after a major snowstorm wreaked havoc in the country but miraculously left the Jewish quarter untouched; the Kovno Purim, 7 Adar II, when the Jews of Kovno were granted numerous rights in 1783 by King Poniatowski (here too, a *megillah* was written, documenting the troubles suffered by the Jews, and their deliverance by the king's edicts); and, most recently, the "Hitler Purim" of Casablanca, marking 2 Kislev (November 11), 1943, when the city was saved from falling into German hands. Here, a "Hitler *megillah*" was written, paraphrasing the traditional one, including the words "cursed be Hitler, cursed be Mussolini," and listing many of the other Nazi and fascist leaders.

Chapter Eleven

Hanukkah

Question   What is the origin of the name of the holiday, Hanukkah?

Answer   The word Hanukkah means "dedication," for the holiday marks the rededication of the Temple after it had been defiled by being used for idolatrous purposes.

Question   What does the holiday commemorate?

Answer   The festival commemorates the victory of the Maccabees over the Graeco-Syrian king, Antiochus Epiphanes. Antiochus, in an attempt to crush the Jews, had forbidden them to practice their religion. A popular uprising ensued, led by Matthias the Hasmonean and his five sons. The members of the family were also known as the Maccabees. The origin of the latter word is obscure (it might mean "hammer"), although it has traditionally been interpreted as an acronym for a Hebrew phrase which would read in translation, "Who is like You among the gods, O Lord."

Question   What is actually celebrated?

Answer   According to the Talmud, "Once the Hasmoneans vanquished [the Graeco-Syrians], they searched and found but a single jar [of oil] with the seal of the high priest that had not been defiled, which contained only enough to burn for one day. A miracle occurred, and they lit with it for eight days. The following year, they established these days as a festival with praise and thanks [to God]" (Tractate Shabbat 21b). Thus we see that the Talmud considers the miracle of the oil the reason for the festival, and rather cavalierly dismisses the military victory. In fact, the only place the military victory is stressed is in the added passage which one recites in the prayers and grace after meals. The Talmud, though, does not lay its emphasis on the military victory, for traditionally Jews do not believe in glorifying war or the results of war.

Elsewhere, the Talmud tells of a certain man whose wife died, leaving him with a nursing infant. All his efforts to find a woman to nurse his child were fruitless. Finally, he prayed to God, and God gave him the ability to nurse his own son. The Sages of the Talmud are divided about how to interpret this story. One view regards the man as having been truly righteous, in that God was even willing to change the rules of nature to enable him to nurse his son. Another view, though, regards the man negatively: had he been really righteous, God would have found him a solution within the realm of natural events, without having to change nature for him. And the same applies in the case of the Hasmonean victory: Had the people been truly righteous, they would have never had to fight in order to emerge victorious.

Question   When is the festival celebrated?

Answer   The festival begins on the 25th day of the Hebrew month of Kislev, which occurs in either late November or in December. It was on this day that the Temple was rededicated.

Question   If the festival celebrates the fact that the oil which was enough for for one day lasted for eight, the miracle only needed for seven days. Why then celebrate eight days?

Answer   This particular question has been asked by some of the greatest scholars, and scores of answers have been recorded. In fact, an entire volume was published carrying various answers to the question. Among the answers given are: a) the oil was not even enough for a single day, so that even the first day was marked by miraculous intervention by God. b) Each day, only one-eighth of the total oil was consumed, so that on each day a miracle occurred in that a supply of oil sufficient for three hours burned for 24 hours. c) The miracle of the oil was indeed only for seven days. The extra day is celebrated to commemorate the military victory of the Maccabees.

Question   How is Hanukkah celebrated?

Answer   Throughout the holiday, *Hallel* is recited in the morning prayers, and the Torah is read each day. The portion read from the Torah describes the dedication (*hanukkah*) of the Sanctuary in the desert (Numbers ch. 7). A paragraph, *Al ha-Nissim*, is added to all the daily prayers and to the grace after meals, describing the deliverance of the Jewish people. The most prominent feature of the holiday is no doubt the lighting of the Hanukkah *menorah* (candelabrum; known in present-day Hebrew as *hanukkiyah*), to commemorate the miracle of the oil.

Question How does one light the Hanukkah candles?

Answer The *menorah* has receptacles for eight candles, plus a ninth, higher one, known as the *shamash*. On the first night of Hanukkah, after having recited the appropriate blessings, one lights the extreme right-hand candle. On the next night, there are two candles, placed at the extreme right of the *menorah*, but the first candle lit is the one closest to the left (i.e., in the second position from the right). This system is used throughout: each night, a new candle is added to the left of the ones which had been lit the previous night, but the candle lighting is from left to right.

Question Are there any other views of how to light the Hanukkah candles?

Answer The Talmud records a dispute between the School of Hillel, which ruled that one begins with one candle and adds a candle each day until eight are reached, and the School of Shammai, which ruled that one lights eight candles the first day and decreases one each day, until one lights a single candle on the last day. Of course, as we saw in earlier chapters, the law is generally in accordance with the School of Hillel. The Talmud then goes on to explain that the School of Hillel bases itself on how many days have already gone, whereas the School of Shammai refers to how many are still left. Allegorically, there are those who see the School of Hillel, whose ruling we follow, as teaching us an important moral lesson – that a person should always build on his past so as to go on to ever greater heights.

Question What are the blessings recited before lighting the candles?

Answer Throughout Hanukkah, one recites two blessings: "... Who has commanded us to light the Hanukkah light," and "... Who performed miracles for our fathers during those days at this time [of the year]." On the first night, one also adds the *She-heheyanu* blessing, recited on the first day of each festival (and also when wearing a new substantial piece of clothing for the first time or eating a fruit for the first time that season): "... Who has kept us alive and sustained us and permitted us to remain to this time."

Question The first blessing includes the words, "Who has commanded us to light the Hanukkah light." I can understand the formulation of "Who has commanded us" in regard to laws stated in the Torah, for they are indeed God-given, but how can we use that formulation in regard to a law which was clearly instituted by the Sages rather than God Himself?

Answer This question touches on a basic principle of Jewish belief – the relationship between God and man once the Torah was given at Sinai. Judaism believes that the Torah is not a static document – although there were Jewish heretical sects that did not hold that belief. Instead, it believes that there is a dynamic relationship between the Torah text, as given by God, and the Sages in interpreting the text to each age. This, though, is not a blank check. Certain parameters have been laid out – what one might well call cardinal principles – and all interpretation must proceed within these parameters. Given these limits, the Sages of each generation thus assume the role of interpreting God's will to their generation. And this means that whatever they decide is to be considered in accordance with God's will – even if it is His *ex post facto* will. By the same token, any decision taken by the Sages affecting the Jewish people as a whole – and in this case we are referring to the celebration of Hanukkah by lighting the candles – is considered, as it were, to have come from God Himself, through His interpreters. We are thus entitled to recite "Who has commanded us" even though it was the Sages who instituted this *mitzvah* of lighting candles on Hanukkah.

Question   What is sung after the Hanukkah candles are lit?

Answer   It is a well-nigh universal custom among Ashkenazic Jews to conclude the candle lighting with the singing of *Ma'oz Tzur*, a song of customarily of six stanzas (although the sixth is often omitted in prayerbooks), where the opening letters of the first five stanzas spell out an acrostic of the author of the song's name, Mordecai, and the last verse has the acrostic *hazak*, i.e., "be strong." Each stanza describes a different episode in which the Jewish people were saved, including, for example, the story of Esther and Mordecai. The last verse has a reference to a certain *admoni*, or "redhead," this being a reference to the German Emperor Frederic Barbarossa, "the Redbeard" (1121-1190) who caused the Jews of his time great grief. The traditional melody, in various transfigurations, has been used by different groups and religions, with numerous sets of words, and has been traced back to the 13th century in Germany.

Question   Where should the *menorah* be placed?

Answer   The *menorah* should be placed at the front of one's home, where all can see it, for this "publicizes the miracle." It must be placed no lower than 32 inches from the ground and no more than 30 feet above it. Normally, lighting the *menorah* at the front of one's homes should not present a problem – at least not in our days, but there were times when Jews were forced to light the *menorah* inside their homes because of the danger of being attacked by non-Jewish mobs.

Question Are there any preferences in the choice of candles or fuels for the *menorah*?

Answer Ideally, one should use olive oil with wicks, because that was the fuel used in the Temple. Many people prefer to use candles, because they are not messy – as oil has a tendency to become. Modern-day rabbis have discussed the use of electricity, but the majority do not approve of this method.

Question Who must light Hanukkah candles?

Answer Strictly speaking, only one *menorah* must be lit by each family. The custom, though, is for at least each adult male to light his own *menorah*, and in many families women light their own *menorahs* as well.

Question What is the purpose of the *shamash* candle?

Answer The word *shamash* is usually translated as "sexton" or "assistant." The *shamash* is meant to "serve" the other candles. For example, it is the *shamash* which is lit first, before the blessings are recited, and it is used to light the other candles. The *shamash* also serves another purpose. By Jewish law, one is not permitted to derive benefit from an object used for ritual purposes. In this case, it would mean, for example, that one is not permitted to read by the light of the Hanukkah candles. By allowing the *shamash* to burn alongside the other candles, one is not benefitting solely from the light of the Hanukkah candles, but from both sources of light – the forbidden and the permitted – and that is then permitted. This also explains why the *shamash* candle is generally placed higher than the other candles, for this ensures that its light predominates.

Question How long must the candles burn?

Answer The candles must burn for at least half an hour during the evening hours. The definition of "evening hours" for our purposes is from nightfall on "until people are no longer walking about outside." As the purpose of lighting the candles is to "publicize
the miracle," it is logical that the candles should be burning while there are people around to see them. Interestingly enough, the Edison movie theater in Jerusalem was once the source of a rabbinic decision in this regard. One of the greatest rabbis in the State of Israel, who lived a few blocks from the Edison, was asked to define what is meant by "until the people are no longer walking about outside." He defined it simply – as the time when the last

showing at the Edison theater ended! Now, there is no doubt that a rabbi such as this, of the old school, never in his life entered a movie theater, but he was realist enough to use it as the basis for a decision affecting Jewish law. Of course, this decision was for a given city and a given era, and each city – probably each neighborhood – would have its own criteria in this regard.

Question Are there any differences in lighting the candles Friday evening?

Answer As Jewish law forbids lighting anything on the Sabbath (for these purposes, defined as beginning at sunset), one cannot light the candles at nightfall as on other days. Instead, one must light the candles before sunset, but must ensure that they are large enough to burn through twilight and for at least half an hour into the night. Generally, the standard Hanukkah candles burn almost exactly half an hour, and that is clearly not enough. It is thus advisable to use Sabbath candles for the Hanukkah candle lighting on Friday. Of course, if one is using oil, he simply has to ensure that the lamps are filled more fully than on other days.

Question What is this I hear about gambling on Hanukkah?

Answer You heard right. Hanukkah is the one time a year that Jews, of even the most religious homes, have engaged in gambling, but certainly not in any terms that we consider gambling today. To this day, it is customary for families to gather around the table each evening, and to roll the four-sided Hanukkah *dreidel*. The rules are simple: each person places the same sum in the pot (generally, the stakes are matchsticks, but more adventurous homes may use pennies). The *dreidel* is then spun by each person in turn. Depending on the results of the roll, the person either: a) receives the entire pot, b) receives half the pot, c) wins nothing and loses nothing, or d) is forced to add to the pot.

We should also mention that, surprisingly, there are two types of *dreidels*, one type used in Israel and one throughout the rest of the world. The reason is self-explanatory. In Israel, the four sides have the Hebrew letters *nun, gimmel, heh, peh*, which stands for *nes gadol hayah poh* – "a great miracle occurred *here*." Outside Isral, the last letter is *shin*, an acronym for the phrase, *nes gadol hayah sham* – "a great miracle occurred *there*."

Question Why gambling? What has gambling have to do with the holiday?

Answer As with many Jewish customs, the answer is lost in antiquity, but Jewish tradition does give us a beautiful answer, building as it does on historical fact. We know that Antiochus Epiphanes forbade Jews to observe the commandments or to study the Torah, under pain of death. For the Jews, though, one could as soon live without Torah as a fish can live without water. Thus they still devoted their time to Torah study, but they took precautions to ensure they were not caught. They would keep their *dreidels* on hand, just in case any informers chanced to walk by. This way, they could always act as if all they were doing was to indulge in a little harmless gambling to pass away the time.

Question   Are there any special foods for Hanukkah?

Answer   Hanukkah is not for dieters! The emphasis of the holiday is on oil – the oil used to light the *menorah* in the Temple – and as a result the traditional foods of Hanukkah are fried in oil. Different communities have different customs. Ashkenazic Jews often make potato *latkes* (fritters) fried in oil. Sephardic Jews specialize in jam-filled doughnuts, fried in – well, by now you know what they are fried in. Neither *latkes* nor doughnuts are what one might call dietetic foods.

Question   Where does the custom of gifts on Hanukkah originate from?

Answer   On Hanukkah, it was the custom of parents to give their children small amounts of money, known as Hanukkah *gelt*, or Hanukkah money. There was certainly nothing like the lavish production we have today, where some parents try to ensure that each of the eight days of Hanukkah the children will receive a new gift. This orgy of giving is evidently a direct response to the proximity of the Christmas season. In Eastern Europe, from which the ancestors of most American Jews immigrated, there was almost no social interaction between Jews and non-Jews. The two religions had almost nothing to do with one another, and there was thus very little (if any) cross-pollination of ideas between the two. In the western world, on the other hand, where the members of the different religions all mingle freely, there has been a tremendous degree of adaptation and "borrowing" between the different religious groups, and the idea of the exchange of gifts on Hanukkah is no doubt part of that adaptation.

Question   Does Hanukkah mark the end of all the joyous holidays until Purim, about 2 1/2 months later?

Answer   As far as the major holidays are concerned, that is indeed the case, and the next period of the year is probably the quietest as far as the Jewish calendar is concerned. There is, however, one minor holiday that breaks up the time period, and that is Tu bi-Shevat.

Question   What is Tu bi-Shevat?

Answer   Tu bi-shevat is a minor holiday, the only required observance is a few small changes in the daily prayer services. The holiday nevertheless has a rich tradition of its own. Coming as it does toward the end of winter, it is the harbinger of spring. Officially, it is the New Year for Trees.

Question   Why would trees need a New Year?

Answer   There are a number of laws that apply to trees, including some related to the first four years after they are planted. For example, one may not eat the fruit of a new tree during the first three years, and in ancient times the fruit of the fourth year had to be taken to Jerusalem to be eaten there. Today, in the absence of the Temple, the fruit of the fourth year too may not be eaten. But how do we know how old a tree is? The answer is Tu bi-Shevat. On Tu bi-Shevat, every tree is considered to have become a year older. Thus, the New Year for Trees.

Question   Are there any particular customs on this day?

Answer   In order to celebrate this New Year, it is customary to eat different kinds of fruit, especially fruits of the species with which Eretz Israel is blessed. In kabbalistic circles, there is a custom to try to eat no less than a hundred different kinds of fruit on this day! In Israel, schoolchildren throughout the country go out and plant trees on Tu bi-Shevat, thus aiding the country's afforestation efforts.

Chapter Twelve

Fast Days

Question How many fast days are there in the Jewish calendar, and what are their dates?

Answer Over the course of the year there are no less than six fast days: Tzom Gedaliah (3 Tishrei – September/October), Yom Kippur (10 Tishrei – September/October), Asarah be-Tevet (10 Tevet – December/January), Ta'anit Esther (13 Adar – February/March), Shiva Asar be-Tammuz (17 Tammuz – June-July), and Tisha be-Av (9 Av – July-August).

Question What is the purpose of the fast days?

Answer The fasts have one common aim, regardless of the reason for the institution of the particular fast: to bring people to introspection and to repentance. Without this, the fast has not achieved its purpose.

Question What is the duration of the fast days?

Answer All the fasts, except for Yom Kippur and Tisha be-Av, last from dawn to nightfall of the day in question. Yom Kippur and Tisha be-Av last from sunset of the previous day until nightfall, or about 25 hours.

Question Who instituted the fast days?

Answer Whereas Yom Kippur is a Torah-decreed fast day, all the others were instituted by the Sages in memory of specific historic events.

Question What does each fast day commemorate?

Answer Tzom Gedaliah (the Fast of Gedaliah) commemorates the killing of the Jewish governor of Eretz Israel, Gedaliah, after the first exile in 586

B.C.E. As a result, the remaining Jews in Eretz Israel were all sent into exile as well.

Yom Kippur is the day upon which the fate of the entire world fate is decreed for the coming year.

Asarah be-Tevet was the day upon which Jerusalem was besieged by Nebuchadnezzar, prior to the fall of the First Temple. It is also the day proclaimed by the Israeli Chief Rabbinate as *Yom Ha-Kaddish*, the memorial day for the six million Jews murdered in Europe by the Nazis.

Ta'anit Esther (the Fast of Esther) commemorates the three days that Esther fasted before daring to enter King Ahasuerus' private chambers uninvited.

Shiva Asar be-Tammuz is the day the walls of Jerusalem were breached by Nebuchadnezzar.

Tisha be-Av is the day that both the First and Second Temples were destroyed.

Question Why are Yom Kippur and Tisha be-Av 25-hour fasts, rather than merely from dawn to nightfall?

Answer Yom Kippur is a day decreed by the Torah. As such, it begins at sunset and continues to the following nightfall, just as with every Sabbath and festival. Tisha be-Av, on the other hand, is considered the day of the greatest tragedy of the Jewish people, for it was following the destruction of the Temple that the Jewish people went into exile. It is thus understandable that it lasts for a full 25 hours.

Question Who must fast?

Answer By Jewish law, every adult, both male (13 and older) and female (12 and older) is required to fast. Where there are medical contraindications, eating may be permitted. Understandably, Yom Kippur, as the only fast day ordained by the Torah, is the one where there is the least leniency in this regard. Nevertheless, where a person's health may be in jeopardy if he or she fasts, the person may be permitted to eat. Such a decision should only be made after consultation with one's rabbi and physician.

Question What is forbidden on the fast days?

Answer On the four minor fasts (that last from dawn to sunset), one is only forbidden to eat and drink throughout the time period. On Yom Kippur and Tisha be-Av there are five prohibitions: 1. eating and drinking; 2. applying lotions to the body; 3. washing (except for the minimum needed by Jewish law, as when one wakes and after going to the bathroom); 4. wearing shoes that contain leather; and 5. sexual relations.

Question What is *bein ha-metzarim*?

Answer The term *bein ha-metzarim* – "between the straits" – is the name given to the period of time beginning with 17 Tammuz and ending 9 Av, the three week period between the time the walls of Jerusalem were breached in 586 B.C.E. until the First Temple itself was burned. This is the saddest time of the Jewish year. Beginning with 17 Tammuz, various restrictions are gradually added, culminating on 9 Av. For example, throughout the three weeks one is not permitted to have a haircut (and according to many opinions, to shave). No weddings are celebrated, and one does not visit places of entertainment. Beginning with 1 Av, it is customary not to eat any meat or drink wine (except on the Sabbath). Finally, from the Sunday preceding 9 Av (i.e., during the week of Tisha be-Av), one is forbidden to bathe or shower (except where absolutely essential).

Question Are there any other fast days?

Answer The above six are the only ones that are required by Jewish law. There are others, though, which were customary in various communities. For example, among Ashkenazic Jews it was customary to fast on three days – a Monday, Thursday and the following Monday – after the Sukkot and Passover festivals. As these festivals are both extended periods of rejoicing, the fasts were meant to atone for any sins one might have committed under the influence of the joyous time. To this day there are Ashkenazic synagogues which still recite the special *selihot* (penitential) prayers on those days, although there are very few people who actually fast on them. In Eastern Europe, there were especially pious people who would fast each Monday and Thursday throughout the year. And then there are the special fast days.

Fast days are a common Jewish response as an attempt to forfend a calamity. Thus, the Mishnah describes the exact procedures to be followed when there is no rain. Integral to this procedure is a fast by the entire community. By the same token, when Jewish communities were faced with troubles such as epidemics, forced conversion, etc., they would introduce city-wide fast days. As recently as World War II, the rabbinate in the United States and in other countries proclaimed fast days because of the destruction of European Jewry.

We should also mention one other fast day: the Neturei Karta, the most vehemently anti-Zionist ultra-Orthodox group (basically *hasidim* of the Satmar group) marks Yom Ha-Atzma'ut – Israel Independence Day – by holding a fast day and reciting penitential prayers for the "grievous sin" of the Jews in proclaiming their own state. It is this group which annually places full-page ads against Israel on the country's independence day.

Chapter Thirteen

The Life Cycle

The Brit Milah

Question What is the *Shalom Zakhar*?

Answer Among Ashkenazic Jews, it is customary, on the first Friday night after a male child is born, to gather at the parents' home, where the *Shema* is recited, Torah thoughts are expounded, songs are sung in honor of the newborn infant, and refreshments are offered. The Talmud mentions that the newborn male infant brings peace to the world, and this may have something to do with the origin of this custom. Others state that the origin of this custom lies in the belief that the presence of an uncircumcised Jewish male in the house is an invitation to the evil angels to cause trouble. The *Shalom Zakhar* is meant to fend off any such trouble.

Question What is the Hebrew term for the act of circumcision?

Answer The full Hebrew term for the circumcision is *brit milah*, which means "the covenant of the circumcision." Generally, the ceremony is referred to as the *brit* or *bris* (Ashkenazic pronunciation).

Question Why are Jewish male infants circumcised?

Answer The Bible commands, "This is My covenant which you shall keep, between Me and you and your progeny after you; every male child among you shall be circumcised" (Gen. 17:10). Circumcision marks the covenant, dating back to Abraham, between God and what later became the Jewish people. Circumcision has always been accepted as the one distinguishing mark of Judaism. Even secular Jews, who may keep none of the other religious commandments, have made it a point to have their children circumcised. Interestingly, a new specialty has developed since the Soviet Union opened its doors and allowed Jews to leave. In the Soviet Union itself, it was almost impossible for Jews to arrange for circumcision, and only the most hardy and brave were willing to risk it for their children. Now that many of these Jews have left the Soviet Union, they have sought to be circumcised. This has resulted in a need for specialists in adult circumcisions.

Question   What does the circumcision consist of, and when it is performed?

Answer   The circumcision consists of the removal of the foreskin, and is supposed to be performed on the eighth day after the child's birth (i.e., if a child was born on a Saturday, the circumcision is held on the following Saturday). If a child is underweight or jaundiced, the circumcision is postponed until his doctor finds that he is ready for the operation. Where the child is really sick, Jewish law requires one to wait for seven days after the doctor pronounces him well enough to undergo the circumcision. Here, we have a cardinal principle of Judaism: as the Sages put it, basing themselves on the verse (Lev. 18:5), "You shall live by them" (i.e. the Torah laws): "You shall live by them, and not die by them." In other words, the maintenance of human life takes precedence over all the commandments, except for three. And these three are self-explanatory: a person may not save his life if the only way he can do so is by violating the laws of murder, idolatry or sexual immorality.

Question   Why the eighth day?

Answer   The Torah does not offer us any explanation for the choice of this day, and there is no rational reason that we can give for the choice. By the same token, if any other day had been chosen, we could have asked the same question. We thus have to assume that this is in the category of *hukim* – those laws not given to man to understand. Interestingly enough, there have been medical studies that have shown that the newborn infant's blood clotting mechanism does not stabilize until the eighth day. A coincidence? Maybe...

Question   Are there any health benefits involved in circumcision?

Answer   Nowhere in the Torah are we given any health reasons for the operation. Statistical research, though, has shown that when a male has been circumcised it decreases his chances of certain types of cancer, and – even more surprising – the chances of certain types of cancer in his mate. It is thus not surprising that the vast majority of males in the United States are circumcised. The latter type of circumcision obviously differs in certain elements from the Jewish ritual, and its rationale is different.

Question Who are the main participants at circumcision ceremony?

Answer Besides the infant and his father, there are the *mohel*, who is the person who actually performs the circumcision, and the *sandek*, who holds the child during the circumcision. People often refer to the *sandek* as the child's godfather. To be the *sandek* is considered a great honor, and the role is often assigned to one of the child's grandparents or to the family rabbi or another prominent rabbi. Especially among Ashkenazic Jews, it is customary for various people to be honored by having them carry the baby to the ceremony.

Question What is the significance of the special chair – often an ornate one – present at the circumcision?

Answer The chair is known as *kiso shel Eliyahu*, Elijah's chair, and by tradition the prophet Elijah attends every circumcision. The Talmud gives a reason for Elijah's attendance: Elijah complained, "the people of Israel have abandoned Your covenant [*brit*]" (1 Kings 19:10). God rebuked him for maligning the Jewish people, and decreed that he should attend each circumcision and personally witness that the Jews keep God's covenant to this day. Before being placed on the *sandek's* lap, the child is placed on Elijah's chair for a moment in order to invoke the prophet's blessing.

Question What text is intoned at the circumcision?

Answer Both the *mohel* and the father of the child recite certain blessings, the father's blessing, for example, concluding, "who has sanctified us with His commandments and commanded us to bring him [the child] into the covenant of our father Abraham." According to some rites, the *She-heheyanu* blessing is also recited. After the operation, prayers are said for the child's welfare, and a wish is expressed that "just as he entered the covenant, may he enter the study of Torah, the wedding canopy, and good deeds." A blessing is also pronounced over a goblet of wine, which the father drinks. A cloth is often dipped in the wine and placed in the infant's mouth. Talk of starting them young! It is as this time that the child is given his formal Hebrew name.

Question What does "formal Hebrew name" mean?

Answer Throughout the generations, before last names were instituted, Jews have always been known as "so-and-so, son of so-and-so," as, for example, "Isaac, son of Abraham." It is this name which is used in all cases of Jewish ritual: for calling the person to the reading of the Torah scroll, on the *ketubah* – the Hebrew marriage document, and eventually on the person's tombstone. Since the emancipation of the Jews, many Jews have had two different first names: the one on their birth certificate, generally one in use in their mother country, and their Jewish name. Thus, an Irving might have the Hebrew name of Yisrael. It has been a sign of Jewish pride in the last decades for many Jews to give their children only one name, the Hebrew one, that being the one appearing on the child's birth certificate. (This used to present problems in France, because the law there until the 1960s only allowed a parent to choose a name from a special government-approved list of names.)

Question Why is the ceremony always followed by refreshments or a meal?

Answer Judaism lays great store on the concept of the *se'udat mitzvah*, the meal celebrating a religious event, and the *se'udat mitzvah* itself is considered to be a religious ritual. Thus, it serves a double purpose: it allows the family and friends to celebrate the event together; while at the same time making of the commonplace act of eating a celebration of God's goodness to us, thereby elevating the meal itself into a service of God.

Pidyon ha-Ben

Question What is a *Pidyon ha-ben*, and to whom does the law apply?

Answer Originally, at the time the Jews left Egypt, the priesthood was meant to belong to the firstborn of each family. Because of the sin of the Golden Calf, the firstborn, who had participated in the worship of the Golden Calf, were replaced by the tribe of Levi, who had not participated. (The *kohanim* – "priests" – of today are the descendants of Aaron, Moses' brother, of the tribe of Levi.) The firstborn nevertheless retain a certain vestige of this special sanctity, and must therefore be "redeemed." (*Pidyon ha-ben*, translated literally, means "the redemption of the son.")

The ceremony generally takes place in a gathering of family and friends. The father brings the child to any *kohen*, and then declares that this is the firstborn son of the mother. He mentions that the Torah has commanded that the firstborn be redeemed. The *kohen* then gives the father a choice: "Which do you prefer? To give me your firstborn son, who has opened the womb of his mother, or to redeem him for five *shekels*, as required by the Torah?" The father, rather naturally, replies that he prefers to redeem the child. He then pronounces a blessings: "... who has commanded us concerning the redemption of the son," and *She-heheyanu* – "... Who has kept us alive, sustained us

146 THE JEWISH PRIMER

and brought us to this season," after which he hands the *kohen* the value of five *shekels* in silver coins. (Israel has minted special silver coins to be used just for this purpose.) In the United States, one normally uses five silver dollars, but it is important to ensure that the coins used are of the era when silver was still used. Modern-day "silver" dollars are an amalgam of inexpensive metals. After accepting the money, the *kohen* waves it over the child and states, "This in place of that," and he then blesses the child with the wish that in the future he will enter into the study of Torah, into the marriage canopy, and into the performance of good deeds. After that, he pronounces the priestly blessing: "May the Lord bless you and protect you. May the Lord direct His presence toward upon you and be gracious unto you. May the Lord make His countenance shine upon you and grant you peace" (Num. 6:24-26). The ceremony is generally followed by a *se'udat mitzvah* – a festive meal.

Question Who is considered a firstborn for these purposes?

Answer The Torah gives a simple definition of the firstborn: "Everyone that opens the womb" (Num. 18:15). Thus, it must be the first child of the mother, *provided* that the child was born naturally (i.e., not through Caesarean section), so that "the womb was opened." (There is a rabbinic debate whether a second child, born naturally after a first delivery by Caesarean section, must be redeemed.) The law only applies to males, for only they were eligible to work in the tabernacle. If the first child born was a girl, the family does not have a *Pidyon ha-ben*. After all, any boy born afterwards did not "open the womb." Furthermore, as the Levites were exchanged for the firstborn, Levite firstborn do not need to be "redeemed," for their sanctity has remained to this day. By the same token, the firstborn of families of *kohanim* (priests), do not need to be redeemed, because the *kohanim* are a sub-branch of the Levites, descended from Aaron. Even further, if the mother of the child is the daughter of a Levite or a *kohen*, her firstborn son does not need to be redeemed. Summing up, then, a firstborn must be redeemed provided that it is a boy, that he was delivered naturally, and that his father is not a Levite or *kohen* and that his mother is not the daughter of a Levite or *kohen*. All in all, then, one can see that very few children need to be redeemed – especially in those Jewish communities where there is a high birthrate.

Question When does this ceremony take place, and why then?

Answer The ceremony takes place on the 31st day after the child's birth (or any time afterwards if for some reason it was not held on the right day). As the ceremony involves money, it is not held on the Sabbath or festivals.

✦ *Instruments for* Brit Milah *and a prayer book for the ceremony; 18th-19th centuries.*

ברוך אתה יי׳ אלהינו מלך
העולם אשר קדשנו
במצותיו וצונו על המילה׃
זה הכסא של אליהו
זכור לטוב

Unlike circumcision on the eighth day, for which we cannot find any specific reason, there is a logical explanation for the choice of the 31st day. The Talmud tells us – and remember that at the time infant mortality was common – that until an infant has lived for 30 days, there is no presumption that it is viable. (This has certainly ramifications in Jewish law. For example, the laws of mourning do not apply upon the death of an infant within its first 30 days.) Once the child has survived for 30 days, it is presumed to be viable. Hence the *Pidyon ha-ben* on the 31st day or thereafter, once we have established that this is indeed a viable child.

Bar Mitzvah

Question What is the Bar Mitzvah?

Answer Bar Mitzvah is the ceremony which indicates that a Jewish male has become a member of the adult congregation in every sense of the word.

Question What is the significance of this in practical terms?

Answer It means that from now on the young man can be counted in a *minyan* (prayer quorum) in the synagogue, and can be one of the three males needed for the grace after meals to be recited collectively. It also means that the young man has to assume the responsibilities of being an adult, as, for example, praying regularly, keeping the Sabbath, fasting on fast days, etc. By Jewish law, too, once a young man is Bar Mitzvah, he may enter into various legal contracts – including marriage! He can also be called to testify in a Jewish court of law. Of course boys under Bar Mitzvah age are also taught to pray and observe the commandments, but the reason is educational; the laws are not binding until they become Bar Mitzvah.

Question When does the Bar Mitzvah take place?

Answer The Mishnah tells us, "At the age of thirteen, one is obliged to observe the commandments" (Avot 5:25). This is the average age when puberty is assumed to begin. Girls, whose puberty begins earlier, must observe all the commandments from the age of twelve. (We will discuss the Bat mitzvah further on in this section.)

Question How is this transition from being a child to being an adult marked?

Answer Traditionally, the young man attends the synagogue on one of the days on which the Torah is read – Sabbath, Monday or Thursday – and is honored by being called up to the Torah, this being a public demonstration that he has entered the stage of manhood by Jewish law. His father then makes a declaration thanking God for having "released me from the obligation for this young man," in that the Bar Mitzvah boy is considered to be an adult.

Where possible, the boy himself reads the Torah portion, and in most cases will read the *haftarah* if there is one that day. It is also customary for the boy to begin laying *tefillin* a short time before his 13th birthday, in order to become competent at something he will do for the rest of his life.

That is the sum total of the Bar Mitzvah. In fact, in earlier times – and we are talking decades, not hundreds of years, ago – the Bar Mitzvah often consisted of no more than the young man being called to the Torah and his father supplying a bottle of liquor and a few cookies to the regular worshippers present. The young man might also be called upon to give a Torah thought to those assembled in the synagogue.

Question What is the origin of the Bar Mitzvah ceremony as we know it today?

Answer As we have pointed out, almost all of today's ceremony is a recent innovation, and some of this development seems to have been more a question of "keeping up with the Cohens" than of Jewish tradition. It is unfortunate that so many families feel that they are forced to lavish ever more and more elaborate receptions, regardless of what that does to their finances. It reminds one of an aphorism I once heard: "The fear of Heaven of previous generations has been replaced by our fear of what the neighbors will say."

They tell a story of a father who decided he was going to have a Bar Mitzvah that would put all his friends to shame. Chartering a jet, he flew the family and their friends to Nairobi, Kenya. From there, they embarked on a jungle safari, the culmination of which was to be the young man reading the Torah in the middle of Kenya's largest jungle. As they were snaking single file down the jungle trail, their native guide came to a halt. "What's the delay?" the father asked impatiently. "Sorry sir," the guide replied, "we have to wait for the Bar Mitzvah ahead of us to move off the trail."

Question What do the words Bar Mitzvah mean?

Answer Literally, the words translate as "son of the commandment," in the sense that the young man is now obliged to keep the commandments. It thus seems more than strange that certain Bar Mitzvahs are celebrated in ways which are not only non-Jewish, but even anti-Jewish, as, for example, with a non-kosher dinner. A wag once stated that the problem with some of these parties is that "they have everything *bar* the *mitzvah!*"

Bat Mitzvah

Question What does the term Bat Mitzvah mean?

Answer It is the feminine form of Bar Mitzvah, meaning "a daughter of the commandment," and indicates the time when a young girl become an adult according to Jewish law. Girls become Bat Mitzvah at the age of 12.

Question How is the Bat Mitzvah celebrated?

Answer Historically, as little as the celebration of the Bar Mitzvah involved, the celebration of the Bat Mitzvah involved even less. In fact, until this century, the very idea of celebrating a girl's Bat mitzvah was unknown. As this is a modern institution, the Bat Mitzvah has developed along various different lines. To some of the Orthodox stream, there is still no event marking the girl's entry into the adult fold. Among the more modern Orthodox stream, the Bat Mitzvah may be celebrated by having a party for family and friends, at which the young lady may make a speech or offer Torah thoughts. In some synagogues, the father of the girl is honored by being called to the Torah reading. Or the young lady's Bat Mitzvah may be acknowledged by a presentation to her by the congregation. Among the non-Orthodox, there has been a tendency in recent years to have girls celebrate their Bat Mitzvah the same way boys celebrate their Bar Mitzvah, by being called to the Torah and chanting a portion in it. As the Orthodox believe that women should not be called to the Torah, they are obviously opposed to such practices.

Unfortunately the practices of the Bat Mitzvah have all too often been following closely on the heels of the Bar Mitzvah, with the event becoming a major social function. It is a pity that communities do not unite to moderate the celebration of the Bar Mitzvah and Bat Mitzvah, and to have them assume rational proportions.

Marriage

Question What is the Jewish position on marriage?

Answer The first commandment in the Torah is considered to be to "be

♣ *"A Jewish Wedding"; painting by Moritz Oppenheim, Germany, 19th century.*

fruitful and multiply." Judaism thus regards marriage as the ideal state, and one who fails to marry or who refrains from marriage is not considered to be more pious thereby; on the contrary, the person is considered to have negated one of the most fundamental of Jewish laws. In fact, the Sages tell us, when a person comes up for judgment after his death, he will be asked: "Did you get married?" "Did you raise a family?" There are numerous sayings by the Sages extolling marriage. Thus, we are told, "A man who does not have a wife is not a proper man," and "A man who has no wife lives without joy, without blessing and without goodness" (Yevamot 62b).

Question What is the minimum age for marriage according to Jewish law?

Answer By Jewish law, a male has to be 13 and a female 12, that being the age when the individual is considered to be an adult and able to take legally binding decisions. The rabbis, though, have generally insisted on marriage at a later age than that. Ideally, according to *The Ethics of the Fathers*, one should marry at the age of eighteen. Israeli law generally requires individuals to be 17 years of age, but there are exceptions, as, for example, where the female is pregnant.

Question Whom is one forbidden to marry?

Answer Jewish law does not consider taking a partner from outside the faith a legally binding marriage. Various other relationships, of an incestuous nature, cannot result in a legally binding marriage. These include with parents, step-parents, grandparents, between siblings, and between a nephew and his aunt. Jewish law, though, does not forbid the marriage of an uncle and his niece or of first cousins. A man may not marry his wife's sister as long as the wife is still alive. Rabbinic law extends various of the prohibitions for further generations, for example forbidding marriage with one of a person's great-grandparents or with step-grandparents.

There are also certain marriages which, while legally binding, are nevertheless forbidden. An example of this is the prohibition against a *kohen* – a member of the priestly clan – marrying a divorcee. The priests, as the ones who served God directly in the Temple, are subject to various rules which apply only to them, signifying the higher standards required of them by their position.

Question Does Judaism believe in monogamy?

Answer Strictly speaking, Judaism permits polygamy, and, of course, we have various Biblical accounts of this, such as with Jacob and, of course, King

Solomon and his 1,000 wives. By the time of the Talmud, though, it would appear that monogamy was the norm, and none of the Sages listed in the Talmud is noted to have had more than one wife. This tendency toward monogamy was enshrined in Jewish law by Rabbenu Gershom (11th century C.E.), who forbade the taking of more than one wife. His prohibition, though, was only accepted by the Ashkenazic Jews, and indeed there were Sephardic and Yemenite Jews who had more than one wife. In fact, there are cases of polygamy in Israel to this day, where men from various North African countries or Yemen, who had more than one wife, moved to Israel with all their wives. While Israeli law forbids a man from marrying a woman if he is already married, it did not require these men to divorce wives they had married before moving to the country.

We should also note one other provision of Jewish law, which allows for bigamy under certain rigorously defined circumstances. If, for example, a woman has become insane and cannot accept a divorce from her husband (and accepting the divorce means having the mental capacity of understanding the implications), the court has the right to rule that the man may marry a second time, even though he has not divorced his first wife. Of course, he is still obligated to support his first wife and this provision does not allow him to live with both women at the same time. In order not to abuse this condition, the man cannot marry a second time until he has been given the *written* permission of 100 rabbis to this step – a long and arduous process.

Question What does the Jewish wedding consist of?

Answer While those who attend a wedding may think of it as a single ceremony, generally lasting between twenty minutes to half an hour, what they are really seeing is two separate ceremonies, one known as the *kiddushin* (or *erusin*) and the other known as the *nisu'in*, both of which we will describe below. In fact, at the time of the Talmud, a year usually elapsed between the two ceremonies, during which time the groom had the opportunity to set up his home for his bride. Let us examine each of these elements:

Kiddushin – Literally, the word means "sanctification," in that the groom "sanctifies" the bride to himself as his wife. The name itself is significant, implying marriage as a holy act. The basic part of this ceremony is the giving by the groom to the bride of an object in front of two valid witnesses (we, of course, use a ring), and the bride's acceptance of it as a sign of her acquiescence. In ancient times, the couple would then return to their respective homes until the *nissu'in* a year later. During this year, they were forbidden marital relations. On the other hand, *kiddushin* is far more than the engagements of our days, and the only way it can be terminated (short of one of the parties dying) is through a formal divorce.

Nissu'in – Literally, "elevation." This is the stage when the groom takes the bride to himself as his wife in every way. Seven special blessings are recited and are followed by *yihud* ("privacy"), whereby the bride and groom are sequestered alone together for a few minutes, thus symbolizing the groom's bringing the bride into his home as his wife.

The ceremony itself, though, which is performed in the presence of at least ten adult Jewish males, is more elaborate than the mere giving of the ring and the *yihud*. The act of *kiddushin* is preceded by two blessings over a cup of wine, one the standard blessing over wine and the other concerning the ceremony itself. Both the groom and bride then drink of the wine. The groom places a ring on the bride's right forefinger, while he recites (in Hebrew) "You are consecrated to me according to the laws of Moses and Israel." Where the groom does not know the Hebrew formula, the rabbi will read the Hebrew words out one by one, and the groom will repeat them. (Many rabbis read out the declaration word by word even for learned bridegrooms, so as not to shame the ignorant ones.) In reality, that ends the *kiddushin*.

To mark a break between the *kiddushin* and the *nissu'in*, the *ketubah*, which we will describe below, is read at this point. The *nissu'in*, which follows, consists of the recitation of seven blessings over a second cup of wine (because we must remember that this is a separate ceremony), one of them the blessing over wine and the remaining six dealing with marriage as such, including prayers for the young couple's happiness throughout their lives. The bride and groom then sip the wine from the second cup. The ceremony generally ends with the groom breaking a glass with his foot, as a sign that all our joyous moments are incomplete as long as the Temple in Jerusalem lies in ruins. (Some grooms even place a little ash under their headgear before the ceremony, as a sign of mourning for the Temple.) It has been said that the groom breaking the glass also serves as another symbol: that it will be the last time in his marriage that he puts his foot down!

Question   What is the *huppah*?

Answer   The *huppah* is the bridal canopy, under which the marriage ceremony takes place. Nowadays, it generally consists of an embroidered cloth held on four staves, but it can even be a *tallit*, a prayer shawl. The *huppah* is, of course, symbolic. Before the bride comes down the aisle, the groom is already under the *huppah* waiting for her. It is as if the *huppah* is the groom's abode, and when the bride comes under the *huppah*, it is as if she is entering his house, to be his wife. (This is also the symbolism of the *yihud*, mentioned above.) We should note that in popular speech, the word *huppah* is often used to denote the actual wedding ceremony, as opposed to the reception and festivities which follow.

Question What is the *ketubah*?

Answer The *ketubah* is a document, signed by two witnesses before or during the marriage ceremony, depending on custom, in which they testify that the groom has undertaken to support his wife during their marriage and to pay her a specified amount should the marriage be dissolved through divorce or through the groom's death. According to Jewish law (later amended by the same Rabbenu Gershom mentioned above, as we will see), a husband has the right to go to a Jewish court of law – a *bet din* – and have it write up a divorce document, a *get*, regardless of whether the wife is willing to be divorced or not. Once the *get* is given to the wife, she is divorced. By Jewish law, the husband does not even need a reason, and may even state, as the Talmud notes, that the reason is because his wife burned the food. Rabbenu Gershom, though, enacted a decree that forbids a man to divorce his wife against her will. In any event, in order to prevent husbands from taking this step precipitately, the *ketubah* was instituted. What the *ketubah* does is to impose a financial obligation on the husband (or his estate, should he die before the wife), should he divorce her or die. This financial obligation can be quite considerable, and was meant to serve as an inducement for the husband not to treat lightly the idea of divorce. In any event, the *ketubah* is read at the wedding, informing everyone of the obligations the groom has accepted upon himself in the marriage.

Question Why does the groom sometimes wear a white garment over his suit during the wedding ceremony?

Answer The garment, known as the *kittel*, is the same one many married men wear during the prayers on Yom Kippur, the Day of Atonement. The day one gets married is considered by Jewish law as equivalent to Yom Kippur, in that one atones for all one's sins and, as it were, begins a new life, free of sin. The *kittel*, then, symbolizes the beginning of that new, pure life. One may also note that it is customary for both bride and groom to add a special section in the afternoon service they recite on the day before their wedding, this being the same section one adds in the afternoon service preceding Yom Kippur. In this, they confess all their sins and ask God for atonement. There is also a custom for both to fast on the day of their wedding until the wedding ceremony.

Question What is the *ufruf*?

Answer It is customary, among Ashkenazic Jews, for a bridegroom to be called up to the Torah on the Sabbath before his wedding. The word *ufruf* simply means "being called up." The *ufruf* is a festive occasion, and it is the custom, immediately after the groom has recited the concluding blessings on the Torah reading, for him to be pelted with candies (supplied by him and his family – talk of masochism!), symbolic of the sweet life everyone wishes the couple. There is generally a wild scramble among the children present to grab as many of the candies as possible. Among Sephardic Jews, the equivalent ceremony occurs on the Sabbath *following* the wedding.

Question Why isn't the bride present at the *ufruf*?

Answer There is an ancient Jewish custom for the bride and groom not to see each other for the last week before the wedding, and thus the bride cannot be present at the synagogue service. It is a custom, though, for the bride to celebrate at her own home with her friends on that Sabbath.

Question What is the significance of the groom's veiling of the bride before the wedding ceremony?

Answer We are told that when Eliezer, Abraham's servant, brought Rebeccah back as a bride for Isaac, Rebeccah veiled her face as soon as she saw Isaac in the distance. The Jewish custom, known as the *badecken* (Yiddish for "covering") recalls that event. In fact, it is customary at the *badecken* for those present to bless the bride with the same blessing given Rebeccah by her relatives before she left them: "Our sister, may you become the mother of thousands of ten-thousands."

Question In many Jewish weddings, the bride walks around the groom a number of times (three or seven) before the actual wedding ceremony begins. What is the significance of this act?

Answer This custom traces back to a verse in Jeremiah, "A woman shall go around a man" (31:21). Various symbolisms have been attached to this custom, as for example, the bride's declaration, as it were, that from then on the groom will be at the center of her existence.

Question Sometimes, the parents escorting the groom and bride down the aisle carry lighted candles. What does this symbolize?

Answer By Jewish tradition, when God gave the Jews the Torah on Mount Sinai, the Jewish people were "married," as it were to God. Now, we are told that at the time of the giving of the Torah there was lightning, and the lit candles thus are a reminder of the earlier "wedding."

Question   During many wedding receptions, various guests may perform what might be called "circus" acts before the young couple, such as juggling, acrobatics, etc. What is the origin of this custom?

Answer   The Talmud lays great stress on the importance of adding to the young couple's joy at a wedding, and these are all ways to entertain the bride and groom. We are also told that the bride must be praised to the groom, so that he will appreciate her all the more. Here we come to an interesting discussion in the Talmud. According to the School of Hillel, one should praise the bride to the groom in the most glowing of colors: "Beautiful and charming bride!" The School of Shammai, though, disagrees, and states that one must tell the truth regardless: "The bride as she is," without going into superlatives which are untrue. The final ruling is in accordance with the School of Hillel, because, as this school explains it, one does not badmouth something a person has bought once he has already bought it! Incidentally, one of the most popular songs at weddings, *Keitzad merakdin lifnei hakallah*, enshrines the School of Hillel's words: "How does one dance before the bride? Beautiful and charming bride!" It is reported that at a certain wedding, while everyone was singing *Keitzad merakdin*, the bride's brother went over to her and told her in a stage whisper, "Aren't you grateful that we rule in accordance with the School of Hillel and that you have to be praised regardless?"

Question   What are the *sheva berakhot*?

Answer   Translated literally, the words mean "seven blessings," and indeed the phrase refers to the seven blessings recited under the *huppah* as part of the marriage ceremony. The phrase as used, though, has a more inclusive meaning. Jewish law requires a newly married couple – if at least one is being married for the first time – to celebrate their marriage for a total of seven days. Throughout these seven days, the couple will generally have at least one festive meal daily, at which ten adult Jewish males are present. If there are ten males present, the grace after meals is followed by the reciting of the same seven blessings as at the wedding, although in a slightly different order (the blessing over wine is now the last rather than the first blessing). Often, different members of the party will be honored to recite the different blessings. At the conclusion of the seven blessings, both the bride and the groom partake of the wine. The festive meals in the first week after a couple's marriage, are all known as *sheva berakhot*, obviously because the seven blessings are repeated at the end of the meal. There is one special require-ment in order to hold *sheva berakhot*: at least one of the males present has to be *panim hadashot* – a "new face" – namely a person who did not attend the wedding or any of the previous *sheva berakhot* meals for this couple. It is not uncommon for a couple to be married in one city, and then to fly to another city (or even country) for the *sheva berakhot* celebrations.

Question What is the Jewish attitude toward sex in marriage?

Answer Judaism believes that sex is an integral part of marriage, even to the extent that it is one of the three obligations a husband has toward his wife; the other two are to feed and clothe her.

Question Must sex be only for procreation?

Answer While Judaism is opposed to contraceptive measures (see Chapter 16 – Medical Questions), it does not regard sex as being only for procreative purposes. Thus a husband's "obligation" is not suspended during his wife's pregnancy or cancelled if she is found to be barren.

Question What is this I hear, though, that there are times when sex is forbidden between husband and wife?

Answer Indeed, Judaism believes that when a woman has her monthly period she becomes ritually impure (as noted elsewhere, the entire realm of ritual purity and impurity is beyond man's understanding); at that time she is referred to as a *niddah*. When her menstrual period begins, a woman may not have sexual relations with her husband until she has completed a purification process lasting seven days after the conclusion of her monthly period. (She must observe five days for her monthly period, even if menstruation lasted less than five days.) At the end of this time period of at least 12 days the woman must immerse herself in a *mikveh* – a ritual bath – and the couple is permitted to resume sexual relations. Thus, in essence the couple must remain apart for a minimum of 12 days (possibly longer if menstruation lasts longer than five days) during each monthly cycle.

Question Are there any benefits to such an arrangement?

Answer As pointed out by Rabbi Norman Lamm in his *A Hedge of Roses*, the enforced abstinence each month helps to keep the romance between the couple perpetually fresh. Each month is, as it were, a new start.

Question What is the penalty for a couple that ignore the laws of *niddah* and that have sexual relations without the wife's going to the *mikveh*.

Answer The Torah tells us that the punishment for this sin is *karet* – "cutting off" – a punishment which God, not man, inflicts. Incidentally, the same punishment is prescribed in the Torah for a person who eats on Yom Kippur.

Question Do Jewish women still keep this ritual?

Answer Indeed hundreds of thousands do. We have accounts of women who travel many hundreds of miles to visit the closest *mikveh*. And these are not isolated instances. Nowadays, almost any city with a decent-sized Jewish population has its own *mikveh*.

Question How important are the laws of *niddah*?

Answer The laws of *niddah* are of the utmost importance. Jewish law, in fact, states that the *very first* public building to be erected in a town must be a *mikveh* – not a synagogue, not a yeshivah.

Question If the marriage does not work, is it difficult under Jewish law to obtain a divorce?

Answer Under Jewish law, should the parties both agree that they wish to be divorced, the process itself is a simple matter. All that is needed is for a scribe to write out the specific formula of divorce and for the husband to hand the document to his wife. As we pointed out above, though, this may not be done without the wife's consent, and the husband has the legal obligation to pay the wife whatever he promised her in the *ketubah*. Matters can, however, get messy if there is a disagreement between the two regarding such matters as child custody or the division of property. As by Jewish law the husband must be the initiator of the action and the wife must be willing to accept the divorce, it is obvious that no divorce can result where either partner refuses to acquiesce to it.

Question How about a civil divorce?

Answer Jewish law accepts only Jewish divorce (the bill of divorce is known as a *get*) as severing the marriage relationship between husband and wife. Thus it is possible for a couple to obtain a civil divorce and yet to remain married by Jewish law, and vice-versa.

Question What happens if one of the partners is stubborn and refuses to accede to a divorce?

Answer This particular problem is one of the major ones facing contemporary Jewry. For the man in the case, matters are much easier: By Torah law, a man may have more than one wife, and where the Jewish court of law is convinced that the wife's refusal to accept the *get* is unjustified, it can eventually permit the man to marry another woman. This is a very long and complicated process and involves the participation of 100 rabbis. In western countries, the rabbinical courts usually only resort to this process if the wife remarries without receiving a Jewish divorce.

The real problem arises where the husband refuses, for whatever reason – failure to agree on a settlement or even out of pure spite – to grant his wife a *get*. In such a case, the woman is known as an *agunah* (i.e., "chained"). As Jewish law forbids a woman from being married to more than one man, the woman is forbidden under any circumstances from marrying, even if she is completely blameless.

Question   Have there been any attempts to relieve the situation?

Answer   In answering this question, we must consider two different aspects: what has and is being done in individual cases, and what was and is being done to try to solve the problem universally.

Generally, where the husband's whereabouts are known, every effort is made by the local rabbinic authorities to persuade him to consent to giving his wife a divorce. In Israel, where the rabbinic courts are official arms of the government, a husband who refuses to grant his wife a divorce can be charged with contempt of court and may even be jailed until he finally agrees. Where the husband has fled the country, the rabbinic courts even hire special investigators to track him down, and when they find him, they try to persuade him to grant the divorce.

As to the overall situation, there have been attempts for decades to find some type of halakhically acceptable formulation to be included in the *ketubah*, which will enable the rabbinic courts to solve the problem of stubborn husbands by invoking punitive sanctions, declaring their marriage void or some other such means. Unfortunately, the problem does not lend itself to easy solutions, and there has not been any consensus on a formula that will serve to solve the problem of the *agunah*. After all, it does seem strange to annul a marriage that lasted for years, where children may have been born. Meanwhile the problem remains with us like a festering sore.

We should also point out that it has been the practice for Jewish soldiers to fill out forms supplied by their chaplains, in which the soldier agrees that, should he be missing for a specified period of time, the chaplaincy has the right to issue his wife a *get* as the soldier's delegated representative. Thus, if the soldier is missing in action, after the specified period of time has passed his wife will at least be set free to remarry.

Question What happens if a woman remarries after a civil divorce, even though she has not received a *get*?

Answer In such a case, by Jewish law the woman is considered to be adulterous, since she is co-habiting with a second man even though she is halakhically married to the first one. All her subsequent children are then considered to be *mamzerim*, and *mamzerim* are not permitted by Jewish law to marry other Jews. One can thus see how important it is for a woman to obtain a valid *get* from a properly qualified *bet din* before entering into a second marriage.

Question How does the Reform Movement rule in regard to divorce?

Answer According to the Reform Movement, a civil divorce is sufficient, and no *get* is necessary. Unfortunately, what women who accept this view often do not realize is that by remarrying without a *get* they may have children who will in future years not be able to marry into Orthodox or Conservative families. Thus, by not insisting on Jewish divorce, the Reform Movement has created a situation where there are two classes of Jewish who cannot inter-marry.

Question What is a *mamzer*?

Answer The common English translation of the word is "illegitimate," but the word is incorrect. According to Jewish law, a child born of unmarried parents has no permanent stigma as such, and may marry any other person. The *mamzer* is the offspring of an adulterous or incestuous union.

Mourning

Question What is the Jewish attitude toward death?

Answer Judaism regards the human being as being the only creature who combines in himself elements of the physical and the spiritual, the physical as represented by the corporeal body, and the spiritual by the soul. Whereas the body must eventually return to the dust from which it came, the soul is eternal. The purpose of man's life in the world is to perfect the soul by acting properly. The closer the person comes to perfection in this world, the greater the reward for the soul in the World to Come, as it is called. Two stories may be the best way to illustrate this.

It is told that the saintly Rabbi Israel Meir of Radin, known universally as the Hafetz Hayyim (1836-1933), lived very modestly. Once, a visitor from the United States came to the Hafetz Hayyim's home and was disturbed at what he saw. "Rabbi," he said, "Is that all the furniture you have?" The Hafetz Hayyim responded with a question: "Well how about you, my good man? Is what I see with you all the furniture you have?" "Rabbi," the man replied, "I have no furniture here, because I'm just passing through. I have all my furniture in my home." "The same is true with me," said the Hafetz Hayyim, "I am just passing through this world. All my furniture awaits me in my permanent home as well."

The second story concerns a hasidic rabbi, who lay on his deathbed. His disciples were all about him, and they couldn't help but show the grief in their eyes. The rabbi, though, reprimanded them. "My children," he said, "All my life I have worked for this one moment. Now that it is upon me, should I feel sad?"

Question   Does that mean that one should not mourn the dead?

Answer   Judaism definitely considers mourning to be in place. In fact, as we will see later, it makes provision for different stages of mourning, some of these provisions applying up to a year after the death of a parent. But the mourning is more for the living, who will miss the deceased, rather than for the deceased him- or herself. In fact, among *hasidim*, it is customary to treat the anniversary of the death of a sainted rabbi as a joyous occasion, signifying that the rabbi went to his eternal rest and reward. We should also point out that, while Jewish law makes extensive provisions for mourning, it lays strict curbs on excessive mourning. For example, the Torah specifically forbids one to cut himself as a sign of mourning, a common practice among the Canaanite nations of the time.

Generally, we regard a birth in the family as a joyous occasion, whereas a death is a cause for grief and mourning. Yet, we are told in Ecclesiastes (which, by Jewish tradition was written by Solomon in his old age, after he had experienced all that life has to offer), "It is better to go to the house of mourning, than to go to the house of feasting." As our Sages explain this, when people see a ship sailing out to sea, all are delighted and wish it well, but when a ship comes in to port, on the other hand, it comes in unattended. Logically, though, it should be the other way around, for no one knows what will be the fate of the ship going out to sea, while the ship returning to port after a long voyage has clearly survived the rigors of the trip and has returned safely. By the same token, when a child is born, it is as if it is just going out to sea, and no one knows the course it will take. When a person dies, on the other hand, it is as if the person has now entered the port after life's voyage is over.

Question How about those deaths that we cannot understand? People dying young, people dying after great suffering, infants dying? How does Judaism reconcile these with a compassionate God?

Answer Jewish law requires a person, upon hearing of the death of a close relative, to recite the following blessing: "Blessed are You, O Lord our God, King of the Universe, the True Judge." (Those who hear of a death, but not of a close relative, recite "Blessed is the True Judge.") There is no doubt that – from man's perspective – there are tremendous injustices in the world. Judaism, though, regards this world as only part – and the minor part – of the totality of man's existence. It firmly believes that God's ways are just, and that ultimately each person receives what he deserves. Thus, for example, a wicked person's *punishment* may be that he is rewarded in this world for the good deeds he has performed, at the expense of the eternal reward that he would otherwise have received in the World to Come. Similarly, a righteous person may suffer in this world for his sins, rather than suffer for his sins in the World to Come. But man cannot understand these calculations.

The Talmud tells the story of the learned Bruriah, wife of Rabbi Meir. On one Sabbath, both the couple's sons died. Rather than disturb everyone's Sabbath, their mother had the bodies covered and she did not tell her husband about the great tragedy that had befallen them.

After the Sabbath, Bruriah approached her husband with a problem: "My husband," she began, "I need your advice. Some time ago, a wealthy man deposited some precious jewels with me. Now he wants me to return them. Am I required to do so?" Astounded at this question from his wife, Rabbi Meir told her that of course she had to do so immediately. Removing the cover, Bruriah showed her husband their two sons that had died. Rabbi Meir, totally griefstricken, began to weep uncontrollably. "Husband," Bruriah told him, "Listen to what your mouth said. Years ago, the Holy One, blessed be He, entrusted us with two precious jewels – our sons. Now He has decided He wants them back. Are we not duty-bound to return them to Him when He asks for them?"

Question Turning to the laws involved, what precautions must be taken when a person is about to die?

Answer If a person is on the threshhold of death, one is forbidden to take any action whatsoever that may hasten the death by even an instant, as, for example, even moving one of the person's limbs. As the chief rabbi of Great Britain, Rabbi Immanuel (Lord) Jakobovits, once explained it, human life is of infinite worth. Each instant of life, then, is of that same infinite worth, and if one hastened a person's death by even an instant, it is the same as killing the person. In fact, in order to be sure that one does nothing that may hasten death, Jewish law requires the body of a person who dies not to be moved for an hour after the death, for had there been any vestige of life present, any movement would hasten death.

Question What rituals are prescribed after the person is definitely dead?

Answer The eyes are closed, the body is reverently laid on the floor and is covered, as a sign of respect. Candles are lit next to the body (the flickering of the candle's flame is symbolic of the human soul, as we see in Proverbs 20:27, "The soul of man is the candle of the Lord"). From then until the actual burial, the body is not left alone. Often shifts are arranged of *shomerim* – "guards" – who sit by the body, reciting chapters of the Psalms. Those in the presence of the dead are forbidden to eat or drink, or to perform any commandments, for this is considered to be "mocking the helpless," namely the deceased who is no longer able to carry out any of these functions.

Question What is this about *kohanim* – those of priestly origin – and the dead?

Answer The *kohanim*, who are all direct lineal descendants on their father's side of Aaron, the first high priest, have certain restrictions, based on their religious status. One of these is that they are not permitted to defile themselves ritually by coming into contact with the dead. (We will discuss the question of defilement in the next section.) A person is ritually defiled by either coming into contact with a dead body, being close to one, or being under the same roof (or any other covering, such as a tree) as a dead body. For all but the *kohanim*, becoming defiled presents no problem – there is no law forbidding one to do so. As *kohanim* are forbidden to become ritually defiled, the law is that if a person dies, *kohanim* in the same building must leave the premises immediately, and remain outside the building until the body has been removed. There are exceptions to this rule, though. There are seven close relatives for whom a *kohen* may be defiled: his father, mother, brother, unmarried sister, son, daughter and wife. In the case of any of these deaths, he may remain with the body for as long as he is actively involved in the burial procedure.

We should note that Israeli hospitals generally are built to make provision for *kohanim*, in that the morgue section of the hospital is insulated from the rest of the complex. This way, if a person dies anywhere in the hospital building, the body is removed to the morgue. For the benefit of *kohanim*, the major hospitals, such as the Hadassah Hospital in Jerusalem, have a sign outside the front door indicating whether *kohanim* may or may not enter the building at the time. Generally, if there is a death, the sign advising *kohanim* not to enter will be posted for less than an hour, until the body has been moved to the morgue.

We should note another aspect of the law as it applies to *kohanim*. As *kohanim* cannot come close to a dead body, they are not permitted to walk within the rows of graves in a cemetery. In order to enable *kohanim* to visit the grave sites of their relatives, it is customary for *kohanim* to be buried in the outer rows of each section. This way their relatives can come at least relatively close to the grave site. This custom can often be verified visually when one visits a cemetery, for the graves of many *kohanim* are marked by two hands raised in the priestly benediction, and it is often the graves with this distinctive sign that are on the outer rows. (Another way to verify this custom is to look at the names. The names Cohen, Kohn, Kagan, etc. are all generally indicative of a family of *kohanim*.)

Question   What is this ritual defilement to which the last answer referred?

Answer   Of all the laws of the Torah, the laws of ritual purity and impurity are among the most difficult to understand. Rationally, a person who has come in contact with a dead body or under the same roof as a dead body has not changed in any way. Physically, that is absolutely true. The only possible way to explain it is to realize that we are dealing with a different dimension than the physical. The question of ritual purity and impurity is entirely a question of the spiritual. Indeed, we are told that "the corpse does not cause impurity, nor do the waters purify, but it is a decree of the Supreme King of Kings" (*Pesikta de-Rabbi Kahana* 40a-b). Thus, when dealing with this question, we can only take the laws as we find them, and any attempt to offer a rational explanation is doomed from the outset.

Question   What must the mourners do once their relative is definitely dead?

Answer   At that point, the mourners enter the first stage of mourning, known as *aninut*, each of the mourners being known as an *onen*. Those in *aninut* have but one responsibility – to make all the arrangements necessary for the burial of their loved one. This responsibility takes precedence over all other obligations, thus exempting the *onen* from the performance of all the positive commandments of Judaism. For example, the *onen* is exempted from prayer and from laying *tefillin*.

Question   How long does *aninut* last?

Answer   Theoretically, *aninut* lasts from the death to the burial. As Jewish law requires burial of the dead as soon as possible after death (this being considered a sign of respect), *aninut* is a question of a day or two, at the most. In Jerusalem, for example, the general custom is to bury the dead within the same day, and not to leave a body unburied overnight. Thus, if a person died in the late afternoon, the burial may be held that same night. In such cases, cars with loudspeakers circulate in the neighborhood where the deceased lived, giving details of the funeral. There are, however, exceptions to the laws of *aninut*, and they are entirely logical. Where a person cannot possibly do anything to facilitate the burial, as, for example, if he is in another country or the death occurred on the Sabbath, he is required to observe all the laws, including that of prayer.

Question Returning to the question of burial, what other procedures are followed?

Answer Jewish communities throughout the world generally have an organization named the Hevrah Kadisha – the Holy Society – which deals with preparing the dead for burial. The people involved are generally volunteers, and the work is considered to be especially meritorious. Our Sages tell us that doing something to aid in the burial of the dead is the highest degree of acts of lovingkindness to our fellow-man. In every other case, when we help another, there is always the possibility that that person may help us in return at a later time, and this, in a way, diminishes the completeness of our good intentions. Only in the case of the dead can there be no such ulterior motive of any kind. Thus, aiding in the burial is known as *hesed shel emet* – true lovingkindness.

The first step in the preparation for burial is the *taharah* – "purification" – in which the body is washed completely, so that it may return to its maker as it arrived. It is then enclosed in a plain linen shroud. In the case of a man, the shroud is covered with his prayer shawl. In most places, it is then placed in a plain wooden coffin. By Jewish law, the shrouds and the coffin must be as plain as possible. This rule was instituted in Talmudic times because, as we are told, the funerals kept getting more and more lavish, to the extent that the expenses became exorbitant. Then as now, people had to keep up with the Cohens even in matters as sad as this! As a result of the high cost of burial, there were even cases where the relatives simply abandoned the dead body. It was as a result that the Sages instituted the provisions mandating simplicity. We should thus note that the modern-practice of lavish, felt-lined coffins is completely at odds with Jewish law.

Question What was that veiled reference in the last answer to the use "in most places" of a coffin?

Answer   In Israel, indeed, it is the custom in almost all cities to bury the body directly in the earth without a coffin. There is certainly no Jewish law requiring the use of a coffin. In fact, according to Jewish law, even where a coffin is used, it must have holes bored in it to enable the earth to seep through and come in contact with the body. In military funerals and those of people whose bodies have been mutilated in an accident, coffins are always used.

Question   What is the procedure at the funeral service proper?

Answer   The funeral generally begins with eulogies for the departed. There are certain festive dates of the year when eulogies are forbidden, in which case the speakers will limit themselves to short remarks about the deceased. After this, all the close relatives of the deceased (parents, siblings, children, spouse) stand, and each rends his/her garment as a sign of mourning. This action is known as *keriyah* The tear is made on the upper garments, in the case of men all upper garments so as to expose the chest, and in the case of women only the outer garment. For parents, the tear is on the left side of the garment, opposite the heart, and for any other relative on the right side of the garment. At the time, the mourners recite the blessing, "Blessed are You, O Lord our God, King of the Universe, the True Judge," thus accepting God's verdict, as it were. Whereas the tear made for another relative may be completely repaired after thirty days of mourning, that for a parent may never be.

The body is now taken to its final resting place. Psalms are recited as the procession makes it way to the burial site. The procession halts periodically, and the mourners recite the "mourners' *Kaddish*" (see below). In many communities, it is customary to place a little sack of soil from the Land of Israel in the grave. After the body is placed in the ground, various people take turns in shovelling in the earth to cover the body. Finally, a prayer is intoned asking the deceased to forgive anyone that may have wronged him or her at any time.

After the funeral is over, all but the mourners form two rows. The mourners then walk between the rows, and as they pass each person, they are comforted with the traditional Jewish message of condolence: "May the Almighty comfort you among the other mourners for Zion and Jerusalem."

It is customary for those who have been at the cemetery to wash their hands before entering any home, and cemeteries generally offer facilities for washing one's hands.

Question   What is the *se'udat havra'ah*?

Answer   When the mourners return home from the cemetery, their closest neighbor brings them a meal, consisting of bread and hard-boiled eggs. This is known as the *se'udat havra'ah*, or "meal of condolence." The egg, being rounded, symbolizes the ongoing cycle of human life.

Question What are the stages of mourning after the burial?

Answer For all mourners, there are two basic periods of mourning: the first seven days, known as *shivah* (the word simply means "seven"), and the first thirty days, known as *shloshim* ("thirty"). For one's parents, there is a third stage, lasting for a full year. The way the laws are set up shows a clear understanding of the psychological needs of the mourner, with the greatest display of mourning during the first seven days, and lesser degrees of mourning as time goes on.

Question What are the rules regarding *shivah*?

Answer During the first week of mourning, the mourners may not sit on any chair or sofa of normal height. They are not permitted to either bathe or shower, nor cut their hair (men may not shave). Nor may they change their outer garments. Throughout this time, they must wear the garment which was torn at the time of burial. Mourners may not wear any footgear which contains leather. Mourners are also not permitted to study Torah or to engage in their occupation during *shivah*. Marital relations are forbidden throughout this time. All three daily prayer services are held at the home of the mourners, and neighbors, friends and relatives make up the rest of the *minyan* or quorum. At each prayer service, those in mourning for parents recite the mourners' *Kaddish*, a practice they will maintain for eleven months. Visitors at the *shiva* conclude their visit with the words, "May the Almighty comfort you among the other mourners for Zion and Jerusalem." We should point out that the mourners never actually "sit *shivah*" (as it is known) for seven full days, for a number of reasons: The day of the burial is considered to be one of the seven days, even if the funeral took place just before sunset. Since mourning is not permitted on the Sabbath, the mourners attend the synagogue as usual on that day, but it is counted as one of the seven. On the seventh day, the mourners "get up from the *shivah*" soon after the morning prayer service.

Question What are the laws regarding *shloshim*, actually the remaining 23 days after *shivah*?

Answer During this time, the mourner may not have a haircut and men should ideally not shave, if possible. The mourners may not attend any joyous event, such as a Bar Mitzvah, wedding, or concert. Nor should they listen to music during that time. Males who are in mourning for parents must recite the *Kaddish* at all three daily synagogue services.

Question How about the laws regarding mourning for parents, which apply for a full year?

Answer Except for the restrictions on cutting one's hair, which are relaxed after the thirty days, all the rules of *shloshim* listed above apply for the full year in the case of the loss of a parent. *Kaddish*, though, is only recited for eleven months, as will be explained later. Throughout the year, the mourner is also not permitted to wear any new clothes. Mourners in the year after the death of parents may attend the actual wedding ceremony, the *huppah*, but not the reception that follows it. Generally speaking, the principle is that mourners should not participate in any joyous event, even a social event such as a party.

Question As mentioned earlier, those in mourning are required to recite the mourners' *Kaddish*. What is this prayer, and what does it have to do with the dead?

Answer The mourners' *Kaddish* is the prayer said by men in mourning for parents for 11 months at each of the daily prayer services. Those who read the translation of the words of the prayer (all except the last line are in Aramaic) soon realize that it has nothing to do with death or the deceased. Instead, it is a prayer of praise for God. As has been said, the *Kaddish* is not meant to serve as a prayer for the deceased, but as a pledge by the living. Even though one's dear one has departed, the mourner, by attending the prayer services and reciting the *Kaddish*, pledges to continue in his observance of the commandments and in the ways of his ancestors. Thus the mourner is, in effect, proclaiming that the living chain of Judaism continues on.

Question For whom does one say *Kaddish*, and when?

Answer As mentioned earlier, the Torah lists seven close relatives for whom one mourns: father, mother, sister, brother, son, daughter and spouse. *Kaddish* is recited for all of the above, at the funeral itself and thereafter at all prayer services for the period specified (11 months for parents and 30 days for all others, if they left no sons). In addition, the *Kaddish* is recited at all prayer services on the Hebrew calendar anniversary of the death (the so-called *yahrzeit*) each year. It is also customary for the mourner to lead the prayer service, if he is capable of doing so.

Question   Why is there a difference in the length of time that one recites *Kaddish* for one's parents and the time one recites it for other close relatives?

Answer   The Torah lays great stress on honoring one's parents, for having brought the person into the world. Part of this honor is expressed in reciting the *Kaddish* at all the prayer services for the 11 months following the burial. One may also note that it is possible for a person to have more than one of any other type of relative, except for a father and a mother. Thus it is only for one's parents that the mourner's *Kaddish* is recited for almost a year.

It is told that when Rabbi Abraham Isaac Kook, the chief rabbi of Palestine (d. 1935) lost his mother, all the efforts by his friends to console him were unavailing. Finally, a personal friend of his came to him and told him: "Rabbi, as chief rabbi of all of Palestine and rabbi of Jerusalem, aren't you overdoing things a little?" Tearfully, the rabbi turned to him and answered: "You forget that with all the titles I have acquired, no one else called me 'my son'."

Question   Why is the term for *Kaddish* for one's parents eleven months rather than a year?

Answer   Our Sages note that the souls of all those who have departed must spend a limited time to purify them of all their sins before entering the everlasting bliss of the World to Come. The most evil person spends twelve months in this purification process. Jewish belief is that reciting *Kaddish* helps the person through that process. If one would recite *Kaddish* for twelve months for his parents, he would be implying that the deceased is totally evil. In order to avoid this implication, the Sages set 11 months as the time one recites *Kaddish* for a parent.

Question   What rules apply to mourners after the period of mourning is over?

Answer   Whenever mentioning one's deceased father, one adds the words *zikhrono li-verakhah* ("may his memory be a blessing," or alternately, *alav ha–shalom*, "peace be upon him"), and when mentioning one's deceased mother, the term is *zikhronah li-verakhah* (or *aleha ha-shalom*). On the anniversary of any close relative's death (known among Ashkenazic Jews as the *yahrzeit*), it is customary to light a special candle which will burn for the entire 24 hours of the anniversary and for males to recite the mourner's *Kaddish* at all the synagogue services of that day. In many communities the mourner acts as the cantor for the prayer services of that day. It is a general practice to honor the mourner on the Sabbath preceding the *yahrzeit* by calling him to the Torah reading. It is also customary to remember one's departed family at *yizkor*, as we will see below.

Question What is *yizkor*, and when it is observed?

Answer The word *yizkor* means "May He [i.e., God] remember," and refers to a special prayer which one recites for each member of one's immediate family who is dead. The prayer is recited after the *haftarah* reading on four days of the year: on Yom Kippur, Shemini Atzeret (the eighth day of the Sukkot holiday), the last day of Passover (i.e., the seventh day in Israel and the eighth day elsewhere), and on Shavuot (on the single day of Shavuot in Israel and on the second day of the festival elsewhere). At that time, it is often customary for all those who do not need to say the prayer (i.e., whose parents are still alive) to leave the synagogue, although there are rabbinic authorities who rail against this practice. During the *yizkor* time period, those who have lost loved ones recite a prayer for each person individually, mentioning him or her by name, and pledging a contribution to charity in memory of that person. The individual *yizkor* prayer is often followed by collective prayers: for deceased members of the congregation, for those killed in the Holocaust, and for those who died in defense of the State of Israel.

It is customary to light *yahrzeit* candles on the afternoon before each *yizkor* day, and to have the candles burn throughout the day, just as on the *yahrzeit* day.

Conversion

Question Before discussing how a person converts to Judaism, shouldn't we first discuss what makes a person a Jew?

Answer Absolutely. According to Jewish law, a person born of a Jewish mother, or a non-Jew who has undergone the formal process of conversion, is considered to be a Jew.

Question Is that a universally accepted definition?

Answer In recent years, the Reform movement has advocated a new position – one that goes entirely against Jewish law and a tradition of thousands of years. According to the Reform movement, not only is a person with a Jewish mother to be considered Jewish, but the same is true for anyone with a Jewish father (the so-called "patrilineal" amendment). As can be understood, the Orthodox oppose such a change totally, seeing it as the absolute abrogation of Jewish law. (We should note parenthetically that at a recent meeting of the Conservative Rabbinic Assembly, about 30% of the rabbis present voted to accept the patrilineal clause, and this may be the forerunner of the adoption of this change within the Conservative movement in the next few years.)

Question What is the Jewish attitude toward conversion?

Answer One cannot speak of one Jewish attitude toward conversion, as there have been different views at different times. There were even times when the non-Jewish inhabitants of the Israelite country were forcibly converted. And history showed that the Jews had nothing but trouble from these forced converts. Jewish practice for the past thousand years or more has been to discourage people from converting. In fact, by Jewish law a person desiring to be converted to Judaism must be actively discouraged. This includes making him aware of the many obligations that Jews must fulfill and informing him of the low status of Jews throughout the world. (The latter was certainly true throughout the world until almost modern times. And in our generation we have the example of Hitler, who killed anyone who was even but a quarter Jewish – including Jews who had converted to Christianity.)

Question What happens if the person persists in the desire to become a Jew, in spite of the efforts to discourage him?

Answer If the rabbi who is involved becomes convinced that the person is sincere in this desire, he will prescribe a course of study for the person to follow. The person will also be asked to gradually observe more of Jewish ritual. When the rabbi feels that the person is ready for conversion, he will convene a *bet din* (court) of three rabbis, generally including himself, and the applicant for conversion will be questioned closely. If the three rabbis agree, the person will undergo a conversion ceremony to Judaism.

Question What is the conversion ceremony?

Answer Conversion consists of two or three parts: the person must accept the Jewish faith voluntarily and audibly, must be immersed in a *mikveh* (ritual bath), and, in the case of a male, must be circumcised. The new convert will generally be given a new Hebrew name. "Ruth," for example, is quite common among female converts, as Ruth – the ancestor of King David – was a convert.

The ceremony makes the person a full-fledged Jew, with all the rights and all the obligations involved. This is a one-way street. Once a person has been formally converted, any attempt to leave the Jewish religion is considered to be unavailing – just as a person who is born a Jew by Jewish law cannot possibly leave his religion.

Question Is not circumcision for an adult male a painful procedure?

Answer That may be true, except that most American males, at least, are circumcised soon after birth for hygienic reasons. Where a non-Jewish male was circumcised in such a manner that he would by Jewish law technically be considered to be circumcised (this is not always the case), all that is needed is the extraction of a single drop of blood from the penis with the clear intention of doing so for ritual circumcision. The man is then considered to be ritually circumcised.

Question Are there other methods of conversion to Judaism?

Answer Here we touch upon a very sore point, which, probably more than any other, has been a tremendous source of friction between the Orthodox rabbinate and the other groups. Orthodoxy believes that the procedure prescribed above is necessary. Any attempt to modify any of the two or three steps involved must thus result in an invalid conversion. Now, the Reform movement as a whole has dispensed with both the requirements of immersion in the *mikveh* and ritual circumcision. All it requires of those wishing to join the fold is a commitment to Judaism. The Orthodox obviously feel that such a conversion does not meet the requirements of Jewish law. The Orthodox will generally reject Conservative conversions as well, although there are exceptions, where the conversions of specific Conservative rabbis may be accepted. The Orthodox rejection of Conservative conversions generally hinges on the clause requiring the person to commit himself to Judaism. The Orthodox, who feel that the Conservative movement violates various specific rules of Jewish law, feel that a commitment to observing Jewish law as practiced by the Conservative movement is tantamount to the acceptance of only certain parts of Jewish law. Yet Jewish law requires the prospective convert to accept Jewish law in its entirety, without exception. Orthodoxy further objects to the fact that many Conservative rabbis will accept converts of any of the streams – even those converted by the Reform movement without a pretense of following Jewish law – as converts in good standing, as part of their belief in the need to preserve Jewish unity. To the Orthodox, this means that there are rabbis of the Conservative movement who are willing to accept people who – under even their own guidelines – are not Jews, and to consider them as Jews in every sense of the word, including in questions of marriage, etc.

Question Why does Orthodoxy require its converts to observe all aspects of Jewish law? After all, the majority of the Jews in the world today do not do so.

Answer Many years ago, this exact question was asked of the late Rabbi Isaac Herzog, the chief rabbi of Israel. Rabbi Herzog had a very cogent and succinct reply: "Judaism already has enough law-breakers," he replied, "and there is no reason why we should add to the ranks of those who violate the law."

Question Is there any difference between Israel and other countries in regard to conversion to Judaism?

Answer In Israel, unlike in other countries, there is less emphasis on discouraging people from joining the Jewish people. After all, a Jew living in Israel hardly feels himself to be a member of a minority living among a non-Jewish majority. In Israel, in fact, the rabbinate conducts official courses for prospective converts, of about six months' duration. Most of these are held in religious kibbutzim. At the end of the course, each prospective convert appears before a *bet din* made up of three rabbis sent by the chief rabbinate, and only those satisfying the *bet din* of both their sincerity and their basic Jewish knowledge are permitted to convert.

Question How about converting *from* Judaism?

Answer As we briefly noted earlier, Jewish law does not recognize such a thing as converting from Judaism. A person who is a Jew has absolutely no way of becoming non-Jewish. Even one who is baptized as a Christian remains a Jew – albeit a Jew who has sinned and is sinning, in that he does not observe Jewish law.

Question Well, how about the "Jews for Jesus," who claim that they do observe Jewish law?

Answer "Jews for Jesus," even if they were to observe every single law on the books (which they do not), would still be considered to be heretics, for one simple reason: A Jew may not believe in the Trinity. (According to many rabbis, a non-Jew who believes in the Trinity is not violating the Noahide provision requiring all of mankind to believe in the one God, but all agree that the standards demanded of a Jew in this regard are higher, and the Jew's belief in the One God must be absolute and exclusive.) Even to believe that the true messiah has already come is heresy as far as Judaism is concerned.

Question   What is the status of a new convert to Judaism?

Answer   A person who converts to Judaism is considered to be like a newborn child, so that even blood relationships are considered to have ceased. There is no doubt, though, that the new convert must still respect his parents, etc.

Chapter Fourteen

Clothing

Question Does Judaism have what one might call a "dress code"?

Answer Rather than a single code, Judaism has a number of these, each serving a different purpose. Thus there are certain restrictions under the laws of *tzeniut* (modesty), while other aspects of what the Jew wears relate to symbolism, custom, or various aspects of Jewish law.

Question Do these rules apply in our days as well?

Answer A basic fundamental of Judaism, enshrined in Maimonides' *Thirteen Principles of the Faith*, is that Jewish law is eternal, and is applicable to all times. Due to various circumstances, many Jews have abandoned many of the rules which will be discussed below, but that does not make them any less applicable.

Question What are the laws regarding *tzeniut*?

Answer Judaism requires more of women than of men under the rules of modesty. In fact, except during prayers, there are few restrictions for men. In the case of women, on the other hand, they are required to be covered from the neck to the knee, and to have sleeves to the elbow. (Certain groups within Judaism, the *hasidim*, for example, adopt an even more stringent ruling, requiring women to have sleeves to the wrist and to wear stockings. Some go even further than that and demand that the stockings have a seam, so that it is clear that the woman has her legs covered.) The laws of *tzeniut* also require a married woman to have her hair covered. How this is done is a question of law, custom and taste. It is generally agreed that a hat or scarf that covers most of the hair fulfills the law. There are communities where women wear a wig (a *shaitel* as it is often called, that being the Yiddish for a wig), but others oppose it, claiming that a wig is almost like wearing no hair covering.

DEAR VISITOR, YOU ARE QUITE WELCOME TO MEAH SHEARIM, BUT PLEASE DO NOT ANTAGONIZE OUR RELIGIOUS INHABITANTS BY STROLLING THROUGH OUR STREETS IN IMMODEST CLOTHING. OUR TORAH REQUIRES THE JEWISH WOMAN TO BE ATTIRED IN MODEST DRESS. MODEST DRESS; DRESS SLEEVES REACHING UNTIL BELOW THE ELBOWS, (SLACKS FORBIDDEN), STOCKINGS, MARRIED WOMEN HAVING THEIR HAIR COVERED, ETC., ARE THE VIRTUES OF THE JEWISH WOMAN THROUGHOUT THE AGES. PLEASE DO NOT OFFEND OUR RESIDENTS AND CAUSE YOURSELF ANY UNNECESSARY INCONVENIENCE. WE BEG YOU NOT TO INFRINGE UPON OUR WAY OF LIFE AND "HOLY CODE OF LAW". WE BESEECH YOU TO USE DISCRETION BY NOT TRESPASSING OUR STREETS IN AN UNDESIRED FASHION. THE MEN ARE REQUESTED NOT TO ENTER BAREHEADED. THANKING YOU IN ADVANCE FOR COMPLYING WITH OUR REQUEST, AND WISHING YOU BLESSINGS FROM ABOVE FOR YOUR GOOD DEEDS. COMMITTEE FOR GUARDING MODESTY, MEAH SHEARIM AND VICINITY, JERUSALEM, THE HOLY CITY.

MODEST DRESS
DRESSES
AND
SKIRTS
REACHING
UNTIL
BELOW
THE KNEE

✦ *Notice in Me'ah She'arim, Jerusalem, requesting women to dress modestly."*

Question Where else does Jewish law enter into the "dress code"?

Answer One of the provisions of Jewish law is that men may not wear women's clothing and *vice-versa*. The logic for this is obvious – it prevents a person from "passing off" as a member of the other sex. This law, as we will see in the next answer, has implications in our own times.

Question Where does custom enter into the picture?

Answer A simple example of this is slacks for women. Until relatively recently – within the past few decades – no woman would wear slacks of any kind. Under the circumstances, for a woman to wear slacks was forbidden by Jewish law, for slacks were considered to be male apparel. Yet even this was relative. In Yemen, for example, women would normally wear a type of trouser under their dresses, that being the style. Some of the Yemenite women who came to Israel wear this type of trouser to this day under their dresses. The question, though, which has arisen today is whether women may wear slacks in our times, for it is quite common for women to wear them today. Although few prominent Orthodox rabbis have been willing to commit themselves to permitting slacks, Rabbi Ovadyah Yosef, former Sephardic chief rabbi of Israel, has ruled – and this is only a relative ruling – that it is preferable in terms of Jewish law for a woman to wear pants than to wear a mini-skirt.

Question Are there any other restrictions on what women may wear?

Answer The Talmud frowns on women wearing red clothing, regarding red as provocative and attracting attention. In Jerusalem's Me'ah She'arim quarter, the home of the *haredi* (literally [God]-"fearing") community, where the most ultra-Orthodox live, signs are pasted up periodically stating that women may not wear red clothing. These signs also, on occasion, state that women may not wear high heels, because the noise of the heels can attract undue attention. We may mention, parenthetically, that there have even been signs in Me'ah She'arim calling for storekeepers to have separate shopping hours for men and for women, to prevent the sexes from mixing.

Question Many male Jews wear a little skullcap – the *yarmulke* – on their heads What is the origin of wearing the *yarmulke*?

Answer In reality, the *yarmulke* (or *kippah*, as it is known in Hebrew) as such has no significance. Its importance stems from what it symbolizes. Since Talmudic times, at least, it has been a Jewish custom for males to wear a head covering. During Talmudic times the head covering was worn during prayer, Torah study, when eating, and when reciting blessings. The pious would wear a head covering throughout the day. The head covering symbolizes man's submission to God, serving, as it does, to remind him that there is Someone above him. Since the Middle Ages, at least, the custom has been for men to wear a head covering throughout all waking hours. Orthodox Jews and many Conservative Jews still observe this custom.

Question The male members of the ultra-Orthodox community seem to wear clothing very different from that worn today. Why is this so?

Answer This community's members believe that Jewish law requires Jews to refrain from following the customs of the non-Jews. Thus, they reason that wearing the style adopted by everyone else is following a non-Jewish custom. Besides the obvious difference in the style between these clothes and contemporary fashions, there is also another, not quite as obvious difference: As we know, men's clothes are made with the buttons on the right and the buttonholes on the left. Women's are the other way around. With the members of the ultra-Orthodox community, in addition to the difference in fashion, one can also note that the buttons of the jacket are on the left, and the buttonholes on the right.

Question So how about those Jews that do not dress differently from everyone else? Are they violating Jewish law?

Answer Judaism, a religion with a history spanning over 3,000 years, is far from monolithic. While there is agreement among Orthodox rabbis about the basic fundamentals (e.g., the prohibition against driving a car on the Sabbath), there are many areas where there are legitimate differences of opinion. In this case, for example, the majority of great Orthodox scholars have ruled that the law against not following non-Jewish customs does not apply to clothing styles. They regard the prohibition as only applying to those non-Jewish practices which are of a religious or even a pagan origin, as, for example, displaying a Christmas tree.

Question Is there any significance in the men's different clothing styles seen in the ultra-Orthodox communities?

Answer Generally each hasidic group, under its own spiritual leader, has a specific set of clothes. Some, for example, wear pants that extend only below the knee and have black stockings which reach to the knee. Others may wear full-length trousers. As the groups see it, their clothing is like a type of "uniform," for they serve in "God's army," as it were. Those who are "in the know" can generally identify which hasidic group a man belongs to by his garb.

They tell the story of a member of the ultra-Orthodox world who flew in to a town in the deepest South to collect money for his yeshivah in Brooklyn. As he began walking down the street in his long black coat and wide-brimmed hat, a number of youngsters, who had obviously never seen a *hasid* before, began following him. Finally, exasperated, he turned around and asked them: "What's the matter? Haven't you ever seen a Yankee before?"

Question   Sometimes, one sees a hasidic Jew wearing a round fur hat. What is the derivation of this hat, and when is it worn?

Answer   The fur hat, known as a *shtreimel*, was originally worn by members of the Polish nobility. The hat was taken over by the hasidic Jews (not all hasidic sects, though, wear the *shtreimel*) after the Poles had stopped using it, and of course they are the only ones who wear them today. The different hasidic sects also have different shaped *shtreimels*. Again, those who are in the know are able to identify the individual's association by the shape of his *shtreimel*. The *shtreimel* is only used on festive days, such as on the Sabbath and on holidays, but is also worn, for example, by a groom at his wedding and in the first week after his marriage. During the intermediate days of festivals, the Jerusalem zoo is filled with visitors from the ultra-Orthodox sections of the town – many wearing *shtreimels*! In case you are curious, there are specialists who prepare these hats, the method of their manufacture being a family secret, handed down from generation to generation.

Question   Some of the ultra-Orthodox men in Jerusalem wear striped yellow robes. What is the significance of these clothes?

Answer   To answer this question, we have to go back in history to the 19th century. At the time, there were two groups of Jews living in Jerusalem: the Sephardic and the Ashkenazic. The Ashkenazic Jews wanted to build a magnificent synagogue, and borrowed a great deal of money from the local Arabs to do so. Unfortunately, there was a depression, and the Ashkenazic Jews defaulted on their loans. As a result, they were banished from Jerusalem. A few of the Ashkenazic Jews, who wished above all else to live in Jerusalem, then began wearing the clothes of the local Sephardic populace to mask their Ashkenazic background. And the Sephardic dress at the time was a yellow striped robe. In other words, the robe, which is only worn by a very few of the ultra-Orthodox Ashkenazic Jews today traces back to 19th century Sephardic dress!

Question   Are there any restrictions about the fabrics used?

Answer   In general, one may use any type of fabric for clothing. The Torah, though, does have one clear restriction, in that it forbids any garment to be made of a mixture of wool and linen (Lev. 19:19). Such a mixture is known as *sha'atnez*. This law is one for which the Torah offers no explanation whatsoever, and any attempt to explain it rationally is futile. In fact, the law of *sha'atnez* is generally considered as one of the classic examples of those laws known as *hukim* – statutes beyond man's capacity to understand.

Question   What is included in the prohibition of *sha'atnez*?

Answer   Any garment which contains both wool and linen, whether woven together or merely sewn together, is forbidden. There is no prohibition against wearing two garments at the same time if one is of wool and the other of linen.

Question   How can one tell if clothing is *sha'atnez*?

Answer   A listing of the composition of the fabric is not sufficient, because, for example, linen is often used as a stiffener in the collar of suits. In order to enable Jews not to violate this prohibition, a special laboratory (known, appropriately enough, as the "*Sha'atnez* Laboratory") was founded in Brooklyn, NY, where, by means of chemical tests, those parts of the garment which might be linen (primarily the lining) are analyzed. Where the garment is found not to contain linen, a seal of approval is sewn into the garment, generally near the label. If the garment does contain linen, the linen is removed and is replaced with a different fabric. Similar laboratories are now active in many cities where there is a large Jewish population, most of the people working in them having been trained in the *Sha'atnez* Laboratory or by people who trained in it.

Question   Is there any religious significance in the beard and long sideburns that many Orthodox men wear?

Answer   Well, yes and no. On the one hand, the Torah forbids one to shave one's beard. The prohibition, though, only applies if two conditions are met: the beard is cut close to the skin, and the shaving is done by a blade that actually touches the skin in the process. A safety razor, as can be seen, meets both conditions, and, as such, is forbidden by Jewish law. If only one condition is met, though, Jewish law does not forbid one to shave. For example, one may use a depilatory, because it only meets the conditions of a close shave, without meeting that of a blade touching the skin. A more practical suggestion, though, is the electric shaver. As the actual cutting edge does not touch the skin, the blade being behind a protective screen, Jewish law does not forbid its use. There are nevertheless those who prefer not to use an electric shaver, as they regard the wearing of a beard as one of the signs of the Jew for hundreds and hundreds of years.

As to the sideburns, generally known by their Hebrew name, *peyot*, these too trace back to Torah law. In Leviticus 19:27, we are told, "You shall not round the corners of your head." What this means is that one cannot take a haircut similar to a monk's tonsure, where all the hair is shaved off the face so as to leave a circle of hair on the head. Instead, the sideburns have to be left growing until the cheekbone. The hair does not have to be long: the law only requires that it be long enough that one can grip it between one's thumb and forefinger. Among *hasidim*, the custom has been not to cut these sideburns at all, and, in fact, to curl them.

Those who have seen religious Yemenite Jews may have noticed that they too wear curled sideburns, and many wonder what the origin is of their custom. After all, it would seem highly unlikely that they would have any contact with the Eastern European *hasidim*. Indeed, the two have nothing in common. One of the kings of Yemen, in order to force the Jews not to mingle with the Muslims, forced the Jews to grow their sideburns long. At first, the Jews resented tremendously and resisted this attempt to single them out. Eventually, though, the long sideburns became a badge of honor, and even when the Jews were given the opportunity to discard them, they elected to wear them as a sign of their Jewishness.

Chapter Fifteen
Dietary Laws

Question Jews are not permitted to eat a cheeseburger, even when both the meat and the cheese are kosher, because they are forbidden to eat meat together with milk. What is the reason for this prohibition?

Answer As our Sages tell us, there is no possible logical explanation; it is one of those laws known as *hukim* (pronounced *chookim*), which the human mind cannot understand. As has been said, "If a person could understand everything that God does, he would be God." It has been suggested that all the *hukim* have a single underlying purpose. The prohibitions against theft or murder are rational; a person who refrains from stealing or killing is not necessarily showing by his actions that he wishes to obey God. A person who does not violate the *hukim*, on the other hand, even though he does not understand why these actions are prohibited, is showing that he really wishes to obey God. In essence, the *hukim* may almost be considered as touchstones for Jewish religious practice.

Question Why are Jews forbidden to eat certain specific foods, such as shellfish?

Answer We must first point out that the Torah restrictions are not limited to fish, but extend to every species of living creature. In regard to mammals, for example, one may only eat the meat of an animal which chews it cud *and* has split hooves, such as cattle and deer. Thus pig is forbidden because, while it has a split hoof, it does not chew cud. In regard to seafood, the Torah offers the following definition: "These shall you eat of all that are in the waters: whatsoever has fins and scales in the waters... them shall you eat. And all that does not have fins and scales... they shall be an abomination unto you" (Lev. 11:9, 10). The Torah makes absolutely no attempt to give a rational explanation for these prohibitions, and we certainly cannot give an authoritative explanation is the Torah does not. At best we surmise about possible rationales, knowing full well that we cannot "second guess" God, as it were.

While we are about it, we should mention that the Torah specifically permits the eating of certain species of locusts – a high protein food if ever there was one. As most groups of Jews have not eaten locusts for countless generations, the identifying marks of the kosher species of locusts have been forgotten. As a result, most groups of Jews simply forbid the eating of all locusts. The exception to this rule is the Yemenite Jews, who from time immemorial have eaten locusts, and who have definite traditions about the identifying signs of the kosher species.

Question Is it not possible that the reason for the laws regarding forbidden animals is based on hygienic reasons? After all, improperly cooked pork can lead to trichinosis and there are numerous health hazards with shellfish.

Answer There have been numerous attempts to give the different prohibitions pertaining to food a health rationale. Even Maimonides gave such explanations, but he made it quite clear that his explanations were only *possibilities*. The trouble begins when a person decides unilaterally that a certain health reason is *the* rationale for a Torah law. This line of thinking was especially common among members of the Reform clergy at the turn of the century and even beyond. The general pattern adopted went something like this: a) The reason why the Torah forbids the eating of X is because of the following sanitary concern (e.g., trichinosis). b) In our times, given the fact that we have improved our system of storage, cooking, etc., that concern is no longer valid, and, for example, if pork is cooked properly, the trichinosis germs are destroyed. c) It therefore follows that the original prohibition no longer applies, and there is no reason why the food cannot be eaten in our days.

Unfortunately, this whole argument is based on specious logic, for the simple reason that Premise A, the "reason" why the Torah forbade the particular food, is never stated anywhere in the Torah. When the Torah forbids eating specific foods, it almost never gives a reason why. In fact it is quite laconic in its statements: "You shall not seethe a kid in its mother's milk" is an example, and that is the origin for the prohibition against mixing meat and milk.

What happened, unfortunately, was the creation of a paper tiger: "The Torah's reason for the prohibition is..." In the light of this, we can understand why many prominent rabbis have been violently averse to offering explanations for Torah commandments in those places where the Torah does not do so itself. In fact, those traditional rabbis that do offer explanations for various commandments always stress that their explanation is a *possible* one, and one certainly cannot construe any Jewish law from it. Even logically, this is true. After all, if each person may construe the meaning of each law as he sees fit, there are very few laws which cannot be so construed and rephrased, thus making a mockery of the entire basis for Jewish law.

Actually, the classical Jewish commentators agree that the laws concerning kosher and non-kosher food do not have any rational basis *that a human being can understand*. Their purpose, so we are told, is to show the Jew's obedience to God as God, even where the human intellect cannot comprehend why He decreed any specific law.

Question Why do you say that the Torah "almost never" gives a reason why certain foods are forbidden? Are there exceptions?

Answer There is one exception to this rule, and that is in regard to blood, which Jews are forbidden to consume. In regard to this, we are told, "You shall not consume blood, because blood is the life force" (Deut. 12:23). Thus, the consumption of blood might almost, as it were, be considered to be like eating an animal which is still alive.

So strong is this prohibition against blood, that one is required to remove the blood from meat before one is permitted to eat the meat. This can be done in one of two ways: a) by soaking the meat in water; then salting it with coarse salt, which draws off the blood; and finally washing off the blood-soaked salt; or b) by roasting the meat over an open flame, so that the blood can drain off into the fire. Incidentally, as liver is saturated in blood, it can only be made fit for consumption by the second method.

Question What restrictions are there about fowl?

Answer Unlike the case of animals and fish, where the Torah indicates general *rules* of what is permitted and what is forbidden, in the case of birds the Torah merely lists birds which may be eaten and those which may not be eaten. It has been surmised, from a study of the list, that the Torah forbids birds of prey as a whole, among others, to the Jew. Interestingly enough, one of the birds that is forbidden is the stork, in Hebrew the *hasidah*. The word means "the merciful creature," and our Sages tell us the bird received its name because "it is merciful to its fellows." That being the case, one should wonder why the stork is not considered to be a kosher species. One of the rabbis gave a beautiful homiletic explanation of what the problem is with the stork: it only cares about its own, but ignores the rest of the world. That is not true mercy.

We may note that Rabbi Isaiah ha-Levi Horowitz, known as Shelah (16th-17th century) feared that the turkey is not permitted. While not wishing to declare a blanket prohibition against the fowl, he did forbid his descendants to eat it, and to this day there are descendants of his who will not eat turkey.

Parenthetically, we may note that the modern Hebrew name for the bird (it was unknown in ancient times) is *tarnegol hodu*, which would translate as "Indian chicken," thus switching the locale from Turkey to India.

Question   Why do some people wait three hours after eating meat before drinking milk, while others wait six hours?

Answer   We have to differentiate here between the various levels of Jewish law. The highest level is that contained within the Torah itself; below it are those laws ordained by the rabbis; and finally, there are various customs which arose over the ages. If these customs remain in effect for a considerable period of time, they attain the force of law.

As to the case of meat and milk, Torah law, as deduced by the Sages from a triple repetition of a verse, forbids only three specific actions: 1. cooking meat with milk; 2. consuming meat together with milk; 3. deriving benefit of a mixture of meat and milk (e.g., by selling it). The rabbis extended the rules – which originally applied only to meat from cattle – to include fowl as well. Whereas by strict rabbinic law one would be permitted to have milk immediately after meat, the Talmud mentions customs of waiting a period of time – usually from one meal to the next – between the two (one rabbi would wait 24 hours between them!). As the amount of time one must wait is not a question of law but of custom (albeit a custom which by now has attained the force of law), there are different customs as to how long one must wait; i.e., as to what is considered the accepted time lapse between meals.

Question   With the prohibition involved of mixing meat and milk, how many sets of dishes must the Jew maintain?

Answer   First, one must have two entirely separate sets of dishes, silverware and pots, one for milk foods and one for meat foods. If a meat dish is used with milk products, or *vice-versa*, the dish can no longer be used. In some cases it can be kashered (purged) and then restored to service, while in others it must be disposed of. The details involved in such questions are quite technical, and specific questions in this regard are generally addressed to one's local rabbi.

In addition to these two sets of dishes, people often keep a few pots and other items for cooking and eating foods which are *pareve* ("neutral"), being neither meat nor dairy. This includes items such as fruit and vegetables, pasta, eggs and fish. While all of these items can be cooked in either a meat or dairy pot, people sometimes prefer to use a *pareve* pot.

And then there is Passover, when *all* the dishes, silverware and pots are changed, so add at least another two or three sets. And, of course, one may always have separate sets of dishes and silverware for weekday use and for festive occasions such as the Sabbath. All in all, space is generally at a premium in the kosher kitchen.

Question With all the modern humane methods available for slaughtering animals, why does Judaism insist on using a method thousands of years old?

Answer Strictly technically, as with all the laws dealing with kosher foods, the reason why Jews use the traditional method of slaughter, by slitting the animal's throat, is because that is what Jewish law, which it regards as of Divine origin, demands.

Furthermore – although strictly speaking this is irrelevant – ritual slaughter has been shown to be one of the most humane – if not the most humane – methods for slaughter. First, the knife used must be razor-sharp. The *shohet* – ritual slaughterer – must ensure that there is not the slightest nick in the blade, and he is required to test for this by running the sides of the blade down his nail. An incentive to ensure that there are no nicks is that any animal slaughtered with a knife containing the slightest nick renders the meat non-kosher. Even further, if the *shohet* does not carry out the act in one smooth operation, the slaughtering is considered to be invalid, and the meat is not kosher.

Thus the actual slaughtering itself is carried out by the *shohet* with a swift motion that must cut through the majority of both the wind and food pipes. Studies done in Cornell University, in fact, whereby electrodes were attached to the brains of animals before they were slaughtered, indicated that animals slaughtered in the traditional Jewish way lost consciousness instantaneously, thus feeling no pain whatsoever.

Question Are there any other provisions in slaughtering animals?

Answer Simply because an animal has been slaughtering ritually and all the provisions of the law governing the slaughter have been followed, does not make the animal's meat kosher. After the animal has been slaughtered, the *shohet* has to check that it was healthy. (In fact, the traditional name for the occupation is *shohet u-bodek* – "ritual slaughterer *and* checker.") Should the animal be found to be terminally diseased, its meat is not kosher, and cannot be eaten. For this law, the definition of "terminally diseased" is any physical defect which would lead to the animal's death within less than a year. While the Talmud lists a number of symptoms of terminal disease, most of these are sufficiently rare not to need checking. Thus, only one major area is checked, that being the lung. Should the animal be found to have a perforated lung, it is not kosher.

As the laws of slaughtering and checking animals are extremely complex, it has been Jewish practice for hundreds of years for those wishing to work as a *shohet* to be of impeccable character and to pass both theoretical tests in the Jewish law involved and practical tests in sharpening and checking the special knife, slaughtering properly, and checking the animal's lungs afterwards, whereupon they are granted a written license to practice as a *shohet*.

There is a story told of a man in the Old Country who had decided to become a *shohet*. As he began studying, he realized more and more the responsibility of the *shohet*, for one who slaughters improperly can cause tens of Jews to sin by eating non-kosher meat. Finally, he decided that he was unable to assume such a great responsibility, and he discontinued his studies. When he went back to his rabbi to tell him the news, the rabbi asked him: "Well, what will you be doing instead to earn your living?" The man told him that he had decided that he would be a *melamed* – a teacher of small children. "What gives you the idea," the rabbi asked him, "that teaching little children is a position of less responsibility than slaughtering a cow?"

Question   What is the so-called "kosher milk" that is sold in various cities? How does this vary from the regular milk one buys?

Answer   By its nature – short of chemical analysis – it is difficult to differentiate between pure cow's milk and milk adulterated with water or even milk of a different species of animal. As the rabbis were afraid that cow's milk might be adulterated by milk from a non-kosher species of animal, they forbade Jews to buy any milk unless the milking had been supervised by Jews. The so-called "kosher milk" is simply regular milk obtained through a special distribution network to ensure supervision against adulteration with non-kosher milk. Many religious Jews will drink only this milk. Rabbi Moses Feinstein, probably the greatest rabbinic authority of our generation, permitted the use of any milk in the United States on the grounds that the various state departments of health and agriculture test milk regularly, so that farmers are unable to adulterate their milk with a foreign substance. The same would thus apply in any country where there is similar government supervision of milk production.

Question   How about "kosher wine"? What makes wine kosher or not kosher?

Answer   As with the case of milk, wine as such should be kosher, for the ingredients are generally kosher. Drinking wine, though, has traditionally been associated with conviviality and the breaking down of barriers between people. The Sages felt that if Jews mingled too freely with non-Jews – and drinking together epitomizes the camaraderie between people – it might lead to intermarriage. In order to ensure that Jews would maintain a certain necessary reserve, the Sages simply forbade them to drink any wine that had been manufactured, bottled, or even handled by a non-Jew. This prohibition served as an effective barrier against Jews mingling too freely in non-Jewish society.

In passing, we can note that the tremendous growth in interest in wines in the United States has not passed the Jewish population by, and today it is quite common for kosher wine corporations to arrange to have wines produced according to Jewish law in such places as Spain, Italy and France.

Question What is considered as wine under this ordinance?

Answer Jewish law includes any beverage made of grapes in this prohibition, including, among others, wine, grape juice, champagne and brandy. In fact problems may even arise with grape soda, if the flavoring is real rather than artificial.

Question How can one tell if any given food is kosher?

Answer In earlier times the question seldom arose: foods were either clearly kosher or clearly non-kosher. Whatever one bought generally came in its natural state. With the advent of modern food production, where reading the ingredients of a processed food often requires at least a master's degree in chemistry, it has become a real problem to identify those foods which are kosher and those which are not. At first, those companies interested in adding the Jewish trade thus approached individual rabbis to offer supervision over their products. While there are still various individual endorsements of products, the trend in the last decades has been for organized bodies of rabbis to offer rabbinic supervision of various products. This frees the individual rabbi who supervises the plant from being beholden to the owner of the plant. While there are different organizations supplying such rabbinic supervision, each with its own copyrighted symbol of kashrut, the largest and oldest such organization is the Union of Orthodox Jewish Congregations of America (known as the Orthodox Union), which is the lay counterpart of the Rabbinical Council of America. The Orthodox Union, with its copyrighted symbol of a letter U surrounded by a circle (referred to colloquially as "OU"), is a universally accepted national body which offers endorsements on thousands of products, thus assuring the Jew in the smallest town of the United States a goodly number of kosher products. (In our travels, our family once passed through Fargo, North Dakota, where we found cans of kosher meatballs on the shelves – and they surely were not stocked for the Jews of the area!)

Question   What significance is there to the letter K on some products?

Answer   Some companies use the letter K on their products to indicate that their product is kosher. As one cannot copyright a letter of the alphabet, any company – whether under rabbinic supervision or not – can print a label with the letter K on it. Thus the letter as such is of limited informational value.

Question   As US law requires the labelling of ingredients, can one not just examine the list of ingredients to find out if a product is kosher or not?

Answer   Logically, this would seem like a sound suggestion. The problem, though, is that the US law allows for what one might call "loopholes" – at least as far as Jewish law is concerned. For example, ingredients that are less than 2% of the product often do not need to be listed. Again, US law has an "emergency" provision, where, under certain circumstances, substitutions may be allowed for a very limited time, without the company needing to change its label. For example, if the product's label states that it contains vegetable shortening and this is temporarily unavailable, US law would permit a temporary substitution of animal shortening. Thus, the list of ingredients, as such, cannot be used to ascertain whether a product is kosher. Of course, if the product is under rabbinic supervision as indicated by the label, there cannot be any substitution of non-kosher ingredients for the kosher ingredients.

Chapter Sixteen

Medical Questions

As we have so often reiterated in this volume, Jewish law is timeless and has answers for all of life's dilemmas. Probably in no other area has this been as apparent in recent years as in that of medicine. As technology advances, it presents new questions and new problems: When does life begin and when does it end? These and other topics are discussed in this chapter. We must point out that many of the questions discussed below are the source of a great deal of rabbinic debate, and very few of them have unequivocal answers. What the chapter has attempted to do in the circumstances is to give an indication of what might be called the "mainstream" opinions on the topics. In the final analysis, though, one should consult with a competent rabbinic authority before determining any specific course of action.

Question   According to Jewish law, when is a fetus considered to be alive?

Answer   Forty days after conception is the time when a fetus is considered to be alive. This, of course, has implications for questions relating to abortion, etc., as will be seen below.

Question   What does Jewish law have to say about birth control?

Answer   Generally, Judaism is opposed to birth control, for the very first commandment in the Torah is to "be fruitful and multiply." However, there are nevertheless exceptions. The Talmud, for example, stipulates three conditions under which a woman may insert some type of tampon before intercourse in order to prevent pregnancy. The conditions are: where the wife is under age (i.e., under the age of 12); where she is pregnant; or where is nursing. In the first case, pregnancy is seen as a possible danger to the mother, in the second to the fetus (although there is still debate to this day whether a woman can become pregnant a second time during a pregnancy), and in the third to the infant, in that the mother's milk might dry up.

In general, then, birth control is not viewed as a blanket *carte blanche*, but as a procedure permitted (and, according to some views, required) where pregnancy may result in danger to the mother. Examples of danger to the mother are discussed in the questions regarding abortion (see below), and – understandably – the rules governing when birth control methods may be used are more lenient than those governing the termination of pregnancy. Each case, though, has to be examined on its own merits.

Question What rules govern the use of birth control where the circumstances warrant it?

Answer According to Jewish law, the commandment to "be fruitful and multiply" applies (which may be surprising to many) to males and not to females. Women are not obligated to become parents. For a male to fulfill this commandment, he has to father at least one boy and one girl. Thus, as a general rule, should there be need for birth control it should be the female who takes the necessary measures. After all, if a man takes any preventive measures, he is deliberately thwarting a commandment of the Torah, while this does not apply to women. We should also point out that many rabbinic authorities are more lenient in permitting the use of birth control after the male has fulfilled the commandment to be "fruitful and multiply," i.e., where he already has a son and daughter.

Question What logic is there in having only the male commanded to "be fruitful and multiply"?

Answer Whenever one attempts to offer reasons for a law where the Torah does not offer any of its own, one treads on dangerous ground. At the risk of sounding sexist, though, the author would like to offer a possible explanation. Traditionally, it has been the women who have provided the stability of the home, while men have often been the ones to "sow their wild oats." Women are thus far more desirous of children, with or without any specific commandment. Thus, when the Torah commanded men to father children, it in effect forced them to settle down and make a home for themselves, rather than acting "fancy free."

Question How about sterilization? Is it permitted under any circumstances?

Answer Here, too, one must differentiate between men and women. Under no circumstances does Judaism permit the sterilization of the male, for such an act is a deliberate thwarting of the man's obligation of procreation. As to whether the prohibition applies to women as well, the answer is by no means clearcut. Some authorities hold that the sterilization of women is also forbidden by Biblical law, while others regard it as forbidden only by rabbinical law. Where pregnancy can pose a danger to a woman's health, sterilization may be permitted.

Question   What is the Jewish law regarding abortion?

Answer   As a general rule, Judaism is strongly opposed to abortions, regardless of how much or little time has passed since conception. Under certain circumstances, which we will describe below, abortion may be sanctioned by Jewish law, in which case it is preferable to have the abortion take place within 40 days of conception. There are instances, however, when abortion may be permitted within the first trimester and even to the end of the second trimester.

Question   What are the criteria for permitting abortion?

Answer   Jewish law regards the life of the mother as supreme, if for no other reason than that she is definitely alive while the fetus may or may not live. Where giving birth to a child can pose a life-threatening health hazard to the mother, the Jewish authorities concur that the fetus is to be sacrificed for the sake of the mother. The rationale advanced by Maimonides (1135-1204) for this ruling is one that has been accepted by most rabbinic authorities since that time. According to Maimonides, when a fetus poses danger to the mother, it must be considered to have the status of a "pursuer," and according to the Torah, should no other way be available to stop the pursuer, one is permitted to save a person by killing his pursuer.

While there is universal agreement about a life-threatening pregnancy, other, less threatening situations have been the cause for much rabbinic debate. Some rabbis have taken a more stringent view, and have not permitted abortion in any but a clearly life-threatening situation, while others have adopted a more lenient view as to what is considered to be danger to the mother. An example of a rabbi who has advocated the lenient view is Rabbi Eliezer Waldenberg, a leading contemporary Israeli rabbinic authority, who is even willing to take into account such factors as the extreme emotional distress of the woman.

Question   Under what circumstances may abortions be performed beyond 40 days after conception?

Answer   According to Rabbi Waldenberg, should there be a substantial risk that the fetus will be born with a deformity which will result in a life of suffering, one may have an abortion until the end of the first trimester. Further, if amniocentesis has shown that a child will definitely be born with Tay-Sachs disease, a disease which inevitably leads to a child's death within the first few years of life after a long and painful process of degeneration, Rabbi Waldenberg permits abortion until the end of the second trimester.

Question How about difficulties in the birth process that may pose danger to the mother's life?

Answer Up to the time that an infant is born, the mother's life takes precedence. The question that then arises is when birth is considered to have taken place. According to Jewish law, once the infant's head and a majority of its body have passed out the birth canal, it is considered to have been born. Thus, until that time the mother's life takes precedence over that of the infant, and the infant's life may even be sacrificed to save the mother. Beyond that point, both are considered to be of equal standing, and neither may be sacrificed for the sake of the other.

Question What is Tay-Sachs disease?

Answer Tay-Sachs is a particularly agonizing form of disease. It is a hereditary condition, and is always fatal. While the newborn child appears to be developing normally for the first six months, a regression begins at that time, as the nervous system ceases to develop. The child deteriorates rapidly, and dies at the age of three or four. It has been shown that Ashkenazic Jews in particular have a high incidence of Tay-Sachs disease. Where both the father and mother are carriers of the disease, each pregnancy has a one in four chance of resulting in a child with Tay-Sachs.

In order to avoid the problem of Tay-Sachs, many American Jewish communities have adopted a screening process, whereby young adults are tested to see whether they are carriers or not. A computerized list is kept of the results, and should a young man and young woman wish to marry, the screening can point out whether or not they are both carriers. Statistically, it is believed that one out of every 30 Ashkenazic Jews is a Tay-Sachs carrier (among non-Jews the figure is 1 in 300), so that the chances among Ashkenazic Jews of both parents being carriers are thus 1 in 900.

Question Is there a Jewish position about smoking?

Answer As Judaism strongly forbids any human being from intentionally harming himself, it certainly has much to say about smoking. Its views have generally reflected those of the medical community. Thus, when no one was aware of the possible harmful effects of smoking on the individual, the only discussion in the rabbinic literature on the subject concerned the question of whether one is permitted to smoke on the different festivals (except Yom Kippur, where one is not permitted to light a fire). The question revolves about an interesting analogous situation quoted in the Talmud. Thus the Talmud mentions it was a common practice to light incense in order to perfume one's clothes. The question that then arises in the Talmud is whether one may carry out such an action on festivals, and the Talmud specifies that such an action is permitted on festivals only if the majority of people customarily act in this way. Thus the early questions on smoking on festivals often revolved about the percentage of people that smoke, for if only a minority of people smoke, one might be forbidden to do so on the festivals.

Recently, as evidence has mounted about the danger involved in smoking, there has been a marked change in the way it is regarded. Evidence of this change can probably be seen best in the different yeshivah study halls, where the yeshivah students spend most of their day. Up to as little as a decade or two ago, the smoke in the study halls was so thick that a respirator would have come in handy. At the time, even many of the great rabbis were addicted, and it was hard to find anyone to forbid the practice. Today, though, most of the yeshivot have forbidden smoking in the study halls, and those who wish to smoke must leave the hall to do so. In fact there are rabbis today who have ruled that one is forbidden to smoke at all, for a person who smokes is like one who attempts suicide!

In passing, we should note that, while the percentage of people smoking has declined steadily (in the United States it is now down to about 1/3 of the population), one place where the percentage seems to have increased is among the *hasidim*. There are those who say the reason for this is a simple one: among the *hasidim*, one's life is completely mapped out: what to wear, what to eat, where to go, and so on. Such amusements as movies or television are forbidden. Smoking is thus one of the few avenues where the young *hasid* can express himself. At the same time, though, we should note that among *hasidim*, women are strictly forbidden to smoke, smoking being considered an exclusively male pursuit. Incidentally, according to some recent ultra-Orthodox rulings, women are also not permitted to drive a car, this too being an exclusively male preserve. (Of course, if we all refrained from smoking and driving, that would certainly increase the longevity in the world, so these women have a good thing going!)

Question How about alcohol?

Answer Much of Jewish ceremonial includes the use of wine: the *Kiddush* on the Sabbath and festivals, weddings, circumcisions, the redemption of the firstborn, etc. In fact, the Jewish male gets his first sip of wine at his circumcision, when he is all of eight days old! Thus, Judaism is certainly not opposed to drinking. While the Torah makes provision for a Nazirite – a person who refrains from consuming anything derived from the grape and from cutting his hair – the same Nazirite must bring a sin offering at the end of the period of his Nazirite vow. According to some rabbis, a Nazirite has sinned in that he refrained from enjoying the fullness of the world given to man by God.

On the other hand, Judaism is strongly opposed to excessive drinking. Thus, even though one is supposed to drink more on Purim, all leading authorities agree that one should not drink to the extent where he is unable to recite the prayers and blessings with the proper concentration. Along these lines, Nahmanides (1194-1270) explains the verse, "You shall be holy" (Lev. 19:2), to mean that one must remain within the spirit of the law and not only within the letter. And one of the examples he gives to illustrate his point is that even though the Torah permitted one to drink, one may not drink to excess and become drunk!

Question How about drugs?

Answer There is universal condemnation among all rabbinic authorities of the use of "mind-enhancing" drugs. First, all drugs – without exception – have been shown to have potential harmful effects on the body, if not necessarily directly, then in the chromosomes of the reproductive system. Thus, using drugs violates the prohibition against harming one's own body – the body which is only on loan from God. Second, as with alcohol, the use of drugs inhibits one's performance of the various commandments and prayers, and as such alone would be forbidden.

Question What is the Jewish attitude toward medicine?

Answer The use of any measures to alleviate disease is not something taken for granted by the Talmud. After all, a case can be made (as the Christian Scientists argue) that disease is something caused by God, and man may have no right to intervene in attempting to "bypass," as it were, God's designs. To counter this view, the Talmud quotes a verse in the Torah regarding a person who harmed another, where the law is that "he shall cause him to be healed" (Ex. 21:19). From this, the Talmud deduces that one has the right to practice medicine and to seek medical advice.

Regarding this deduction, the story is told of a noted rabbi who was gravelly ill. A doctor was called in and told the rabbi that he had very little time to live. Confounding the experts, the rabbi recovered, and one day he bumped into the doctor. The doctor, amazed at the rabbi's recovery, couldn't understand where he had gone wrong in his diagnosis. "The problem, doctor," the rabbi explained to him, "is that you weren't doing your duty, and that is why your diagnosis failed. The Torah teaches us, based on the verse 'he shall cause him to be healed,' that a person has the right to practice medicine in order to heal others. Nowhere in that verse is there any indication that a doctor has the right to despair and to pronounce that a person is about to die!"

The institution of the rabbinate as a full-time position is only a relatively recent one in Jewish life. Prior thereto, rabbis would earn their living in different occupations, and, indeed, many of the greatest rabbis, including Maimonides, Nahmanides and Ibn Ezra earned their livelihood as doctors. Maimonides, in fact, was the court physician in Egypt.

A story is told about the beginning of the *Haskalah* ("enlightenment") era of the 1800s, when various Jews in Eastern Europe turned to European culture as the panacea to the Jewish problem. Often, the adoption of European culture meant the discarding of all that was sacred in Judaism. The battle between the members of the *Haskalah*, known as the *maskilim*, and the rabbinate was thus a fiery one, a real battle of different cultures. There is a story told of a *maskil* who once complained to the local rabbi: "The trouble, Rabbi, is that the rabbis today only know the Talmud and nothing else. Why don't we have rabbis today such as Maimonides and Nahmanides, who were great Talmudic scholars yet were foremost doctors of medicine?" "You are absolutely right," the rabbi replied. "The problem is that the generations today are not as the previous generations. After all, why don't we have great doctors of medicine, such as Maimonides and Nahmanides, who were at the same time great Torah scholars?"

It is obviously a question of perspective ...

Question   Are all medical procedures permitted?

Answer   The question is obviously a broad one, and cannot be answered with a simple yes or no. In general, though, those medical procedures needed to heal a person are normally permitted. Where the procedure is not necessarily medically indicated, as, for example, cosmetic plastic surgery, matters are not that simple. Nor are experimental medical procedures permitted except under very carefully delineated guidelines.

Question   What is the problem with cosmetic plastic surgery?

Answer   One of the prohibitions of the Torah is against inflicting injury on oneself. Thus, for example, a person is forbidden to cut himself "just for the fun of it." Where there are medical grounds for such an action, as, for example, where a person needs to undergo surgery, the prohibition does not apply. Obviously, where a person wishes to undergo cosmetic plastic surgery just in order to look more pretty, it hardly qualifies as a sufficient reason to void the prohibition of needless injury. Of course, where cosmetic plastic surgery is needed for a person to be able to lead a more normal life or to alleviate a major psychological disturbance, there is reason to permit such surgery.

Question How about experimental medical procedures? What is the Jewish attitude toward such?

Answer After carefully examining the literature on the subject, Chief Rabbi Lord Immanuel Jakobovits of Great Britain, in his magnificent work, *Jewish Medical Ethics*, arrives at the following "tentative conclusions" about the subject:

a) One may only use an experimental procedure if there is some chance – even if it is remote – that the person will benefit from the procedure.

b) If a person is terminally ill, one may use any type of procedure, tried or untried, if there is no tested procedure available to save that person.

Question How about experiments on animals?

Answer Millennia before animal suffering became an issue, the Talmud wrote of the prohibition against causing *tza'ar ba'alei hayyim* – pain to living creatures. In the Torah, for example, we find a prohibition against muzzling an ox which is working on the threshing floor, for it is torture for the animal to see the grain all about it without being able to eat any. The Torah prohibition against having animals of two species hitched up together has also been explained as being forbidden because of the added burden placed on the weaker species in trying to keep up with the stronger species. Yet Judaism does not forbid animal experimentation, provided that it is meant to aid human life. Thus, as one rabbi explains it, as much as Judaism is against causing pain to animals, saving human pain must be considered to be of greater importance. What all rabbinic authorities stress, though, is that in every experiment involving animals, every attempt must be made to limit the pain as much as possible.

Question How about transplants?

Answer When Israel's first heart transplant was performed, a leading rabbi proclaimed that the doctor who had performed the operation had been guilty of "double murder" – of the person whose heart had been removed, and of the one into whose body the heart had been transplanted. At that time, when such transplants were experimental and almost never succeeded, the rabbi may have had a point, in spite of his hyperbole. Today, though, where such operations are almost commonplace and there is a reasonable chance that they will be successful, most rabbinic authorities approve of them where the transplant is made from a cadaver. That, though, still leaves two other questions which require to be answered: at what point is a person considered to be dead, for only then may organs be removed; and what are the rules about an organ transplant from a living donor, such as the transplant of a kidney?

Question What is the Jewish definition of death?

Answer The Talmud has a classic discussion about this question, but in a somewhat different context. Jewish law forbids a person from digging up rubble on the Sabbath, as such an action is considered to be work. The Talmud presents the following scenario: Let us say that a building collapsed while a person was inside it. May one dig up the rubble to extract the person? The answer is a simple one: If there is even the smallest chance that the person may be alive, every possible effort must be made to try and dig the person out. If it is definitely proven that the person died, no further efforts may be made during the Sabbath to extract the body. Now comes the following question: Let us say that the rescuers dig up the rubble and uncover the person's head. How can they ascertain if the person is alive or dead? The Talmud answers that a mirror is to be held up to the person's nose and if it fogs up the person is alive, whereas if it does not, he is dead. This leads us to a simple definition of life: If a person is breathing, he is alive.

Since that time, as we know, it has been shown that – under certain circumstances – it is possible to revive a person, even after he may have stopped breathing. For example, if a person has suffered cardiac arrest, a fibrillator may be able to restart the heart beat. Given the fact that a definition of death in one era may be superseded by medical technology in a later era, Rabbi Chaim Zimmerman, one of the leading rabbis of our time, has come up with an eminently logical operative definition of death according to Jewish law. According to him, death is a condition which, given the level of medical science of one's time, is one in which the person cannot possibly be revived. Thus, our definition of death may not be the same as that fifty years in the future, and is certainly different from the one in effect fifty years ago.

Question May a live person offer an organ to be donated to another person?

Answer The basic question involved here is the degree of risk to which the loss of the organ will expose the donor. Rabbi Waldenberg rules that where the loss of the organ exposes the donor to life-threatening danger, even if by his action he may save another's life, the action is forbidden. In case of doubt, a group of expert physicians must determine that there is no danger to the donor, before the transplant is attempted.

Question What is the Jewish attitude toward euthanasia?

Answer Judaism is unequivocally opposed to euthanasia, no matter what the circumstances. By Jewish law, in fact, a person who hastens the death of another person by as little as a second is considered to have killed the person. As Rabbi Jakobovits explains it, human life is of infinite worth. As such, each second is also of infinite worth, so that hastening another's death is considered to be murder. As Dr. Abraham S. Abraham puts it so well in his *Medical Halachah for Everyone*:

> This definition is not only a mathematical and logical one, but is based on deep moral ethical judgments. Once one destroys this value definition of human life at the nearness of death, one destroys the absolute value of all life and gives it instead a relative value only – relative to age, health, further use to the community and any other factor one wishes to consider. The moment one is willing to shorten, by however much, the life of a dying patient because it is of no further value, one destroys
> the infinite value of all human life.

On the other hand, Jewish law does recognize certain actions that may be taken which may hasten a suffering person's death. For example, the Talmud notes that Rabbi Judah the Patriarch (editor of the Mishnah) was suffering greatly. One of his servants prayed to God that he die swiftly, and the Sages regard such a prayer as being acceptable. Rabbi Moses Isserles (16th century) ruled that where the chopping of wood outside a dying man's room keeps him from slipping off into death, one is permitted to ask the person to cease chopping wood. This, of course, is a passive, rather than active, action.

Question How about suicide?

Answer As mentioned earlier, man's body is considered to be on loan from God. No person, therefore, has the right to do what he wants with his body, and the decision as to when a person is to die is entirely in God's domain. Should a person commit suicide, it is considered to be an act of self-murder. It is thus understandable that Jewish law decrees that there is no mourning for a suicide and that suicides not be buried alongside everyone else in the local cemetery. Where there is reason to assume that a person committed suicide

while of unsound mind, the rabbis will generally treat the case as a normal
death rather than as a suicide.

Question What is the Jewish law regarding autopsies?

Answer Judaism views the human body as the sanctified receptacle of the
soul. Even after the soul has departed, the body must be treated with
reverence. Generally speaking, then, autopsies are forbidden. There are
exceptions, though. If a medical practitioner can use the results of an autopsy
for the immediate benefit of another person, an autopsy may be permitted.
Thus, for example, organs may only be taken to be transplanted if there are
specific people waiting for those particular organs. Corneas can be donated
for immediate transplanting, but not for storage in an eye bank. By the same
token, an autopsy may be performed if an epidemic is raging and there is need
to determine what is causing the epidemic. Finally, if foul play is suspected,
an autopsy may be allowed in order to aid the police in their investigation.

Question May every Jew become a doctor?

Answer In theory, yes, but in practice there are tremendous problems
where a man is a *kohen* – of priestly descent. By Jewish law, a *kohen* may not
generally come into contact with the dead. This presents a problem – most
rabbis would say an insurmountable one – for any *kohen* who wishes to study
medicine, because the study of medicine includes pathology and working with
cadavers. The same problem, incidentally, may be involved for a *kohen* who
wishes to study dentistry.

Chapter Seventeen

Business and Social Legislation

Judaism has a great deal to say on interpersonal business dealings. In fact, one of the four sections of the *Shulkhan Arukh*, the standard code of Jewish law, is devoted entirely to the topic. In it, or by extension from its laws, one can find answers to modern-day questions, such as the right to strike, monopolistic practices, and the rights and duties of both employers and employees. This chapter will also relate to various questions of social legislation. It will discuss these topics, but will also delve into other areas – not all of which are germane to this day – which will add to the general picture.

Question   What is the Jewish attitude toward an individual striking?

Answer   Interestingly enough, this question is discussed as early as the Mishnah (200 C.E.). There the principle is laid down that a worker has the right to leave his job at any time of the day. This is based on the verse, "They are My servants" (Lev. 25:42), which, our Sages tell us, means that "they are My servants, but not the servants of [My] servants." Thus, no person can be forced to work against his will (with one exception, as will see below). On the other hand, should the workers by their precipitate action cause the employer a loss, as, for example, if he is required to hire other workers at a higher rate to complete the work, the workers who had left their work must indemnify their employer for his losses. In capsule form, this examples summarizes Jewish business law – a finely honed concern for the welfare and justice of all sides to an issue.

Question   Do workers have the right to organize in unions in order to protect their interests?

Answer   Jewish law certainly permits workers to band together for their welfare, but here, too, the different interests of the parties must be weighed. The first chief rabbi of Palestine, Rabbi Abraham Isaac Kook (1865-1935), for example, was asked whether a union may go out on strike. He ruled that the strike is permissible *provided* that the union has first attempted to bring its employer to a court for adjudication of its claims. Only if the employer refuses to come before such a court or to accept its ruling may the workers go out on strike against their employer.

Question   How about teachers going on strike?

Answer   While teachers should be permitted to strike, there have been various rulings by rabbis that those who teach Torah to children may not generally go on strike, for they are depriving their students of Torah study – and Torah study is considered to be the most fundamental and important of all the commandments. Thus Torah teachers may be considered to be offering an "essential service" *par excellence*. Only in the most extraordinary circumstances may Torah teachers go on strike, as, for example, if they have not been paid for months.

In Israel a few years ago, when there was a major teachers' strike that paralyzed all of Israeli education for a few months, the Torah teachers of our children's school continued to hold classes in various synagogues, so that the students would not lose out on their Torah study. In solidarity with the overall strike, though, they refused to accept pay for these sessions.

Question   When, under Jewish law, can a person be forced to work against his will?

Answer   While this law has not applied for millennia, according to Torah law a Jew may be sold into slavery against his will, but *only* if he has stolen an object and does not have the wherewithal to make repayment. A person may have borrowed money from everyone under the sun, may have squandered every cent he ever earned and reneged on his debts, but that does not allow the court to sell him into slavery. Only a thief may be sold. And even here there are restrictions on the court's actions. For example, even though a thief who is caught must by law repay the double the value of what he took as a punishment, a person can only be sold to raise the money to repay the value of the object itself, but *not* in order to repay the penalty involved. For example, if a person stole an object whose value is X dollars and does not have the money to repay it, and if his value as a slave is that same X dollars per year of work, he is sold for one year as a slave, and not for two years. Furthermore, as part of the restrictions entailed in "They are My servants and not servants of servants," no person can be sold against his will for more than six years – and even if the amount he should theoretically repay may be equivalent to 20 years or even more of his labor.

Question What does it mean when we say that a person is a slave?

Answer Probably in no other place can we see so vividly how the Torah has built in checks and balances for the well-being of all sides. On the one hand, as a slave, the person is required to perform whatever work his master imposes upon him; he cannot refuse, for example, to do gardening or whatever else is needed. Nor can he, of course, quit in the middle. On the other hand, it is just because the master has such control over the slave that Jewish law imposes restrictions on what he may assign him. For example, a master may not assign a slave to particularly loathsome work, as, for example, making him clean out latrines. Nor may he assign him "make-work," such as carting rocks from one side of a field to another and then back again. Nor is he permitted to tell the slave, "Work at this job until I tell you to stop." Judaism feels that such an open-ended assignment is unfair to the slave. Instead, the owner must specify that the work is to be done either for X hours, or until a certain amount, for example, has been accomplished. Similarly, a master may not impose work on a slave that is clearly not suited to him, as, for example, asking a male slave to do women's work. Interestingly enough, while a master is forbidden to impose such work on his slave, he is fully at liberty to hire a free man to perform any of these jobs; the point is that where a person voluntarily accepts a job for which he will be paid, it does not matter what the work is, for it is his choice. Only where the worker has no choice does Jewish law step in and limit the assignments given to him.

Question That hardly fits in with the classic view of slavery. What, indeed, is the Jewish attitude toward slavery in general?

Answer According to Maimonides, slavery was a necessary evil tolerated by the Torah because it was the prevalent norm throughout all of the known world at the time. On the other hand, Jewish law so circumscribed it as to make it an entirely different concept from that in the rest of the world. As a simple example, a Roman master had the full right to do whatever he wanted with his slave – just as he would have with his dog. He could harm the slave, maim him, or even kill him if he so desired. If a Jewish master, on the other hand, killed his slave, he would be charged with murder, and if he so much as maimed or otherwise injured him, the slave had the right to sue his master in court and collect damages.

Perhaps the best example of the master/slave relationship in Jewish law is the Talmudic discussion of what happens when the master, for example, has only one pillow. The Talmud starts off by saying that under no circumstances may the master keep the pillow only for himself, for we are told in regard to the slave, "It is well for him with you" (Deut. 15:16), implying that the slave cannot be treated any worse than his master. Thus, the master may not have a pillow if the slave does not have one. Should the master decide that, that being the case, he will simply forgo a pillow and leave the pillow in storage, that is considered by the Sages to be "the attribute of Sodom," for why should a perfectly good pillow go to waste because of the master's meanness? Instead, the law is that if there is only one of any item, the slave gets it and not the owner. Thus it is not surprising that our Sages summed the relationship to the slave up by telling us that "One who buys himself a slave has [in reality] bought himself a master."

Question Going back to contemporary questions, is there a Jewish view about tenure?

Answer According to Rabbi Moses Feinstein, one of the greatest rabbinic authorities of our time, who died a few years ago, Jewish law does not believe in tenure provisions, but for an interesting reason. Simply put, according to Rabbi Feinstein, no person can be discharged if he is performing his work adequately and there is still need for that type of work. Thus, if a school's population dwindles, according to this view, a teacher can be dismissed regardless, whereas he cannot be dismissed just because of some vague dislike or disgruntlement as to his performance. By the same token, according to Rabbi Feinstein, if a person's performance is such that he cannot carry out the function for which he was hired (e.g., a teacher who cannot maintain class discipline), even if the person theoretically has tenure, his employer would have the right to dismiss him.

Question What is the Jewish attitude toward monopolies?

Answer On the one hand, Jewish law gives the members of a particular trade the right to enact regulations that will govern all the members of that trade. Thus, for example, a specific trade group would have the right to decide that none of its members are to work on one particular afternoon each week. On the other hand, the rabbis have always attempted to ensure that this right to band together will not be exploited to the detriment of the public. Thus, for example, as we saw previously in the chapter on the Sukkot festival, when fish merchants abused this privilege and raised the price of their fish without reason, the local rabbi simply forbade all Jews to buy fish until the prices were brought down to a fair level. There is even a case in the Talmud of a certain family, the House of Garmu, that specialized in baking the special thin *matzah*-type bread used in the Temple. As no one else was able to duplicate the process, the family had a monopoly on this production. In an effort to break this monopoly, we are told that the Sages had foreign craftsmen brought in. Unfortunately, the efforts was wasted: the other craftsmen were unable to duplicate the work of the House of Garmu. What is interesting about this case, though, is the active involvement of the Sages to prevent a monopoly from using its position to its advantage and to the detriment of the public.

Question May an artisan or craftsman prevent others from engaging in the same occupation in his city, on the grounds that the others are trespassing, as it were, on his livelihood?

Answer This question is already discussed in the Talmud, and the conclusion of the Talmud is that any person has the right to open his own business where he wishes, even if it encroaches on another's business. In the Middle Ages, though, where many Jews were forced to make their livings by buying concessions for particular occupations from the local authorities, there was the danger that when various people vied for the same concession, the price might become so steep that one could no longer earn a decent living. As a result, various country-wide decrees were issued, especially in Poland, to allow for concessions to be uncontested.

Interestingly enough, even when rabbis were willing to permit individuals in various occupations to prevent others from entering the same fields, the rabbis generally made two exceptions: Everyone has the right to open a school for Torah studies or a synagogue, for the proliferation of such institutions is deemed to be in the public interest.

We may point out that in Jerusalem today there is a rule that no new pharmacy may be opened within a radius of 500 meters (about 550 yards) from any existing pharmacy. The only exception to this rule is in the city center itself, where a "grandfather clause" entitles anyone who already had a pharmacy before this rule was enacted to continue to operate it. Of course, no new pharmacies may open in the city center, because of the "500 meter" rule. Recently, though, there was need for a decision that a Talmudic mind would be happy to grapple with. One of the pharmacies in the center of the city decided to open a branch a few blocks away – also in the center of the city. The other pharmacies all cried "500 meter rule," while the one which wished to open a branch claimed that the branch was just an extension of itself. The final verdict agreed that the pharmacy had the right to open a branch, and now there are two pharmacies with the same name in the city center.

Question Is a Jew permitted to take interest?

Answer The Torah states quite clearly, "Of a foreigner you may exact gain: but that which is yours with your brother your hand shall release" (Deut.

15:3). In other words, Jews may take interest from non-Jews, but not from one another.

Question Is that not downright discrimination?

Answer Although at first blush it may indeed seem so, closer examination shows that the Torah's law is entirely logical and fair. Let us begin with a basic premise: Any law which applies to business must be reciprocal to be fair. Now let us examine the different types of loans that may be arranged:
1. A Jew lending to a fellow-Jew
2. A Jew lending to a Gentile
3. A Gentile lending to a Jew
4. A Gentile lending to a Gentile.

Obviously, the Torah can only control the first two cases – where a Jew is doing the lending. It certainly cannot force a Gentile to lend without interest. Now, if the Torah forced the Jew lending to a Gentile not to take interest, an anomalous situation would arise: Jews lending to Gentiles would be forbidden to take interest, while Gentiles lending to Jews could charge interest. That is obviously unjust. Thus the Torah in essence permitted Jews to collect interest on loans from Gentiles to keep the parity in business dealings. On the other hand, in cases of loans between Jews, where the Torah legislation applies to both sides of the transaction, the Torah forbade one Jew from taking interest from another. And of course, in the case of loans between Gentiles, the Torah permits the taking of interest.

Question Is that the reason why Jews in the Middle Ages were known for being engaged in lending money at interest?

Answer Actually, historically the Jews often became involved in money-lending because the Christian leaders wanted it. The Catholic Church had adopted as part of its canon the prohibition against lending money at interest. Here the situation was reversed, for the Church ruled that the law only applied to loans between Christians, but Jews were permitted to collect interest. As the need for financing became more acute with the development of trade, Jews were sometimes brought into an area in order to ensure that loans could be available to those who needed them for their businesses. For example, Jews were brought into Pisa, Italy, in 1399 just for this purpose, and were permitted to charge no more than 2 1/2% interest per month. Other times, Jews were brought in to counteract the high rates of (by canon law unlawful) interest charged by non-Jews. Thus, in 1420 the city of Florence imported a number of Jews in order to reduce the rate of interest being charged in the city.

Question   If Jews cannot charge one another interest, how does Israel have banks? Are they all violating Jewish law?

Answer   There is one possible way that a Jew may legally receive interest on his money: if he invests it in the business of another, *provided* that the terms of the loan are so constructed as to make him liable to lose money should the business venture fail. In other words, interest is only forbidden where the lender is guaranteed a certain return regardless of whether the person borrowing the money gains or loses money while utilizing the loan. If the lender has the theoretical possibility of not only earning interest but also losing money should the venture fail, he is considered to be a partner in the business venture, with the risks entailed in such. And that is permitted. For a loan to be permitted to pay interest, then, a loan contract, known as a *heter iska* – "permission for a business venture" – must be drawn up, with the above specifications. Every bank in Israel has such a *heter iska* drawn up by the rabbinate, thus enabling it to both lend and borrow funds as required.

Question   What is the Jewish attitude toward physical labor?

Answer   To us, accustomed as we are the majority of Jews being in either the professions or business, it may come as a surprise to know that the Sages were particularly lavish in their praise of physical labor. For example, on the verse, "You shall eat the labor of your hands: happy shall you be, and it shall be well with you" (Ps. 128:2), the Talmud comments, "Happy shall you be in this world, and it shall be well with you in the World to Come." Thus we see that there is value in work itself, the reward being "in the World to Come," as is the case for the observance of all commandments. In fact, we find that the Sages of the Talmudic era were almost all laborers, a classic example being Rabbi Joshua "the blacksmith." In the Talmud we are told of a classic confrontation on this issue between Rabbi Ishmael and Rabban Johanan ben Zakkai. Rabbi Ishmael, basing himself on deductions from various verses, claims that, in addition to Torah study – which he obviously considers paramount – one must also plow during the plowing season, sow, reap, etc. Rabban Johanan ben Zakkai, on the other hand, claims that "If a person plows during the plowing season, sows during the sowing season... what will become of Torah study?" Thus, he advocates that one should spend all his time on Torah study, to the exclusion of all else. As to livelihood, Rabban Johanan ben Zakkai claims that "if a person is worthy enough, his work will be taken care of by others." What is even more interesting in this classic debate is the conclusion reached by the Talmud: "Many did as Rabban Johanan ben Zakkai and were unsuccessful, while many [others] did as Rabbi Ishmael and were successful." There is even an opinion that "Six days shall you labor" is a positive commandment, and that just as one is forbidden to work on the Sabbath, he is required to work on the other days of the week.

Question Why is it that the rabbis of the Talmud all earned their livings in various different occupations, while today most rabbis have no other source of employment?

Answer Of course, the most obvious point is that one cannot possibly compare social conditions 1,500 years ago to today. Nowadays, the position of the rabbi is very different. Today, the rabbi is not only an educator, but he is often a social worker, an administrator of a large complex, the representative of the Jewish community to the general community, and involved in a myriad of other tasks. The job description as such simply does not allow him to devote less than his full time to his community.

Question Isn't there a Jewish law which forbids a person to earn money for teaching Torah? How, then, do rabbis and religious studies teachers collect pay for what they are doing?

Answer The Talmud is aware of this, and mentions an important concept: A person who teaches another Torah may not, indeed, be paid for doing so, but we assume that by teaching another Torah, the teacher cannot earn money in another line of work during that time. Now, a person has the right to be paid for the time he has "wasted," that he could have spent earning money in another field. This is known as *sekhar batalah* – "pay for being idled." Thus rabbis and teachers are not paid for their work as such, but for the time that they spend in their own positions, thereby being unable to engage in other occupations.

Question Does Judaism have anything to say about the desired social order in the world?

Answer In a famous answer to this query, Rabbi Abraham Isaac Kook, first chief rabbi of Palestine, did not give a specific answer to the question. He did, though, state that, whatever the Torah's view may be, it is definitely not one endorsing outright capitalism. In fact, the Torah legislation, given at a time when most people lived off the land, is a model of social justice. One classic example of this is the jubilee year legislation. Under this, no agricultural land could be sold in perpetuity. All land had to return to the original family in the jubilee, which occurred every 50 years. In fact, if a person wished to sell a field, he could only sell the crops which would grown on it until the jubilee year. When this law was enforced, it meant that it was simply impossible for a permanent landless class to emerge. And as long as a family had its ancestral land, it had a way to sustain itself. In that year, too, all Hebrew slaves had to be freed. It was as if the entire country was given a chance to begin again from scratch.

Similarly, the sabbatical year, which occurred every seventh year, included the wiping out of any loans. This, too, enabled a person who had become mired in debt to begin with a clean slate.

Question   What, then, was Hillel's famous *pruzbul*?

Answer   This legal device, recorded in the name of Hillel, has been the cause of a great deal of misunderstanding, primarily among non-Orthodox groups. But first let us find out what the *pruzbul* is. Simply put, it is a legal device whereby a person who is owed money by others turns over his loans to the local *bet din*, the Jewish court of law, before the advent of the sabbatical year. Now, the law is that the sabbatical year cancels all *private* debts between individuals; it does not, however, cancel debts to the *bet din*. Thus, by using a *pruzbul*, a person can, as it were, circumvent the laws of the cancellation of debts in the sabbatical year. The Mishnah tells us that when Hillel saw that the rich – contrary to what the Torah demanded of them – were reluctant to lend money to the poor before the advent of the sabbatical year, he ordered that *pruzbuls* be issued. This, we should stress, was not made as a device to help the rich collect their debts, but as a way to ensure that the poor would not find themselves without any sources for loans. What many do not understand is that Hillel did not, by his action, *change* a Torah law. What he did, instead, is institutionalize a method which had always been valid by Torah law.

Question   What is the Jewish attitude toward giving charity to the poor and needy?

Answer   Interestingly enough, there is no word in Hebrew that translates as "charity." The word that is used in Hebrew is *tzedakah*, which derives from the Hebrew root *TzDK*, a root meaning "justice" or "fairness." This, in a capsule, sums up the Jewish attitude toward charity. Judaism does not regard helping an unfortunate person an act of freewill benevolence by the rich to the poor. Rather, it is the *duty* of those who are better-off to help those that are less fortunate. In fact, the well-off are required to do whatever they can to remove the blight of poverty from the land. This, in fact, is the way Prof. Yeshayahu Leibowitz, one of the greatest modern Jewish thinkers, explains the seeming contradiction between two verses in the same chapter (Ch. 15) of Deuteronomy. There we read, on the one hand, "There shall be no poor among you" (v.4), whereas a few verses later we find, "For the poor shall never cease out of the land" (v. 11). According to Prof. Leibowitz, the first verse indicates man's obligation – namely to try to eliminate poverty, and the second verse tells us that this situation will not come about by itself, as, for example, by a divine miracle, and that we are not to sit by idly and wait for divine intervention. Instead, man must do whatever he can to rectify the situation.

Question   Is there any required amount that a person is required to give for charity?

Answer   Jewish law specifies that one must give a tenth ("tithe") of one's income for charity. On the other hand, one should not give more than 20% of his income – unless he is extremely wealthy – in order not to impoverish oneself, lest he become a public burden. Maimonides, though, states that no person ever becomes impoverished by giving *tzedakah*, nor does one suffer any ill consequences by giving it. In fact, in one of the most famous word plays in the oral law, the Sages tell us, "Tithe [Hebrew: *aser*] so that you may become wealthy [*titasher*]", the implication being that the more one gives to *tzedakah*, the more God rewards one with added income, in excess, in fact of the amount he gave away.

Question   What expenditures are considered to be valid toward the tithing of one's income?

Answer   Of course, certain donations are obvious: to the poor, to health care institutions, to synagogues or to yeshivot, for example. Other permissible expenditures are not as well-known. For example, a person who supports his children beyond the age when they are legally (i.e., by Jewish law) able to support themselves is considered to be giving *tzedakah*. So, too, one may use some of one's tithing money to buy religious books, provided that the books are clearly marked as having been bought with this money, and that the person makes these books available to others. Theoretically, too, one should be able to the percentage of one's taxes that are used by the government for social welfare causes, although, of course, this is not an easy matter to calculate.

Question   Who must give charity?

Answer   Jewish law requires *everyone* to give charity – even a person who is supported by charity must allocate some of what he receives for charitable purposes. The point is that the giving of charity must become an ingrained part of one's being.

Question   Who may receive charity?

Answer   The Talmud – speaking for its time – listed as its criterion for eligibility to receive charity any person whose total assets are less than 200 *zuzim*. A person in that category may collect charity from others. Other categories are also listed by the Talmud, as, for example, who is permitted to dine at the community soup kitchen set up for the poor. Of course, these standards are not readily translatable into our terms, as a dollar amount. After all, as we will see below, poverty is a relative concept, depending on the person and the era. But the principle remains the same – only a person in real need may take *tzedakah*, and, we are warned, any person who takes *tzedakah* when he does not need to, will ultimately be reduced to poverty, so that eventually he will legitimately have to go beg for alms.

Question   How much must a person be given?

Answer   Jewish law lays down an interesting provision – a person should be supported by the local community in a style relative to the one he had been accustomed to. Thus, if a person was a member of the middle class, for example, and suffers a severe financial setback, he has to be given greater support than a person who had been of the lower classes. In essence, then, Jewish law realizes that there is a psychological element in poverty, and that one cannot treat all the poor identically. A modern-day parallel of this, no doubt, is the fact that the average poor person in the United States lives on a standard that is probably higher than that of the overwhelming majority of the members of the middle and upper classes of developing countries. Yet, subjectively, the American feels himself poor.

A story is told about a rabbi who came to the town rich man for a donation for a certain person in need. The rich man asked the rabbi who he was collecting for, but the rabbi refused to tell him. "Rabbi," he said, "I'll give you twenty-five rubles" – a princely sum in those times – "for the person, if you tell me who it is." "No," replied the rabbi," I can't tell you. That's private information." "Well then, if I give you fifty rubles?" "That makes no difference." "And if I make it a hundred rubles?" "You could offer me all the money in the world," the rabbi told him, "but I cannot break my word." "Well, if that is the case, and I see that nothing I can do will make you divulge such information," the rich man told him, "I have a favor to ask of you. When you go about collecting in the town, could you collect for me as well? You see, a few months ago I lost most of my money, but I've been too embarrassed to tell anyone. Now that we are really in serious financial trouble and I see I can trust you, could you please add my name to the list of the needy you're collecting for?"

Question Should a person be embarrassed to accept *tzedakah*?

Answer Jewish law certainly places no restrictions on a person who is entitled to receiving *tzedakah* offered to him. On the other hand, though, a person should try to do everything possible not to have to accept *tzedakah*. Thus, we are told, "[It is better for you to] make your Sabbath a weekday [by not having any of the special delicacies that are customary on the Sabbath] than to have need of your fellow." On the other hand, Maimonides stresses that "whoever needs to take *tzedakah* and cannot survive unless he does so, such as someone who is old or sick or suffering and shuns such aid and does not take it, is considered to be shedding blood and is, as it were, guilty of a capital offence, and the suffering [caused by his refusal to take money] is but a sin and in vain." Yet, Maimonides goes on, one who has the right to take *tzedakah*, but instead prefers to suffer (i.e., where his life will not be endangered by his action) in order not to impose on the community, will not die of old age before having lived to support others from his own assets.

Question Must one give to every person who asks for *tzedakah*?

Answer Generally, a person has the right to investigate before giving *tzedakah*, with one exception: On Purim, the law is that "whoever stretches forth his hand, is to be given [a donation]." Yet, a vivid story in the Talmud implies differently. There, we are told of a certain sage who was asked by a poor man to give him some food. The sage complied immediately, but it took him time to dismount from his donkey and open his bag. By the time he got the food out, the man died. The Talmud then goes on to describe how that sage suffered physically for the rest of his life, a suffering which he accepted without question, for what he regarded as his sin in not having been quicker in dismounting and opening his bag. And that case, of course, was one where no character references were asked of the poor man who later died! At this point, we may point out an interesting comment in the Talmud, which, as it were, is grateful to the fact that there are some people that collect money that are indeed frauds, for this way, when we do not donate *tzedakah*, we have a plea to excuse our action. After all, had all those who come collecting been legitimate, what possible excuse could we have had for refusing anyone?

Question Is there a "best" way to give *tzedakah* to the poor?

Answer Maimonides outlines eight degrees of giving *tzedakah*, ranging from the least to the most preferable. These are:
1. One who gives another begrudgingly;
2. One who gives less than he should, but cheerfully;

3. One who gives after being asked;
4. One who gives before being asked;
5. One who gives without knowing to whom he is giving, but where the recipient knows who the donor was;
6. One who knows who will receive his donation, although the recipient does not know who the donor is;
7. Where neither the donor nor the recipient knows who the other party is;
8. One who enables another person to become self-reliant, either through giving or lending him money.

Chapter Eighteen

Basic Books

One of the most common descriptions applied to the Jewish people is that they are "The People of the Book." And with good reason. Of course, it was the Jewish people which gave the world the Book of Books, the Bible. But even more than that: no other nation has regarded the study of its holy works as the most important of all commandments, and has devoted all of its energies to the study of these works. This chapter will give an overview of some of the most important works of the Jewish people. Readers who are unfamiliar with the terms should reread the sections in Chapter 1 on the Torah, the Talmud and the Midrash, although there will be a certain amount of overlap in this chapter.

Question The Torah refers to the Five Books of Moses. What, though, is the *Tanakh*?

Answer Judaism divides the entire Bible into three major sections: the Torah, the Prophets (both early and latter), and the Hagiographa (literally, "Holy Writings"), which includes, among others, the Five Scrolls, Psalms, Ezra and Nehemiah, and Chronicles. The Hebrew term for Prophets is *Nevi'im*, and that for the Hagiographa is *Ketuvim*. Taking the first letters of Torah, *Nevi'im*, *Ketuvim*, we get the acronym *TNK*, which, with added vowels, gives us the word *Tanakh*. Thus the word *Tanakh* is the Hebrew expression for the entire Bible.

Question How many books are there in *Tanakh*?

Answer By Jewish tradition, there are 24 books in *Tanakh*. These are the Five Books of Moses, Joshua, Judges, Samuel, Kings, Isaiah, Jeremiah, Ezekiel, Minor Prophets (all 12 count as one book), Psalms, Proverbs, Job, Song of Songs, Ruth, Lamentations, Ecclesiastes, Esther, Daniel, Ezra-Nehemiah (considered as one book), Chronicles. The books of Samuel,

✾ *A scribe checking a Torah scroll to verify that it was written correctly.*

Kings and Chronicles are all considered as single books, and are not divided into two parts.

Question Who canonized *Tanakh*?

Answer Actually, by Jewish tradition, *Tanakh* was never canonized as such, in the Christian sense of the term. Various books were recognized as "holy writings," but the process went on for centuries. The earliest ones to debate the issue were *Anshei Knesset Hagedolah* – "The Men of the Great Assembly" – these being the great Torah sages who lived in about 300 B.C.E. Certainly by the beginning of the Common Era the book as we know it today had been canonized.

Question Were there any problems in the process?

Answer Indeed there were. Doubts were cast about the inclusion of a number of the books now in the canon. For example, there were views that the Song of Songs, a seeming love poem between two lovers and which does not even mention God's name, should not be included. The rabbis, though, regarded the poem as an allegory for the love between God and His people, Israel. As Rabbi Akiva put it, "All the books [of the Bible] are holy. But the Song of Songs is the holiest of the holy."

Another book in dispute was Ezekiel, which contains various passages which are at odds with Jewish law, as reflected in the Torah. Ezekiel, for example, states that a priest may not marry either a widow or a divorcee, whereas the Torah only forbids him to marry a divorcee. The Talmud tells us that the Sages were indeed thinking of excluding Ezekiel, until a certain Hananiah ben Yehezkiah shut himself away and reconciled all the differences between the laws in Ezekiel and those in the Torah.

Question We mentioned earlier that the Mishnah was the first authoritative work compiled of the oral law. How is the Mishnah arranged?

Answer As noted earlier, the Mishnah was edited by Rabbi Judah the Patriarch, in about 200 C.E., and was evidently based to a large extent on various written collections of laws of the time. The entire collection was divided into six major sections, known as *sedarim* – "orders" – and these were further sub-divided into a total of 63 *masekhtot*, or tractates.

Question What are the six *sedarim* of the Mishnah?

Answer The *sedarim*, in order, are as follows:

1. *Zera'im* ("Seeds"), which deals primarily with the agricultural laws of Eretz Israel.
2. *Mo'ed* ("Festival"), the laws of the Sabbaths and festivals.
3. *Nashim* ("Women"), mainly the laws of marriage, divorce, and various contracts.
4. *Nezikin* ("Damages"), torts and other financial questions.
5. *Kodashim* ("Holy Things"), the laws of the sacrifices and of the Temple.
6. *Toharot* ("Purities"), the laws of ritual purity and impurity.

While these broad classifications give some idea of the content of the different *sedarim*, we must note that many other topics are covered, some within their proper places within the above parameters, and others located in unexpected places. For example, when reference is made to a certain rabbi's comment on a topic germane to that order, the Mishnah may go on and list other statements by the same rabbi, even though the other statements have nothing to do with this particular order. It is, as it were, almost a type of "stream of consciousness." Similarly, a dispute between the School of Shammai and the School of Hillel may then evince other examples of disputes between the two.

Question What is *Shas*?

Answer The word *Shas* is really an abbreviation of the Hebrew term, *shishah sedarim* – "The six Orders." The word is thus a shorthand way of referring to the entire Mishnah and, by extension, Talmud.

Question What are the tractates?

Answer Each *seder* (singular of *sedarim*) contains a number of tractates, where each tractate deals with a more specific topic. Thus, for example, the *seder* of *Nashim* ("Women") has tractates dealing with marriage, divorce, levirate marriage and the *ketubah* – the marriage contract specifying the husband's obligations to his wife. In modern-day language, one might consider the *sedarim* as six different series, while the tractates are the volumes within each series.

Question As was noted earlier, the Talmud is a compilation of the Mishnah with the addition of written notes of the oral discussions which had revolved about the Mishnah. What language is the Talmud written in?

Answer The Mishnah itself is written in Hebrew. The Talmud, on the other hand, written two or three centuries later, is written in Aramaic, that being the *lingua franca* of the Jews in Jerusalem and in Babylon, where the two

Talmuds – the Jerusalem Talmud and the Babylonian Talmud – were written. As we mentioned earlier, the Jerusalem Talmud was completed in about 400 C.E. and the Babylon Talmud about a century later. Both, though, start with the Mishnah as their base. For a person who knows Hebrew, Aramaic represents a moderate, but hardly insurmountable challenge, for the two are very closely linked, both being Semitic languages.

Question Is there a Talmud commentary on every tractate of the Mishnah?

Answer No; only about half the tractates of the Mishnah also have Talmud commentaries. Essentially, the tractates which were of more immediate importance were the ones upon which the Talmud was composed, but this was relative. For example, the Babylonian Talmud has almost nothing on the *seder* of *Zera'im*, which deals with agricultural laws which are primarily relevant to Eretz Israel, while the Jerusalem Talmud has a great deal on this particular *seder*.

We should also note that there were some Talmud commentaries on the Mishnah which disappeared over the years. The classic example of this is the Jerusalem Talmud on the *seder* of *Kodashim*, the *seder* which deals with sacrifices. From various quotes by early commentators we know that this *seder* existed, but not a single copy has come down to us. The reason for this is simple: Firstly, until the printing press was invited, every book had to be laboriously copied by hand. Obviously, the books which would be copied most would be those which were studied most frequently. Now, in general, the Babylonian Talmud has been the one that is studied most frequently, for a number of reasons: a) It was finally redacted later than the Jerusalem Talmud, b) and, probably related to (a), it is far more comprehensive. Historically, too, we know that the Jerusalem Talmud was composed under extremely adverse conditions, whereas the Jews in Babylon lived in comparative security and comfort. That may also explain why the Babylonian Talmud is so much more comprehensive.

As a result of this, the Babylonian Talmud was copied far more frequently than the Jerusalem Talmud. Furthermore, as very few people studied *Kodashim*, and even fewer the Jerusalem Talmud of *Kodashim*, we can understand that there were very few manuscripts of it in the first place.

But even that does not explain why not a single copy survived. What does explain it, though, is the periodic burning by the Church of all manuscripts of the Talmud. For example, in the late 13th century, there was a public burning of the Talmud of no less than 24 cart loads of manuscripts in Paris. That represented countless thousands of hours of work by scribes. Now, even though the manuscripts had been burned, there were copies of the more "popular," as it were, tractates in other cities. Evidently, though, whatever manuscripts there were of the Jerusalem Talmud on *Kodashim* were all burned, thus leaving an irreplaceable gap in the Jewish bookshelf.

As an interesting footnote, toward the end of the last century, a certain Talmudic scholar claimed he had found a lost manuscript of the Jerusalem Talmud on *Kodashim*, which would make it the greatest find in Judaica for centuries. The greatest Talmudic scholars of the era argued over the authenticity of the copy, until it was proven that it was simply a forgery perpetrated by the "finder." What he had done – and the irony of this is that only a very great scholar could be capable of such a task – was to collect together all the different quotations in secondary sources of what the Jerusalem Talmud had said, and he then wove them together into a unified whole. Thus this episode was transformed from "the find of the century" into "the fraud of the century."

Question Is everything in the Talmud binding on Jews?

Answer The Talmud covers an incredibly vast range of subjects in its 2,700 folio pages (in the Babylonian Talmud), including Jewish law and custom, medical questions, mathematics and countless other topics. It has generally been accepted that those areas of the Talmud that deal with Jewish law are binding, whereas one does not have to accept as binding statements in other fields, such as science, where the Sages obviously were only acquainted with "science" as it existed at their time.

Maimonides, in a brilliant way, disposes of one such topic discussed quite extensively in the Talmud: the various demons that are supposed to frequent the world and cause damage and destruction. This belief was quite widespread among the masses, and led to all types of superstitious practices. (A vestige of these beliefs is to be found in the common Jewish expression, *kein ayin hora* – "No evil eye!") While Maimonides did not wish to state outright that demons do not exist, which would mean disputing the Talmud's statements, he solved the problem admirably by stating simply that a person who ignores the demons cannot be harmed by them. Case closed!

Question If the Talmud was completed by 500 C.E., does that date mark the end of the development of the oral law?

Answer Quite the contrary. After the completion of the Talmud, a new era began, of commentaries on the Talmud, and later even of commentaries on the commentaries, and this is a process which has continued to this very day.

The different commentaries were written with different goals in mind. For example, the commentary of Rashi (acronym for Rabbi Shlomo Itzhaki, 1040-1105), which is printed on each page of the Talmud text, is concerned with clarifying the meaning of the text itself. That of the Tosafists (12th-14th centuries, France and Germany), which is also printed on each page alongside the Talmud text, on the other hand, is more concerned with taking specific points and contrasting them with points in other places, either in the same tractate or in other tractates. By this means, for example, the Tosafists may point out contradictions between two texts, which they will then attempt to reconcile. Then again, other commentators are more concerned with the halakhic implications of the text, i.e., how the particular text affects the *halakhah*. Such a commentary is that by Rif (acronym of Rabbi Isaac Alfasi, 1013-1103), which basically summarizes the Talmudic text, quoting only those views which Rif believes are the *halakhah*. Throughout the centuries, there have been numerous commentaries of all kinds, especially of the first two. The latest, for example, is being written right now on the Babylonian Talmud, by Rabbi Adin Steinsalz of Jerusalem. In it, Rabbi Steinsalz gives a modern Hebrew explanation of the text and supplies biographical, geographic and other notes on the Talmudic passages. To date, about 20 volumes of this monumental work have appeared. Work is apace to have the entire commentary appear in English translation. Rabbi Steinsalz has also just put out the first volume of his commentary on the Jerusalem Talmud, which is the next project he has undertaken.

We should point out that Rabbi Steinsalz comes from a non-religious background and found his way to religion by his own efforts. In his *9 1/2 Mystics*, Herbert Weiner quotes Rabbi Steinsalz's father as having said, "They tell me that a head such as that of my son comes but once in a thousand years – and it was my luck that it had to happen to me!"

Question   What is the responsa literature?

Answer   Throughout all generations, whenever Jews have had questions about Jewish practice, they have written to great Torah authorities to receive their rulings. Generally, the rabbi did not just answer yes or no, kosher or non-kosher, but would give a reasoned halakhic argument to explain why he had ruled as he had. Many of the rabbis kept records of all the questions they were asked and the answers they gave, and either they or later generations would publish these "responsa." Thus, the responsa literature is that body of books of questions and answers in Jewish law. By their nature, these books discuss the most up-to-date questions. For example, one of the volumes of *Igrot Moshe*, by Rabbi Moses Feinstein who died a few years ago, includes questions regarding the use of dishwashers that have been used for non-kosher dishes, purchasing kosher meats in a store that also sells non-kosher meats, the use of an electric water boiler on the Sabbath, and a ruling on women who wish to practice commandments applying only to men.

Question How many volumes of responsa have been published?

Answer We know of at least 3,000 such volumes spanning the last 12 centuries or more, and there were probably thousands of others which remained in manuscript form, often because their authors simply did not have the wherewithal to pay for the printing. One can thus appreciate the importance of this segment of the classical literature.

Question With a body of literature that vast, how can anyone be expected to find information on a given topic?

Answer Throughout the ages there have been extraordinary men that had encyclopedic knowledge of hundreds of such volumes. This was especially true for the great rabbis of each generation who were consulted on halakhic problems by other rabbis and issued rulings in very many areas. But, of course, there were very few such people at any given time. But now modern-day technology has come to our aid.

Question What "modern-day technology" are you referring to?

Answer More than a decade ago, the religious Bar Ilan University of Ramat Gan, in Israel, undertook its "responsa project." To date, more than 300 of the most important responsa books have been keyed in to the Bar Ilan computer. With the use of key words and a very sophisticated search mechanism, a person querying about any topic receives a printout of every responsum in these 300 volumes which discusses the topic. And the project is not only useful to the Torah scholar, for the responsa contain so much more. For example, one can find out from different responsa such information as people's dress, coinage, mercantile systems, and, of course, the use of language in different eras. Thus, for example, a historian may use the search functions of the responsa project to enlighten him on various aspects of a certain era.

Question Does that mean that the responsa project can replace rabbis in deciding Jewish law?

Answer Decidedly not. The material spewed forth by the computer is raw data. It does not take into account such variables as *who* said what, and under what circumstances. Nor can it point out differences in various situations. There is no doubt that the project can help rabbis to reach a decision by supplying them with raw data, but that is as far as it can go. And then, of course, there is the matter of *siyata de-shemaya*.

Question *Siyata de-shemaya?* What is that?

Answer Literally, the term translates as "aid from heaven." Among Torah-true Jews, it is accepted that great Torah authorities do not just rule without any Divine involvement, and that God somehow injects His own presence in the process, to prevent any marked aberration in ruling. Along these lines, the story is told of a great Torah scholar of the last generation who sent a query for a ruling to another great rabbi. In his letter, he asked that the rabbi send a telegram with his answer. The rabbi, of course, was happy to comply. Later, when the two met, the rabbi who had sent the telegram asked his friend what had been so urgent that a telegram had been needed. "Actually," his friend told him, "there was no real urgency as such. I was afraid, though, that if you sent me a long, reasoned answer to my question, I might question some of your logic, or even disagree with it. I knew that if you sent a telegram, you would only write the ruling, with no further amplification. Now, I am convinced that, whether I agree with your logic or not, you have *siyata de-shemaya*, and regardless of the logic, your decision is correct."

Question The responsa literature would appear to be highly diffused. Is there any place where Jewish law is arranged in an orderly fashion?

Answer There are numerous works of this nature. One of the earliest, for example, was that by Maimonides (1135-1204), whose *Mishneh Torah* is a model of clarity and arrangement. Another example was that of Rabbi Jacob ben Asher (1270?-1340), known as *Arba'ah Turim*. About 200 years later, Rabbi Joseph Caro wrote commentaries on both these works, *Kesef Mishneh* on Maimonides, and *Bet Yosef* on *Arba'ah Turim*. Having written on both these major works, Caro then wrote his own code of Jewish law, known as *Shulkhan Arukh*. It is this work which is authoritative to every Torah-observant Jew to this day.

Question Where does *aggadah* fit into this scheme of things?

Answer Actually, it does not. In fact, one of the classical definitions of *aggadah* is that it consists of all texts which are not *halakhah*, and the Talmud and those texts related to it are primarily meant to teach us *halakhah*.

Question What, then is *aggadah*?

Answer As we noted in the first chapter, *aggadah* starts with the same text as the Talmud, i.e., *Tanakh*, but instead of using the text for halakhic purposes, uses it instead for homiletic purposes.

Question Are Jews required to accept everything stated in the *aggadah* as being correct, as they are required to accept everything in *halakhah*?

Answer No less an authority than Maimonides says quite clearly that this is not the case. According to Maimonides, there are three types of people: a) Those who accept every word of the *aggadah* literally. These according to Maimonides, may be considered to have good intentions, but their deeds are not considered to be good. By their actions, Maimonides says, people relate to the Jewish people as stupid and naive, rather than as "a great nation, a wise and understanding people" (Deut. 4:6). b) Those people who use the literal meaning of the text to mock Judaism. These people, says Maimonides, sin in both intention and deed. c) Finally, says Maimonides, there is the third class, that understands that the *aggadah* cannot be accepted literally, and that realizes that it is to be understood allegorically. That, according to Maimonides, is the only proper way to understand the *aggadah*.

Question What is the Midrash?

Answer The word Midrash, as mentioned in Chapter 1, is derived from a root which means to enquire or to investigate. Midrash may be seen as a commentary on the Holy Writ. What type of commentary it is depends on the type of Midrash involved.

Question What types of Midrash are there?

Answer Generally, the *Midrashim* (plural of Midrash are divided into two broad categories: 1. *Midreshei Aggadah* which take verses and derive moral and ethical lessons from them. Included in this category are, among others, *Midrash Rabbah* and *Midrash Tanhuma*. 2. *Midreshei Halakhah* which use the verses to establish various halakhic principles. Works in this category include, among others, *Sifra* and *Sifre*.

Question What is the Kabbalah?

Answer Kabbalah is that branch of the Jewish religious literature which deals with mysticism. From time immemorial, Judaism has had a mystic strain. For example, we have Ezekiel's description of the throne of God. The Kabbalah probably received its greatest impetus with the publication in the 13th century of the *Zohar* (literally "radiance") by Moses de Leon. De Leon attributed the book to a long-lost manuscript that he had found, and he claimed that the book had been written by Rabbi Simeon bar Yohai (2nd century C.E.). After de Leon's death, his widow testified that she had seen her husband writing the volume at night. Be that as it may, whether de Leon indeed had discovered an old manuscript or had written his own work, based on current sources, *Zohar* has proved to be the prime source for kabbalistic studies, and many commentaries have been written on it. For centuries, it was accepted that no one under the age of 40 may study Kabbalah. The hasidic movement, though, brought the study of kabbalah to the masses, claiming that the time has come for this study to be available to everyone.

Chapter Nineteen

Modern-Day Israel

Before discussing Israel today, it would be appropriate to understand the role the Land of Israel plays in Jewish life and tradition. Only this way can we understand what the reborn Jewish State in the Land of Israel means to the Jewish people.

Question What is the basis for the Jewish claim to the Land of Israel?

Answer The claim is a simple one: Almost 4,000 years ago, God promised Abraham that this land would belong to his descendants. And that promise is reiterated throughout the Torah. Rashi (1040-1105), the pre-eminent commentator on the Torah, begins his commentary by asking a simple question: Why does the Torah begin with the account of the creation of the world rather than with the different laws incumbent of the Jewish people? To this, quoting a *midrash*, he responds: The Torah begins with the creation to teach us that God is the Creator of all, and He has the right to parcel out land to whichever nation He sees fit. Thus, says Rashi, the entire account of the creation serves one purpose: to indicate that the Land of Israel belongs to the Jewish people because it was given to them by God.

Question But that was 4,000 years ago, and is it not a fact that the country remained effectively without Jews for over 1,800 years – from the Destruction of the Temple in 70 C.E. until the 1800s? Does that not imply that the Jewish right to the land has lapsed?

Answer The first point wrong with this argument is that throughout the generations there have been Jews living in the Land of Israel, sometimes in greater numbers and sometimes in lesser. To a large extent, this depended on whether the rulers of the country were tolerant of Jews or not. Furthermore, throughout the centuries there were instances of Jews moving to the country from all over the world, even when the trip was extremely arduous and dangerous. One village in the country, Peki'in, claims an uninterrupted Jewish presence from the Second Temple period, and there is clear evidence of a Jewish population in that village since at least the 16th century to the present.

Furthermore, there has never been a time that the Jewish people ever resigned themselves to the loss of their land. Three times a day Jews prayed: "Return to Jerusalem, Your city, in mercy, and build it speedily in our days." In addition, there are references to the Land of Israel in countless prayers and rituals, ranging from the grace recited after meals to the wedding ceremony. Throughout this time, year in and year out, century after century, Jews have mourned for their land and fasted on the anniversary of the day that the Temple fell.

The Talmud and Midrash, too, are replete with references to the Holy Land and the Jewish yearning to return to it. For example, the Talmud mentions that "it is preferable to live in the Land of Israel in a city where the majority of the people are idolaters than to live outside the Land of Israel in a city where the majority are Jews." Another Talmud dictum claims that "one who lives outside Eretz Israel is to be compared to an idolater!" The Land of Israel is indeed central to Jewish life and Jewish law, and one cannot understand Judaism if one does not take that fact into account.

Question What do Jewish thinkers consider as the seminal events of the 20th century?

Answer Without a doubt, two events of the 20th century must be regarded as among the most significant in Jewish history in the past hundreds of years, if not from the time of the destruction of the Temple in 70 C.E. These, of course, are the 1939-1945 so-called Holocaust, and the establishment of the State of Israel in 1948.

Question You seem to have a certain hesitation in using the term "Holocaust." Why?

Answer Unfortunately, the popular term for the unparalleled mass murder of Jews is the word "Holocaust," which, taken strictly, means a burnt offering. The connotation, and this has been expressed in these terms by various non-Jewish theologians, is that this murder was a type of sacrifice on behalf of the rest of the human race. In a way, the term almost legitimizes the act of the murderers; after all, they were, so it would appear, simply carrying out God's mission. It is for this reason that many people have refused to use the term "Holocaust," and instead prefer the use of the Hebrew term *Sho'ah*, which means destruction or catastrophe.

Question How many Jews were murdered in the Holocaust?

Answer Although it is impossible to establish absolutely accurate figures – even with the Nazi obsession with "order" – because many people were simply killed at random without any record being kept, all available evidence points to approximately 6,000,000 Jews having been killed in cold blood, the majority in them in "death factories," whose only product was death. A comparison of the Jewish populations before and after the war in the countries occupied by Germany yields the same general figure.

Question What was the response of the world?

Answer Generally, the response was a thundering silence. Countries that had the facilities refused to take in Jews, and even when there was already documented evidence of the mass murder. During the war years, for example, the United States did not even utilize the full quota allocated for German immigration. Thus, thousands of people that might have escaped the Nazi claws were denied entry into the United States at a time when there were places available by the quota. By the same token, underpopulated countries throughout the world found reasons for not accepting Jewish immigrants. And a last example of this callous disregard for the events going on in Nazi Europe was the persistent refusal of the allies to bomb the rail lines leading to Auschwitz, the biggest murder camp of them all, or to bomb Auschwitz itself, even though United States bombers had bombed other strategic targets in the same area.

Question Is it not true, though, that the Holocaust laid the way to the founding of the State of Israel?

Answer This is indeed most likely the case, for after the war a chastened world realized that as long as Jews did not have a country of their own there was nothing to prevent another *Sho'ah*. Thus, at an unbelievably heavy price – 6,000,000 Jews killed out of the 17,000,000 in the world before the war – the *Sho'ah* can be said to have contributed to the ultimate founding of the State of Israel.

Question How do Jews regard the State of Israel theologically?

Answer On this topic, probably more than on any other, there is a wide range of opinion, from the Neturei Karta ("Guardians of the [Holy] City"), who see the State of Israel as nothing but an attempt by Satan to seduce the Jewish people with the blandishments of statehood, to the extreme religious

♣ *Yad Vashem, Jerusalem: Monuments commemorating the Holocaust.*

nationalist who regards the State as the beginning stages of the ultimate redemption and the coming of the Messiah. In between, there are all types of shadings, such as, for example, those who believe that the State is indeed the Divine will, but who cannot believe that a secular state such as Israel can be considered to be the beginning of the process of redemption. These differences are expressed most clearly on Israel's Independence Day, as will be seen below.

Question How is Israel's Independence Day observed?

Answer That depends on the person's background and convictions. The vast majority of those who are not observant regard the day much as Americans regard July 4 today, with the difference that a goodly number of Israelis today actually lived through the struggle for the State. To them, independence is not just a historical fact, but part of their lives. And remember that many Israelis now living survived the Nazi concentration and murder camps. To them, indeed, Israel's independence means that they finally found a country that they could call their own and where they do not have to live in constant fear. The members of this group will, by and large, spend the day together as a family, often by going on an outing of some type.

Another group, the religious Zionists, regard this day as no less than a modern-day religious festival, and recite special prayers of thanksgiving to God. To them, incidentally, Independence Day is a unique opportunity. In a land where people work six days a week and where the only day off is the Sabbath – when religious Jews will not drive – it is the only day when none of the family are at work, and yet the family may take its car wherever it wishes to go. (Oh, yes – Israel's Independence Day has one thing in common with the July 4 holiday – it is marked by massive traffic jams at the end of the day as everyone returns home form all these outings.)

Then there are the non-Zionist religious Jews, to whom Independence Day simply means nothing. This group, representing probably no more than 5% of the total population, fails to see the hand of God in what happened – even though it is written in the big bold letters of current history.

Finally, there are the extreme anti-Zionists, who represent a small fraction of the total Israeli population, and to whom the day is one for mourning. They, though, have a problem: by Israeli law, all stores must be closed on Independence Day. If their stores do open on that day, they risk a fine. If they remain closed, they seem to imply that the day is special. It would seem like a Catch 22 position in which they find themselves. But never underestimate man's ingenuity. In Me'ah She'arim, the Jerusalem quarter in which many of the members of this group live, all the stores remain closed, but some brilliant PR man arranged to print up labels which are pasted on the stores on that day:

"Closed in protest of the Zionist government." Thus, as we see, they have managed to both have their cake and eat it too!

Question   Are there any other modern-day festivals in Israel?

Answer   Whereas Independence Day is on the 5th day of the Hebrew month of Iyar (generally in April or May), there is one other special day that month – the 28th of Iyar, Jerusalem Day. This day, which is not officially a national holiday, commemorates how the Israeli army, after having been attacked by Jordan in 1967, retaliated and eventually liberated the Old City of Jerusalem. On this day, thousands of school children from all over Israel come to Jerusalem to celebrate its deliverance.

Among the religious, this festival is far less controversial than Independence Day. After all, Independence Day commemorates a political act – the declaration of the State – while Jerusalem Day commemorates the actual victory of Israeli forces, and, by implication, the liberation of Jerusalem from the hands of foreign invader. Thus, many religious Jews who might have reservations about celebrating Independence Day in a religious manner, have no such hesitation regarding Jerusalem Day.

Question   What is Israel's population?

Answer   The latest estimates have the total Israeli population (excluding those living beyond the borders of pre-1967 Israel) as about 4.5 million people, of whom less than 20% are non-Jewish. While the population may be considered tiny in comparison to that of countries such as the United States and the Soviet Union, we should realize that a country such as Norway has only a slightly larger population.

Question   What is the composition of the Jews in the country?

Answer   As Israel is proud to boast, it has within its borders immigrants from over 100 countries from throughout the world, a reflection, of course, of the dispersion of the Jewish people throughout the world. At present, the Sephardic Jews represent somewhat more than half the Jewish population, and Ashkenazic Jews represent somewhat less than half the total.

Question   What is the "Who is a Jew" ruckus in Israel all about?

Answer   As a haven to the Jews throughout the world, Israel makes special provision for Jews who wish to immigrate to it. Under the Law of the Return, every Jew, upon arriving in Israel, has the right to request citizenship. The law also defines who is covered under its provisions: a Jew, defined as anyone with a Jewish mother or who was converted, and any one of a number of close relatives (even if non-Jewish), such as spouse, parent, child, etc. The law, in accepting as a Jew anyone who was converted, allows any convert, regardless of the denomination of the converting rabbi, to enter Israel and acquire Israeli citizenship. For decades, various Orthodox elements have been pushing to amend the law to specify "conversion according to *halakhah*" – Jewish law – which, they believe, will allow only those who underwent Orthodox conversions to be eligible under the law's provisions, in effect "disenfranchising" the Conservative and Reform rabbinates. As the number of converts affected by this change is generally less than ten in any given year, there are those who believe that the struggle is primarily not over "who is a Jew," but rather over "who is a rabbi."

Question Where does this issue stand at present?

Answer As of July 1989, when the Israeli Supreme Court issued a ruling based on its interpretation of the laws of the State of Israel, any person who is a Jew by birth or was converted by *any rabbinate* is entitled to enter Israel under the Law of the Return. As the Minister of the Interior, who represents a right-wing Orthodox party, was not willing to have his name appear on the identity cards (which carry information as to the religion of the bearer) of individuals who have not been converted according to *halakhah*, two changes were introduced in the identity cards now being issued to everyone: a) the minister's signature no longer appears on each card, and b) each card carries a disclaimer stating clearly that the item on "nationality" (which is where the notation "Jew" would appear) is not to be accepted even as *prima facie* evidence about the person's religion. Thus we now have the anomalous situation of an official Israeli document which states that the information on it is not to be accepted as proof of its truth!

At the same time, the Israeli Supreme Court ruled that as the Knesset had empowered the Chief Rabbinate to determine who may conduct weddings in the State, the Chief Rabbinate cannot be forced to accept Conservative and Reform as marriage registrars. Thus, the situation in Israel at present is that for the purposes of the Law of the Return, any person accepted by any of the different streams of Judaism is eligible for automatic citizenship, whereas only Orthodox rabbis – or to be more specific, those accepted by the Chief Rabbinate – are authorized to preside over marriages.

Chapter Twenty

Some Twentieth Century Issues

Question   What is the Jewish view of the discrepancy between the Biblical account of creation and the theory of evolution?

Answer   While there are differences of opinion among rabbis of various streams, one cannot even find unanimity among the Orthodox. There are, though, certain common guidelines that would be accepted by Orthodoxy as such. For example, all Orthodox scholars accept the fact that the Biblical account of the creation is accurate, at least to the extent that it indicates that at a certain point there was a creation, and that this creation was God's handiwork. Now, whether the creation took place in six days, or six periods of indeterminate time, is really irrelevant. As Rabbi Kook put it, the Bible is not trying to teach us history, just as the scientist cannot teach us – at least not empirically – human morals. The Torah's purpose, says Rabbi Kook, is to teach us how to behave, and the right to tell us what is permissible and what is not is predicated on only one basic fact: "In the beginning, God created the heavens and the earth." If God is the creator of all, then He has the right to make whatever demands He wishes on His creatures. To illustrate the difference between the two spheres – the religious and the scientific – Rabbi Kook uses a beautiful example. Imagine, he says, that you see a painting. Your reaction to it will revolve about whether you like it or not, whether it says something to you or does not. You cannot, however – in any rational sense – assign a grade to a painting. No painting can be "87%," as opposed to another which is "92%." Such a rating is meaningless. On the other hand, a person may be given a problem in mathematics, or a series of such problems, and he can either solve the problems or not. Here, it is eminently logical to say that a person received a specific grade on the assignment, but one cannot very well say that the student's response says something to one emotionally. In essence, then, art and science are two entirely different spheres, and one cannot possibly use the same tools to analyze them. And the same applies when one tries to use scientific methods or criteria on the Bible or religious criteria on

234 THE JEWISH PRIMER

science – the two fields are simply different, and each can only be judged in terms of its own, self-contained criteria. For those of mathematical bent, this would be similar to the various different geometries in existence – both Euclidean and non-Euclidean – each of which is correct *within its own parameters*. And then again, the theory of evolution is exactly that – a theory, based on extrapolation of a few thousand years of recorded data back for a million years or more.

Question How about the evidence for evolution as shown in fossils?

Answer If, indeed, God directed evolution along a continuous time period, it would follow that various creatures were created along the way, these now no longer existent. Advocates of the view that everything was created in six days – and here we refer to days in the sense we know them, rather than six time periods of indeterminate length – have an interesting explanation of the existence of fossils, even though, according to them, God created the world in six discrete stages. Imagine, they say, that there were no fossils anywhere. All we would have would be the various species as we see them now, without any possible explanation of how man – or any other creature – had developed. Now, if that had been the case, man would have been *forced* to believe in the existence of God. After all, no other possible interpretation could explain where man had come from. And that would have taken away from man his free will to choose whether or not to believe in God! Thus, the existence of fossils, in essence, gives man the option of choosing whether to believe in God as the creator of all, or to accept the alternate explanation of the world as having evolved by chance.

And that is exactly the choice that man has been given, and taken advantage of. In fact, one might almost say that some people have made a religion of adopting the alternate view to creation by God. Thus, Dr. Harold C. Urey, a Nobel Prize winner in chemistry, was quoted by the *Christian Science Monitor* (January 4, 1962) as having explained the modern outlook to the origin of life as follows: "All of us who study the origin of life find that the more we look into it, the more we feel it too complex to have evolved anywhere." Yet Dr. Urey then added: "We all *believe as an article of faith* that life evolved from dead matter on this planet. It is just that its complexity is so great that it is hard for us to imagine that it did" (*italics supplied*).

Question You mentioned free will in your last answer. What does Judaism believe in the free will/determinism argument?

Answer We are told in Deuteronomy, "I have set before you life and death, blessing and cursing: therefore choose life" (30:19). A statement like that is senseless if man has no free will and all of his actions are determined for him. Judaism is a strong advocate of man's free will and of his ability and need to choose the proper path. Parenthetically, we should note that it has been shown that nature, which turn-of-the-century scientists regarded as being rigidly deterministic, is not so. For example, we know that radioactive materials decay at a certain specified rate – each substance at its own rate. Yet there is no possible way to predict which particular molecule will be the next to decay. There is thus a certain randomness even within the constraints of nature. Another example is what is known as Heisenberg's Uncertainty Principle (note the name!), which states that, below a certain level one is simply unable to ascertain *both* the position and momentum of an object simultaneously. Again, we see that nature is not as deterministic as had been believed. Indeed, facts such as these have caused many scientists to modify the rigidly deterministic view they had had of the entire world, including of man's nature.

Question How about miracles? Are the different miracles in the Bible to be taken literally?

Answer To the determinist of the 19th century, miracles were simply impossible, because the miracle cannot be explained within the natural laws of science. To the Jew, the God who created the world and instituted its various "natural laws" is equally capable of suspending these laws when it suits His purpose. There is no reason for us, therefore, to have to attempt to explain the various recorded miracles as having occurred by natural means – although that is not precluded.

A fascinating story is told in the Talmud about a man whose wife died, leaving him with an infant son. The man was unable to find a wet nurse, so he prayed to God to save his son. God caused a miracle to take place, and the man's breasts produced milk, with which he was able to nurse his son. Some rabbis were impressed at the righteousness of the man, that God changed the laws of nature in order to help him. Others, though, differed vehemently. If the man was really righteous, they maintain, God would have found a way to help him *by natural means*. It was only because he was not that righteous that God had to change the laws of nature in order to aid him. In the final analysis, though, not every miracle involves a change in the laws of nature. Some miracles are strictly within the realm of the laws of nature, but their timing is such as to render them miraculous. An example of this is given above in the chapter on Purim, where we mentioned the case of the Germans in World War II coming across the British water pipeline just at a time that it was tested by pumping sea water through it.

If we wish to sum it up, then, a belief in God should automatically lead one to a belief, at the very least, of the *possibility* of miracles. Those who deny the *possibility* of miracles are not so much denying that miracles are possible as they are denying that there is a God who controls the world.

Question With the recent increase in interest in ecology, does Judaism have anything to say on the issue?

Answer Although the Bible obviously does not use the word as such, there are already provisions in it that show a clear ecological concern. Thus, for example, we are told that if one besieges a city, he is only permitted to uproot non-fruit bearing trees, and must leave the fruit-bearing trees where they are. In fact, the Sages deduce from this law that it is forbidden to destroy anything whatsoever wantonly. Thus, it is forbidden to just tear up a perfectly good piece of paper ifor the fun of it." Judaism would accordingly be opposed to some of the fads America has gone through, such as lighting a cigar with a bank note, or swallowing a goldfish whole.

Another provision in the Torah is that when soldiers go out to war – and one realizes that a person who is engaged in battle will by necessity act in a different manner than he would normally – he must carry with him a type of trowel, so that when he has to evacuate his bowels, he will be able to cover his excrement with dirt. That is surely a provision of an ecological nature.

We also find numerous provisions in the oral law which are meant to protect the wholesomeness of the atmosphere. As an example, the Sages forbade anyone from opening a tannery in the middle of a city, because the smell in it is particularly loathsome and was even considered to be harmful. There is also a discussion among the Sages whether a person may erect a building in such a way that its windows will be able to see into a neighbor's, that being considered to be *hezek re'iyah*, or "damage by seeing," as it were. In this connection, we find an interesting Midrashic comment on the praise that Balaam heaped upon the Israelites in the desert: "How goodly are your tents, O Israel." The Midrash asks, "What was it that impressed Balaam so much?" And it answers: "For he saw that they had pitched their tents in such a way that no entrance faced another," thus ensuring everyone privacy in his comings and goings.

Chapter Twenty-One

Jewish Functionaries

Question What is a rabbi?

Answer The word "rabbi" simply means teacher. And that has traditionally been the primary function of the rabbi, as teacher of his flock. As part of the rabbi's instructional function, it is his duty to rule on questions of Jewish law, as, for example, whether a certain action is permitted or forbidden, or whether certain food is kosher or not kosher.

Question How does a person become a rabbi?

Answer Originally, the authority to rule on Jewish law was conveyed by the laying of the hands by a person that had this authority himself. And this laying of the hands traced back directly to Moses. Later, after the chain had been broken by the Jewish exile, a substitute form was evolved, whereby any rabbi has the right to award any other person that he deems worthy the title of rabbi. The title is generally awarded only after an exhaustive examination on Jewish law and evidence of the person's unblemished moral character. If a person meets these criteria, the examining rabbi will usually indicate his approval by giving the candidate a written document, known as *semikhah* (ordination). The name of the document, incidentally, traces back to the original method of ordination by the laying of the hands, which in Hebrew is *semikhat yadayim*. Of course, where every rabbi has the right to ordain others, the validity of such a document becomes a function of who the person awarding it is. Obviously, *semikhah* from a world-famous Torah authority carries greater weight than does the same from a less learned rabbi.

We should also point out that with the growth of the different rabbinic colleges – and this, by Jewish standards, is a recent phenomenon of the last 150 or so years – has led to a more formal list of requirements by the colleges themselves. For example, various rabbinic colleges today have courses that the prospective rabbi must pass in such areas as homiletics and pastoral counselling, in addition to the basic course matter on Jewish law. The formal rabbinic courses generally require a student to have a B.A. or the equivalent before even beginning to study the specific subject matter, and some rabbinic colleges require prospective rabbis to acquire a masters' degree in addition to their rabbinic studies in order to be ordained. And some of those who are ordained may go on to receive a higher ordination.

Question   What is a "higher ordination"?

Answer   The normal degree awarded to a rabbi is known as *Yoreh Yoreh* – "He may rule" – and is given after the student passes examinations in the laws of kashrut and in a number of other areas of basic Jewish law. This ordination, though, does not allow the rabbi to deal with cases of Jewish civil law, as, for example, ruling in financial disputes. In order to be permitted to deal with such areas, the rabbi has to pass another set of examinations on the pertinent laws, whereupon he is awarded the further degree of *Yadin Yadin* – "He may judge." Some rabbinical colleges, reasoning that the passing of the first set of examinations is an indication that the person has acquired the tools to rule on all aspects of Jewish law, will automatically award their rabbis with a combined ordination, known as *Yoreh Yoreh Yadin Yadin*.

Question   What is a *tzaddik*?

Answer   In order to answer this question, we have to remember the differentiation between the *hasidim* and the *mitnagdim*, a topic discussed at length in the first chapter. For our purposes, we simply have to recall that *hasidim* are a segment of the Ashkenazic Jews, who broke away from the then mainstream. *Hasidim* have different emphases than the other Ashkenazic Jews, the *mitnagdim*, as, for example, laying greater on the mystic, kabbalistic realm.

Now, unlike the *mitnagdim* who stress the individual's direct contact with God, Hasidism regards its leaders as having a special, mystic power, whereby they are able to intervene with God. Hasidism is thus built on the basis of an individual who is in charge of his own flock. That individual is known as a *tzaddik* (literally "righteous one"). The term "rebbi" is also sometimes to denote a hasidic leader. (The term is sometimes rendered as "grand rabbi" in English.) In Hasidism, the post is generally a hereditary one, and when a *tzaddik* dies his *hasidim* will generally accept one of his sons (or, in the absence of sons or of sons worthy of the position, another close relative of the previous *tzaddik*) as his successor.

The *tzaddik's* relationship with his *hasidim* is a very close one, and he is customarily consulted by them before any major decision – getting married, moving from one city to another, accepting a job, or even undergoing an operation. To the *hasid*, the *tzaddik's* word is final, and a true *hasid* will show blind obedience to every decision by his *tzaddik*.

The story is told about a rabbi who boasted that his congregants always obeyed whatever he told them to do. (This story cannot be about a *tzaddik*, because among *hasidim* such behavior is automatic.) When one of his colleagues, who was always at loggerheads with his own congregation, asked the rabbi for his secret, he replied: "It's really very simple. I never tell them to do anything that they wouldn't do anyway!"

Question   What is a *hazan* – cantor?

Answer   The cantor is the person who leads the congregation in prayer.

Question   What are the qualifications for a cantor?

Answer   By Jewish law, the major criterion for a cantor is that he be a God-fearing person, for he must represent the congregation, as it were, in the community's prayers to God. Beyond the obvious need to be familiar with the prayer ritual and the appropriate melodies, there are no special requirements for a person to be a cantor. In most synagogues, in fact, laymen act as cantors at all of the weekday prayer services. On the Sabbaths and festivals, where the service is longer and the melodies more festive, a cantor may be employed to lead the service, and of course in such circumstances the cantor's voice is one of the primary concerns of the synagogue hiring him. Yet there are many synagogues that do not have professional cantors, and different laymen – obviously those with more melodious voices – will be chosen to lead the services on the Sabbaths and festivals.

Again, we should note that various rabbinical colleges today have separate departments where those wishing to become professional cantors are given instruction in such areas as the Jewish law pertaining to leading the prayers and in the traditional melodies for the different days that have been handed for hundreds of years.

They tell of a very pious man who asked his rabbi to intercede with the lay leaders, so that he might assume the position of cantor in the community. When the rabbi presented the idea to the laymen, they dismissed it out of hand: "That man, rabbi, has a voice like a croaking frog," was the way one of the lay leaders put it. "I know," said the rabbi, "but he has all the other qualities necessary for the position: he is God-fearing, prays with great devotion, and knows all the laws. Are we going to turn him down just because we have found a single imperfection in him? How can one possibly find a cantor who meets *all* the qualifications?"

Then they tell the story of a town which did not have a cantor, where various individuals would lead the services on the different Sabbaths and festivals. One particular individual made a point of acting as cantor whenever he could, even though he was absolutely atrocious – his voice a croak, the words unclear and the melody non-existent. One day, after the man had prayed the morning service and gone to extreme lengths in his "singing," while not noticing everyone in the synagogue cringing, the rabbi called him over at the conclusion of the service. "Was there any reason why you had to pray before the congregation today? Is it the *yahrzeit* of any of your relatives?" the rabbi asked him. "No, Rabbi," the man replied proudly, "It was a voluntary act on my part." "Amazing, amazing," said the rabbi. "Imagine how great the Jewish people are! Even when they don't have anything, that doesn't stop them from contributing ..."

Question What is a *shohet*?

Answer A *shohet* is a person who has been granted written permission, known as *kabbalah*, by a rabbi to act as a ritual slaughterer.

Question What must such a person know in order to receive *kabbalah*?

Answer The first requirement that a rabbi should look for is that the person is a God-fearing individual. After all, it is on the *shohet's* word that hundreds, if not thousands, of people will eat what they have been told is kosher food. In addition, the person must know all the laws involved in slaughtering animals and (especially in the case of cattle) in examining them for possible blemishes that may render them unkosher. Then, of course, the person must know the practical aspects of ritual slaughter, one of the most important of which is the preparation of the slaughtering knife so that its edge is absolutely flawless. The edge is tested by running it against the fingernail; if it catches in the slightest anywhere along the way, the knife may not be used, and – if used anyway – renders the animal that was slaughtered non-kosher.

As in the case of *semikhah*, there are two types of *kabbalah*, one permitting the individual to slaughter only fowl, and the other which permits him to slaughter both cattle and fowl. As one can imagine, the slaughtering of cattle requires far more of the *shohet* in terms of skill, learning and experience than does the slaughtering of fowl.

Question What is a *mohel*?

Answer A *mohel* is a person who has been trained to perform *brit milah*, ritual circumcision.

Question   How does a person become a *mohel*?

Answer   Traditionally, a person wishing to become a *mohel* would study with another already in the field. While this is still a requirement today, there are places which require the person to not only study the technical aspects and laws involved, but to have a reasonable grounding in the medical aspects. While there is no such law in Israel, 70% of all its *mohalim* have taken and passed such a course offered by the Ministry of Health.

Question   What is a *rosh yeshivah*?

Answer   The term itself means "head of yeshivah," and indicates that the person is the head of a particular *yeshivah*. In the case of the major yeshivot, where the *rosh yeshivah* has to be one of the leading Torah scholars to have attained such a position, he is generally regarded by the members of the traditional community with a mixture of veneration and awe.

We should note that over the past century or so there has been a marked change in the respective functions of the rabbi and the *rosh yeshivah* in the Torah world. Traditionally, where a town had both a rabbi and a *rosh yeshivah*, the rabbi was the one who was considered the authority of Jewish law and all questions in the field – even by the town *rosh yeshivah* – were addressed to the rabbi. The *rosh yeshivah* was generally regarded as keeping the flame of the theoretical study of the Torah burning, whereas the rabbi was the pragmatist, who took theory and applied it to the infinite problems of day-to-day living.

In the last century, though, there has been a shift, and in our times it is the *rosh yeshivah* that is often the final authority on Jewish law. Many theories have been advanced for this shift. Thus, for example, there are those who believe that the change came about because the modern rabbi – unlike his earlier counterpart – seldom has the time to delve at length into the literature before reaching a halakhic decision. Thus, the rabbis, as it were, simply abdicated the field in favor of the *rashei* (plural of *rosh*) *yeshivah*, who have the time to immerse themselves totally in the study of the law. Others see as a possible reason for the change the fact that the yeshivot themselves have assumed an entirely different role. In former times, a yeshivah would generally consist of a single rabbi and a select group of students who gathered about him. Only in the 1800s did a new model develop, along the lines, as it were, of a school for higher education, with a number of rabbis giving classes and even, possibly, a graded curriculum. Thus, the *rosh yeshivah* was no longer the "head" of a handful of students, but a Torah giant who might have hundreds of students studying in his institution. Thus, in a way, we can see that the shift may have been caused, among others, by the decline in the rabbis' ability to render halakhic decisions and the commensurate increase in the stature of the *rashei yeshivah*.

Question What is a *mashgiah*?

Answer The word *mashgiah* simply means a supervisor, and, indeed, there are two entirely different functionaries who are referred to as *mashgiah*. First, we find the *mashgiah ruhani* – the "spiritual supervisor" – an integral member of the yeshivah staff. It is his responsibility to ensure that the students under his care develop not only intellectually, but also spiritually and morally. Thus, the *mashgiah ruhani* may, for example, keep a running check on the yeshivah students' attendance at the daily prayers and study sessions, and – on a deeper level – may give periodic lectures on different aspects of proper behavior, such as the need to help others or to be compassionate. Generally, the *mashgiah* is a Torah scholar in his own right, whose own exemplary life leads the *rosh yeshivah* to appoint him as the spiritual mentor of the entire yeshivah student body.

The other type of *mashgiah* is the *mashgiah kashrut* – the kashrut supervisor – who is employed to ensure that the food being prepared or served by a particular establishment is kosher. For food to be considered kosher, especially in our days of "high-tech" food technology, a *mashgiah kashrut* is needed at every stage of the food preparation. Thus, if a company manufactures food, its products can only be endorsed as kosher if all the individual ingredients have been certified as kosher. As a simple example, before a product such as tuna fish can be given kashruth endorsement, there is need for a *mashgiah kashrut* to ensure that the fish that is used is only tuna, and that the vegetable oil was made under rabbinic supervision (i.e., with a *mashgiah kashrut* present). Furthermore, if a product uses spices, it may be necessary to send a *mashgiah kashrut* to the source where the spices are manufactured to be sure that there are no problems at that end.

Of course, any establishment which cooks food for retail sale – a restaurant, take-home food store, butcher, etc. – must have a *mashgiah kashrut* to ensure that all the laws are being observed.

The duty of the *mashgiah kashrut* varies with the product involved. For example, dishwashing detergent manufacturers need far less supervision than do restaurants or caterers, for once the ingredients have been ascertained to be kosher, there is very little that can go wrong in manufacturing the dishwashing detergent. The *mashgiah kashrut* in such a case must simply visit the plant from time to time to ensure compliance with the laws of kashrut. On the other hand, a restaurant constantly receives shipments of unprocessed and processed foods and must constantly prepare meals. In such a case, a full-time *mashgiah kashrut* may be needed.

While on the topic, we should note that one of the most important changes in American Jewish life in the United States the past few decades has been in the field of the certification of kashruth. The change from the individual rabbi's endorsement to the endorsement by public organizations is discussed above, in the chapter on dietary laws.

Question What is a *sofer*?

Answer A *sofer* – scribe – is someone who writes the various ritual texts that must be hand-written. These are Torah scrolls (sometimes referred to as *sefarim*), *tefillin* and *mezuzot*, as well as the Scroll of Esther and *gittin*, bills of divorce. The *sofer* is often known as a *sofer stam*, the word *stam* being the Hebrew acronym for *sefarim, tefillin, mezuzot*.

Question What training does a *sofer* need?

Answer First of all, he needs to know the very detailed laws involved. For example, there are very precise laws governing the form of each letter of the alphabet. If even a single letter is incorrect, the entire text is invalid and cannot be used. The *sofer* also must be familiar with the materials which may and may not be used – the parchment, the ink and the quills, and how to use each properly. (Yes, many *soferim* still use feather quills, as they feel they give the best result.) Furthermore, of course, the *sofer* must have a certain artistic skill.

Question How long does it take to write a Torah scroll?

Answer Considering the painstaking care that the *sofer* must take, it is not suprising that a Torah scroll customarily takes about a year to write. That, plus the fact that the parchment must be prepared by hand and has shot up in price in the last two or three decades, explains the high cost of such scrolls today. It is a very great *mitzvah* to write a Torah scroll or to commission a *sofer* to write one. However, because of the high cost, synagogues and other groups often commission the writing communally so that all have a share in the *mitzvah*.

Question What do Jews refer to when they speak of the *mashiah*?

Answer The word *mashiah* means "anointed," and its pronunciation was later anglicized into "messiah." By Jewish belief, the end of the world as we know it will be marked by the advent of the *mashiah*. As to what will actually happen at that time, there are numerous different versions of the sequence of events at that time. Maimonides, in fact, warns of the utter futility of trying to imagine what that time will be like. He does, though, give us a glimmering of what will take place, in the very final passage of his monumental *Mishneh Torah*, and it is appropriate that we too end our work with his inspiring words:

> The Sages and Prophets yearned for the days of the messiah, not so that they should rule over the entire world, and not that they should persecute the heathen, and not that the other nations should extol them, and not that they should eat and drink and be merry; but so that they should be free to study the Torah and its wisdom. Then there will be nothing to disturb this pursuit, so that they will be worthy of the World to Come ...
>
> In that era there will no longer be want or war, envy or rivalry, for good will be abundant and all delicacies will be as freely available as the earth, and the entire world will be preoccupied with the knowledge of God. Israel will therefore be great scholars and will understand that which is now concealed, and grasp the knowledge of their Creator, as much as man is capable of doing so, as it states, "The earth shall be full of the knowledge of the Lord, as the waters cover the sea"(Isa.11:9).

תַּחֲזִירֶנָה לִמְקוֹמָה בִּמְהֵרָה בְּיָמֵינוּ ׃ וֹאֹס קל כטבת אומר רבח והחליבנו

אֱלֹהֵינוּ וֵאלֹהֵי אֲבוֹתֵינוּ יַעֲלֶה וְיָבֹא וְיַגִּיעַ וְיֵרָאֶה

וְיֵרָצֶה וְיִשָּׁמַע וְיִפָּקֵד וְיִזָּכֵר זִכְרוֹנֵנוּ וּפִקְדוֹנֵנוּ וְזִכְרוֹן

אֲבוֹתֵינוּ וְזִכְרוֹן יְרוּשָׁלַםִ עִירָךְ וְזִכְרוֹן מָשִׁיחַ בֶּן דָּוִד עַבְדֶּךְ

וְזִכְרוֹן

★ *The Messiah entering Jerusalem;* Venice Haggadah, *18th century.*

Index